SEP 2007

## Spain Overview

| | |
|---|---|
| —— | Pilgrimage to Santiago |
| —— | Treasures off the Beaten Track |
| —— | Moorish Memories |
| —— | Madrid and More |
| —— | Cradle of the Conquistadors |
| —— | Old Castile / Cantabrian Coast |
| —— | The Costa Brava and Beyond |
| —— | Andalusian Adventures |

0    50    100 KM
0         50        100 Mi

**1**

Santiago de
Compostela

León

**2** Hondarribia
Bilbao
Pamplona
Olite

Seu d'Urgell    ANDORRA    **3**

Aigua
blava

Barcelona

Zamora

Salamanca

Avila

Madrid

Alcañiz

Albarracin

PORTUGAL

Toledo

Cuenca

**6**

Guadalupe

Merida

Ubeda

Seville
Arcos
Malaga    **4**
Jerez    Ronda

Granada

**5**

MOROCCO

# Spain Map 1

- ● Places to Stay
- ▬▬ Pilgrimage to Santiago
- ▬▬ Cradle of the Conquistadors
- ▬▬ Old Castile / Cantabrian Coast

0    20    40 KM
0    20    40 Mi

ATLANTIC OCEAN

PORTUGAL

Ferrol
La Coruna
Vilalba
Castropol
E 70
Taramundi
N634
Villaviciosa
Ribade-sesella
Peruyes
Collia
Covadonga
Oviedo
E 70
Lugo
Santiago de Compostela
N V1
A66
Fuente Dé
Riaño
A9
Cistierna
León
N625
Pontevedra
Orense
Astorga
Mansilla de las Mulas
Vigo
A52
Verín
Puebla de Sanabria
Baiona
A57
A52
N631
620
Benavente
N630
NV1
E80
Tordesillas
NV1-A6
Zamora
Porto
Salamanca
N620-E80
N501
Alba de Tormes
La Alberca
SA515
N110
Guarda
Béjar
Gredos
N630
Jarandilla de la Vera
Navalmoral de la Mata
Cuacos
Plasencia
Yuste
Oropesa
E90

# Spain Map 4

- ● Places to Stay
- ▬ Treasures off the Beaten Track
- ▬ Moorish Memories

0   20   40 KM

0   20   40 Mi

Madrid

Chinchón

E90

E5

N401

N401

NIII

Toledo

CM400

Consuegra

Madridejos

El Tobosco

N420

Campo de Criptana

Tarancon

N400

Cuenca

Tragacete

Ciudad Encantada

N330

Albarracín

Teruel

Castellon de la Plana

Alarcón

Valencia

Balearic Sea

N234

E901

Daimiel

Ciudad Real

Almagro

NIV

Valdepeñas

E5

Desfiladero de Despeñaperros

N322

Albacete

N430

Xátiva

Jávea

E15

N330

La Carolina

E5

N301

Alicante

Bailén

Linares

Ubeda

Baeza

N322

Andújar

Jaén

Cazorla

Murcia

E15

Baena

E902

Alcaudete

N432

N342

Cartagena

Granada

Cortijo Grande

Torre del Mar

Lanjarón

Almuñécar

Orgiva

Salobreña

E15

Nerja

Almeria

E15

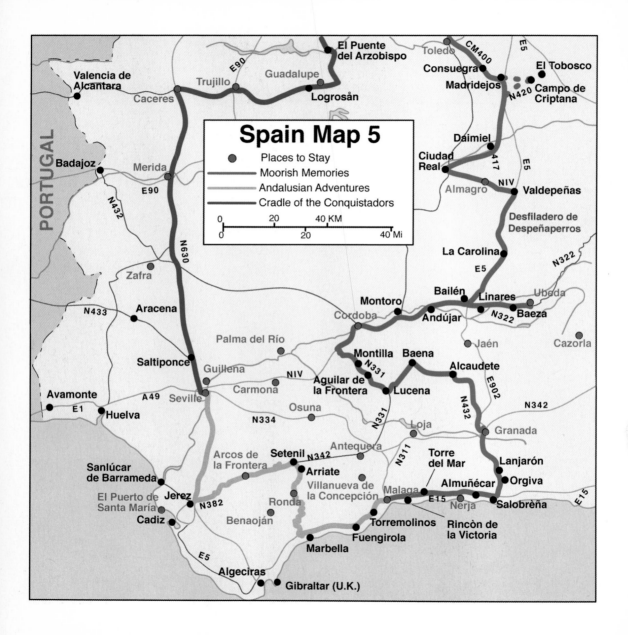

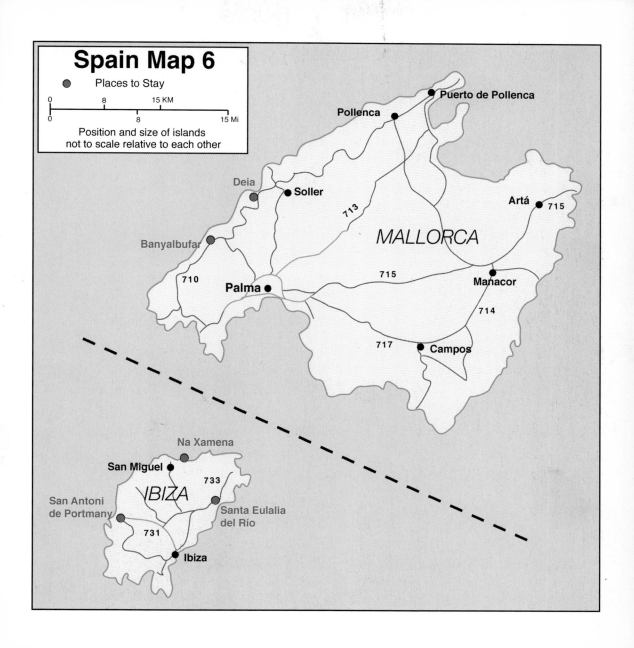

# *Karen Brown's*
# SPAIN
## 2008

*La Residencia Hotel Pampinot*
*Hondarribia*

# Contents

*For Mariela Isabel & Alejandro Rafael*

**Cover painting: *La Residencia Hotel Pampinot, Hondarribia***

*Authors: June Eveleigh Brown, Clare Brown, Karen Brown, Cynthia Sauvage.*

*Contributing author: Lorena Aburto Ramirez.*

*Editors: Anthony Brown, Clare Brown, Karen Brown, June Eveleigh Brown, Iris Sandilands, Debbie Tokumoto, Melissa Jaworski.*

*Illustrations: Barbara Maclurcan Tapp.*

*Cover painting: Jann Pollard.*

*Front photos: Ávila, Besalú.*

*Back photo: Alarcón.*

*Maps: Michael Fiegel, Rachael Kircher-Randolph.*

*Technical support: Andrew Harris.*

*Copyright © 2008 by Karen Brown's Guides Inc.*

*Distributed by National Book Network, 15200 NBN Way, Blue Ridge Summit, PA 17214, USA. Tel: 717-794-3800 or 1-800-462-6420, Fax: 1-800-338-4500, Email: custserv@nbnbooks.com*

A catalog record for this book is available from the British Library.

ISSN 1533-4953

# Introduction

Once you fall under Spain's magical spell, there will be no breaking free, nor any urge to do so—only the desire to return, again and again. However, many seasoned travelers never experience its enchantment, since Spain is considered somewhat "off the beaten path." Outside the major cities, you quickly find yourself away from hordes of tourists and happily immersed in the magic of places that haven't changed for hundreds of years. You will be entranced by the beauty of the landscape, the rich selection of places to see, the diversity of the culture, and the warmth of welcome. We are constantly amazed that more people have not yet discovered Spain's many wonders and hope our guide will entice you to visit. You too will become addicted to its boundless charms.

# About This Guide

Our goal in writing this guide is to share with you the loveliest, historic hotels in Spain and to provide itineraries that will lead you to them by the most scenic and interesting routes. This book is designed for the traveler looking for a guide to more than the capital city and a handful of highlights, for the visitor who wants to add a little out of the ordinary to his agenda. We do not claim to be objective reporters—that sort of treatment is available anywhere—but subjective, on-site raconteurs. We have a definite bias toward hotels with romantic ambiance, from lovely stone farmhouses tucked in the mountains to sumptuous castles overlooking the sea. If you follow our itineraries (each one of which we have traveled personally) and trust in our hotel recommendations (every one of which we have visited personally), you will be assured of Spain's best lodgings while discovering the country's most intriguing destinations.

This book is divided into four parts. At the front a color section, *Maps*, pinpoints the location of each of the recommended hotels and outlines the itineraries. Second, the *Introduction* gives a general overview of Spain. The third section, *Itineraries*, outlines itineraries throughout Spain to help you plan where to go and what to see. The fourth section, *Places to Stay*, is our recommended selection of hotels in all price ranges with a description, an illustration, and pertinent information provided on each one.

## WEBSITE

Please visit the Karen Brown website (*www.karenbrown.com*) in conjunction with this book. Our website provides trip planning assistance, new discoveries, post-press updates, feedback from you, our readers, the opportunity to purchase goods and services that we recommend (rail tickets, car rental, travel insurance, etc.), and one-stop shopping for our guides, associated maps and watercolor prints. Most of our favorite places to stay are featured with color photos and direct website and email links. Also, we invite you to participate in the Karen Brown's Readers' Choice Awards. Be sure to visit our website and vote so your favorite properties will be honored.

# About Spain

Spain is a country with something for everyone: from the birthplace of Don Juan to the birthplace of Hernán Cortés, Conquistador of Mexico, from the tomb of St. James the Apostle to the tomb of El Cid, Spain's medieval epic hero. You can visit the plains traversed by Don Quixote in search of "wrongs to right" and can admire the quixotic architectural achievements of Antonio Gaudí. You can drive the highest road in Europe and visit the largest wildlife refuge. You can see the youthful work of Picasso and the mature work of Salvador Dalí. To cap it all off, there are great beaches, spectacular mountains, stunning gorges, beautiful landscapes, fine dining, and, above all—a warm, welcoming people. Following are some facts about Spain, listed alphabetically.

## AIRFARE

Karen Brown's Guides have long recommended Auto Europe for their excellent car rental services. Their air travel division, Destination Europe, an airline broker working with major American and European carriers, offers deeply discounted coach- and business-class fares to over 200 European gateway cities. It also gives Karen Brown travelers an additional 5% discount off its already highly competitive prices (cannot be combined with any other offers or promotions). We recommend making reservations by phone at (800) 835 1555. When phoning, be sure to use the Karen Brown ID number 99006187 to secure your discount.

## BANKS

Generally, banks in Spain are open from 9 am to 1:30 pm, sometimes 2 pm, Monday through Friday. Some banks (most frequently in larger towns) maintain similar business hours on Saturday. Many, but not all, exchange foreign currency: look for a *Cambio* (exchange) sign outside the bank. Often your hotel or the local tourist office will exchange your dollars, though usually at a slightly less-favorable rate than at the bank.

An increasingly popular and convenient way to obtain foreign currency is simply to use your bankcard at an ATM machine. You pay a fixed fee for this but, depending on the amount you withdraw, it is usually less than the percentage-based fee charged to exchange currency or travelers' checks. Be sure to check with your bank or credit card company about fees and necessary pin numbers prior to departure.

## CLIMATE

There are three distinct climates in Spain, dividing the country in thirds from north to south. The northern area is subject to the moderating Atlantic currents and has a relatively good climate for most of the year—too cold to swim in winter, but seldom bitterly cold either; summer is warm, but never extremely hot. The central plateau is cut off from those moderating currents and has what the Spanish call *nueve meses de invierno y tres de infierno* (nine months of winter and three of hell). The southern third of the country has a more Mediterranean climate: relatively warm, though with damp winters, and often brutal heat in midsummer, which is slightly alleviated along the coastal areas by sea breezes. If you venture to some of Spain's exotic islands, you will find still other climates. In fact, on some of the Canary Islands (just off the coast of Africa), it is so dry that sometimes it doesn't rain for the entire year.

## CLOTHING

Standards of formality can be generalized: In the most elegant city restaurants, dresses and coats and ties are common, though only occasionally required. Skimpy summer attire, though common in resort areas, might make you feel conspicuous elsewhere. When visiting Spain's magnificent cathedrals, it is respectful to cover your shoulders and not wear shorts.

# DRIVING

We always use Auto Europe—a car rental broker that works with the major car rental companies to find the lowest possible price. They also offer motor homes and chauffeur services. Auto Europe's toll-free phone service, from every European country, connects you to their U.S.-based, 24-hour reservation center (ask for the Europe Phone Numbers Card to be mailed to you). Auto Europe offers our readers a 5% discount (cannot be combined with any other offers or promotions) and, occasionally, free upgrades. Be sure to use the Karen Brown ID number 99006187 to receive your discount and any special offers. You can make your reservations online via our website, *www.karenbrown.com* (select Auto Europe from the home page), or by phone (800-223-5555).

DRIVER'S LICENSE: You will need to have a valid driver's license from your home country.

GASOLINE: Gasoline is relatively expensive (at least double the U.S. price) and should be considered in your budget if you plan to drive extensively. Gasoline is available in any small town and at frequent intervals along the freeways. Diesel (called *gasoil* or *gasoleo* in Spain) is considerably less costly. With a little common sense, you should have no trouble finding fuel. Many of the major gas stations accept credit cards—if so, most display a sign with the credit card emblems.

ROADS: Roads in Spain run the gamut from superb freeways to barely two-lane country roads (and, as you might expect, our countryside itineraries find you more often on the latter). Travel on the freeways is swift, but as a rule of thumb, calculate that you will average only about 50–60 kilometers per hour on the country roads. However, the leisurely pace allows you time to enjoy your surroundings as you drive. The personality of the country does not lend itself to an accelerated pace, nor do the itineraries.

There is order to the Spanish road numbers. "A" (A6, for example) indicates freeways. "N" plus a Roman numeral (NIV) indicates major national highways that radiate like spokes from Madrid. "N" with an Arabic numeral (N403) indicates minor national highways that connect the major ones. "C" (C321) indicates regional roads, and two letters (which are the first two letters in the name of the province e.g. TO1234 for Toledo) indicate provincial roads. Their size and the speed possible are usually correspondingly lower as you go down the list from freeways to provincial roads. Roads are constantly being upgraded, so you will encounter many pleasant surprises—a road that looks of questionable quality on a map might turn out to be wider than expected and freshly re-tarred.

Some of the longer freeways are toll roads and every so often require that you pass through a tollbooth. When you enter the highway, usually you will be given a ticket with the point of entry marked and will pay according to the number of kilometers driven when you leave the highway. If you don't know Spanish, look for the amount due on the lighted sign at the booth. While these freeways are excellent and generally uncrowded, the tolls take their "toll" on your wallet if you drive all day on them. Wherever there are freeways, there are also parallel non-toll highways, but you can expect them to double the driving time between two points. Most of the toll stations will take a credit card. This is a great convenience—just one quick swish of your card through their computer and you are on your way.

SEAT BELTS: The use of seat belts is mandatory in Spain, and the law is strongly enforced both in cities and in the countryside, so get into the habit of buckling up when you get into the car.

TRAFFIC: This is never a problem on the freeways; however, on smaller roads it can be ferocious. If you're trying to cover a lot of ground in a given day, we suggest that you try to drive during siesta time—between 1 and 4 pm—when many trucks and buses stop for lunch. In the large cities, unfamiliarity combined with traffic, parking problems, and the fact that almost no two streets are parallel, make driving a trial for all but the bravest of souls. Our preference is to leave the car in the hotel parking lot (or one recommended by the hotel) and take cabs or walk around the cities. Underground public parking areas are common and are designated by a rectangular blue sign with a large white "P." In Madrid and Barcelona try the excellent subway systems (called the Metro and marked with signs bearing a large "M"). If you're stopping to visit a town along an itinerary route, we suggest you park on or near a main square (for easy recall), then venture on by foot into those streets that were never designed with cars in mind. It is not uncommon for parking areas on central streets and plazas to be *vigilados* (overseen) by an attendant, usually wearing something resembling a uniform. He may direct you to a free spot and will approach you after you park—a small tip is appropriate.

## ECONOMY

Though long known as a travel bargain, since its entry into the European Union (EU) Spain has made appreciable progress toward bringing the cost of its commodities (including tourist facilities) closer to the level of other EU members. Tourism accounts for a large share of foreign income, with the number of tourists entering each year exceeding the native population of over 38 million. Fortunately, they don't all arrive at the same time, though the vast majority of visitors come in July and August.

## ELECTRICAL SUPPLY

You will need a transformer plus an adapter if you plan to take an American-made electrical appliance. Even if the appliance is dual-voltage, as many of them are these days, you'll still need an adapter plug. The voltage is usually 220, but in a few places 110 is used. Occasionally a 110 outlet is provided in the hotel bathroom, but these should be used only for small appliances such as electric razors, since they usually can't handle things like hairdryers. Be sure to check with the manager if the outlet is not clearly marked.

*Introduction–About Spain*

## ENGLISH

We suggest you tuck in your suitcase a Spanish phrase book. In the large hotels in the major cities, you will probably never use it, but elsewhere you might find situations where English is not spoken. Most hotels and paradors have someone on the staff who speaks English, but he/she will not always be available. When this happens, just pull out your trusty phrase book and point—Spaniards are friendly and you'll eventually make yourself understood (and probably learn some Spanish while you're at it). If you make advance reservations, be sure to take proof of confirmation and/or vouchers with you: it will save a lot of pointing.

## EURO

All pricing, including room rates, is quoted in euros.

## FESTIVALS AND FOLKLORE

By far the six most internationally renowned Spanish festivals are *Semana Santa* (Holy Week), which is celebrated throughout the country; the *Feria* in Seville (the week leading up to Easter and the second week after it); the *Festival of San Fermín* in Pamplona, which features the running of the bulls (second week of July); the *Fallas* in Valencia (middle of March); the *Festival of St. James* in Santiago (last two weeks of July); and *Carnival* in Cadiz (the week in which Ash Wednesday falls). In addition, every Spanish town has its patron saint, and every saint its day of honor, so there are as many festivals as there are Spanish towns. If you know where you want to go ahead of time, write to the Tourist Office of Spain or the *Oficina de Turismo* (Tourist Office) in the town(s) you plan to visit for a list of festival dates so that you might arrange your visit to coincide with one or several of these colorful events. Be forewarned, however, that hotel space will be at a premium and room rates are almost always more expensive during festival time.

# FOOD AND DRINK

The government rates restaurants from one to five forks: however, its rating system is based on such matters as the number of choices on the menu and the wine cellar rather than the quality of the food, so it can be misleading. For instance, in order to receive three or more forks, the headwaiter must speak English and the menu must be translated into several languages (which often makes for amusing reading)—an achievement that does not reflect upon the dishes served. A modest-appearing and reasonably priced restaurant will often offer good, regional fare.

A very important aspect of dining in Spain is to acclimate yourself to the national time schedule. Breakfast is at the same time as at home. The main meal, however, is almost exclusively eaten at around 2 pm. Most restaurants open around 1 pm and close about 4 pm and it is during this period that they offer their main menu that can be expected to have almost everything on it. They open again at about 8:30 or 9 pm for dinner, which is normally a light meal and is served until 10 or 11 pm, and, often, up to midnight. Traditionally, restaurants have a reduced menu in the evening, although it seems that nowadays more establishments are offering the same fare at night as at midday, as Spain becomes increasingly "Europeanized," a process which is taking place rapidly and, logically enough, from north to south in the country. In Catalonia and the Basque country, you'll find that restaurants close earlier—a fact that astounds even many Spaniards. Restaurants that cater to tourists—such as the parador dining rooms—are the most flexible and will normally offer a full menu in the evening. We feel it is most comfortable to adjust to the Spanish schedule if possible. You may find the service less than perfect if you take a table at a busy restaurant at 2 pm and order only a sandwich, and you may be disappointed if you expect to have a five-course dinner in the evening. Between the *tapas* (munchies) available at all bars at almost all times and the numerous *cafeterias,* where small, quick meals can be had at any hour, you won't starve.

By far the most common type of food on the Spanish menu is the wide variety of seafood. Many of these are totally unknown to most Americans (even where the menu is translated, it doesn't necessarily help). Items such as *angulas* (baby eels), numerous varieties of squid (*calamares*) and octopus (*pulpo*), and shellfish are best viewed as an adventure. You will find many of them excellent and should definitely experiment. Organ meats—such as brains and sweetbreads—are also common and, prepared in many different ways, can be delicious.

If there is any dish more common than seafood, it is the *tortilla española* (Spanish omelet), which is made with eggs and potatoes. It will be found on almost every menu as an appetizer or as a main course for the evening meal. It is also often available as a sandwich (*bocadillo*).

There are a few things you should note about the names of eating and drinking establishments. A *bar* is seldom what we call by that name. It is usually a place where everything from coffee to alcohol is served and is frequented by patrons of all ages. Continental breakfast is served there too, as are pastries and other desserts. Bars often also serve simple sandwiches. A *café* is about the same thing, and indeed, these places are often called *café-bar*—these are the spots that often have tables outside when the weather permits. A *cafeteria* offers a modest but complete menu and relatively fast service. This seldom involves self-service, but provides a less elaborate setting for a meal than the typical restaurant.

Wine is ubiquitous. In the large fancy restaurants, a good selection of imported wines is usually available along with the extensive wines of Spain. In smaller restaurants, the list is mostly Spanish, which is often a rich selection indeed and fun to sample. Probably the best wines come from the Rioja region around Logroño. These are followed by the wines of the Valdepeñas area of La Mancha, which are slightly more astringent. But there are many other smaller wine-producing regions, some of which we'll point out in the itineraries. If you have no particular favorite, you'll rarely go wrong by requesting the *vino de la casa*, often a wine bottled especially for the restaurant, or else a *vino regional* (regional wine), either *tinto* (red), *blanco* (white), or *rosado* (rose), according to your preference.

*Introduction–About Spain*

*Sangría* is a national favorite, made from red wine mixed with fresh fruit and liqueur, with infinite variations on that theme, and served over ice. It's a great thirst-quencher and, even if it doesn't appear on the menu, any place will happily drum up a passable *sangría*.

If there is a drink more common than wine in Spain, it is coffee. Spanish coffee is usually served as what we call espresso in the United States. It is thus a small cup of very strong brew to which most people add a considerable amount of sugar. Here are some of the common terms used in ordering: *café solo*—a demitasse of espresso; *café solo doble*—a double portion of the same; *café con leche*—the same coffee with an equal amount of warm milk added to it; *café cortado*—espresso with just a splash of milk added.

Beer is another favorite, and is always good, sometimes excellent, especially on hot days in a shady plaza. Asking for *una cerveza* will get you a bottle of regional beer or a draught (*cerveza de barril*). *Una caña* will get you a small glass of draught, and the request for *un tanque* will result in a large glass of the refreshing brew.

Another very common beverage ordered in Spanish restaurants is, believe it or not, water: the bottled kind. Though there is nothing wrong with *agua natural* (tap water), *agua mineral* (mineral water) is popular in either *litro* or *medio litro* (liter or half-liter) sizes. It may also be ordered *con* or *sin gas* (with or without carbonation). You'll notice that Spaniards often dilute their wine with it.

Once you leave the large cities and tourist-frequented restaurants, you'll find that menus are poorly translated, or not translated at all. The following list includes some of the terms of traditional specialties to be found on most Spanish menus:

*Desayuno* (breakfast): This may be a continental breakfast, consisting of *pan* (bread) and/or *pan dulce* (sweet rolls) along with *café* (coffee), *té* (tea), *leche* (milk), or *chocolate* (hot chocolate). Many hotels (and all the paradors) offer elaborate buffet breakfasts that include various fruits, cereals, breads, yogurts, cheeses, and meats plus sometimes extras such as *huevos* (eggs)—either *revueltos* (scrambled), *fritos* (fried sunny side up), *pasados por agua* (boiled), *poche* (poached), or in a *tortilla* (omelet).

*Comida* (lunch): This is the main meal of the day for most Spaniards and is taken around 2 pm. It normally consists of several courses: *entremeses* (appetizers), *sopas* (soup, usually of the thick variety), *carnes* (meat dishes), *pescados y mariscos* (fish and shellfish), *postres* (desserts), and, includes of course, *vino*. No one orders all these courses—three is most common.

*Merenda* (afternoon snack): This is taken around 6 pm by many people and may consist of any kind of light food. The most common are *pasteles* (pies or cakes, not usually as good as they look) and *churros* (deep-fried dough, somewhat like a stick-shaped donut) along with coffee or chocolate.

*Tapas* (hors d'oeuvres): This is as much a social tradition as a kind of food and is a feature of after-work bar hopping. Since the variety of *tapas* is apparently infinite, a good method is to search out a bar where they are on display so you can point to what you want. Also available at this time (8 to 10 pm, more or less) are *raciónes* (orders, approximately), which are the same things, but in larger portions (a ración will be a plateful of meatballs, for example, whereas a *tapa* will be just a couple of tapas).

*Cena* (supper): This meal has traditionally been taken in Spain after 10 pm and is a light meal (one course of the same kinds of things as at lunch). Due to Spain's increasing contact with the rest of Europe in the last decade, customs are changing somewhat. Especially in the larger cities and along the French border, you'll find people eating earlier and restaurants offering a more complete menu at night. Most of the paradors and hotels begin serving the evening meal anywhere from 8 to 9 pm.

*Aceite* (olive oil): About the only kind of oil used to cook with in Spain and used in many, many dishes.

*Carne* (meat): *Ternera* (technically veal, but really closer to what we call beef) comes in *chuletas* (veal chop, but similar to a T-bone steak if it's thick), *solomillo* (sirloin), *entrecot* (rib eye), *filete* (thinly sliced and pan fried), and *asada* (roasted). *Cerdo* (pork) and *pollo* (chicken) are also commonly found on menus. In central Spain, *cochinillo asado* (roast suckling pig) is a common specialty.

*Ensalada mixta* (tossed green salad): Besides lettuce, this usually contains any or all of the following: olives, tomato, onion, tuna, hard-boiled egg. But remember that there is only one salad dressing in the entire country: *vinagre* (vinegar) and *aceite* (olive oil).

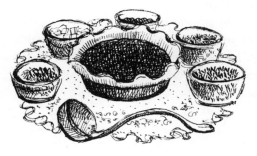

*Gazpacho:* Another justifiably famous Spanish dish, this is a cold, tomato-based soup with various spices and olive oil, and garnished with bits of bread, bacon, green onions, celery, crumbled egg, etc. You are usually given a choice of garnishes at the table. Gazpacho is one of Spain's Moorish legacies, and has multiple variations even though it is usually called *gazpacho Andaluz*, which is the most popular kind. One common variation in the south is *gazpacho de almendras* (almonds), which is white and has thinly sliced almonds floating on top and raisins in it, but tastes pretty much like the regular kind. The soup is an absolutely wonderful cooler if you've been out in the summer heat seeing sights all morning.

*Jamön serrano* (cured ham, similar to prosciutto): A favorite of most Spaniards as a *tapa*, *a bocadillo*, or as an added ingredient to another meat dish. There are many varieties and qualities, and you'll see them hanging from the ceiling in bars with little cups to catch the juice so it doesn't fall on the customers. *Pata negra* (literally "black foot," a darker variety) is considered the best.

*Paella:* Probably Spain's best-known dish, it has as many variations as there are Spanish chefs. Based on saffron-flavored rice and olive oil, it may contain any kind of fish, shellfish, chicken, sausage, green peas, beans, bell peppers, or any combination of these. Because it is complicated to make, it may be offered for a minimum of two people; the menu may warn you that there will be a 20- to 30-minute wait if you order it. Connoisseurs will tell you not to order it in the evening because it will be left over from lunch; but, in our experience, better restaurants make it fresh to order.

*Pescados y mariscos* (fish and shellfish): *Rape* (angler fish), *merluza* (hake), *mero* and *ubina* (sea bass), *lenguado* (sole), and *trucha* (trout) are the common fish varieties. *Pez Espada* (swordfish, also called *aguja* and *emperador*) is often offered thickly sliced like steak and can be superb. *Gambas* (shrimp), *langosta* (a small variety of lobster), *langostino* (large prawns), *almejas* (clams), and *mejillones* (mussels) are common shellfish. In the northern part of Spain there are also *vieiras* (scallops), *centollo* (spider crab), and *changurro* (sizzling crab casserole). A *zarzuela* is a commonly offered fish stew and has the usual infinite number of variations. Although not native to Spain, salmon is popular and frequently found on the menu.

Preparation: Many of the terms describing preparation are relatively meaningless because they simply refer to the origin—*a la Bilbaína*, for example, means Bilbao style, but it never seems to mean the same thing twice. A few terms that are reliable: *al ajillo* (sautéed in garlic), *a la plancha* (grilled), *al pil pil* (sautéed with garlic and olive oil, often with hot pepper), *frito* (fried), *cocido* (stewed), *a la brasa* or *a la parrilla* (charcoal broiled), *en brocheta* (skewered), *al horno* (baked in the oven), and *asado* (roasted).

## GEOGRAPHY

Few people realize that Spain, tucked away on the Iberian Peninsula, is actually one of Europe's largest countries (second only to France). Also surprisingly, Spain boasts one of the highest average elevations in all of Europe (second only to Switzerland). To continue its accolades, Spain has the highest capital in all of Europe—Madrid. Plus, Spain is tops in other areas: her rich, red soil is perfect for growing olives and her gentle hills are conducive to the production of grapes.

## GOVERNMENT

The current government of Spain (dating from 1975 when Franco died) is a constitutional monarchy similar to Great Britain. The monarchy is hereditary and is balanced by a parliament (called the Cortés). The president is elected in somewhat the same fashion as the British prime minister. The traditional regions, such as Catalonia and Andalusia, which grew up during the Middle Ages, have been granted a degree of self-control that might be compared to the powers held by the states in the United States. Strong regionalist identification has always been, and still is, characteristic of Spanish politics.

## HISTORY

EARLY PERIOD: Traces of cave-dwelling prehistoric man—Neolithic, Megalithic, and Magdalenian—have been discovered all over the peninsula. Around the 6th century B.C., the area was widely inhabited by the Celts from the north and the Iberians from Africa. The Phoenicians, the Greeks, and especially the Carthaginians founded ports at Cadiz (1100 B.C.), Málaga, Huelva, and Ampurias (north of Barcelona). As a result of the Second Punic War (2nd century B.C.), the peninsula became a Roman colony.

ROMAN PERIOD: Hispania was the most heavily colonized of all Rome's dominions and, thus, the basis for modern Spanish culture. Its language, legal system, and religion all spring from that 600-year period. A number of Roman emperors were born in Spain of either Roman or Hispanic parents, and Julius Caesar himself served there and learned the art of bullfighting. When the entire Roman Empire was overrun by the Germanic tribes from the north, Spain suffered the same fate.

VISIGOTH PERIOD: By the 5th century A.D. the Visigoths had subdued the peninsula almost completely (the Basque area was an exception) and had adopted Roman Catholicism as their own. Their feudalistic system saw the origin of the traditional

Spanish regions as kingdoms were combined and divided over the next centuries. Their political system involved a monarch who served at the pleasure of the feudal lords and was thus subject to considerable instability as the kaleidoscope of dynastic unions changed constantly. This characteristic strife provided the opportunity, in 711, for the Moors (Islamic Africans) to invade and sweep across the peninsula from south to north in the space of two decades.

MOORISH PERIOD: The Moors were tolerant people and allowed a diversity of religions to co-exist. At that point in history, they represented the highest level of civilization in the western world and contributed greatly to Spanish culture—still evident today in Spanish architecture, painting, philosophy, and science. Córdoba, by the 10th century, was perhaps the most advanced city in Europe. Nevertheless, the Spanish Christians regrouped in the inaccessible mountains of Asturias to launch a crusade to retake their country from Moslem domination, an endeavor that was to last almost eight centuries.

RECONQUEST PERIOD: Legend has it that a Christian leader named Pelayo set up the Kingdom of Asturias after the first defeat of the Moors at Covadonga in 718. The Christians finally established their capital at León in 914. Under their control were Asturias and part of Burgos. The remains of St. James the Apostle were discovered in Galicia, and he became the patron saint of the Reconquest, as well as an object of devotion for millions of pilgrims who made the difficult journey along The Way of St. James (through France and across northern Spain) to venerate the holy remains. The pilgrimage to Santiago de Compostela is still made, albeit by more modern means. By the 11th century, as the frontier between the territories of the Christians and the Moors moved slowly southward, it became fortified with castles and, through various marriages and intrigues, the Kingdom of Castille (the name comes from "castle") had come into existence. During approximately the same period, the Basques began their own process of reconquest that included Catalonia and the eastern coastal areas. During this period, border battles were constant, both between the Christian kingdoms and between the Christians and the Moors.

By 1248, the Castilian campaign had recaptured most of southern Spain from the Moors, including Seville, conquered by Ferdinand III (later to become known as St. Ferdinand). Castile, now united with León, included most of the western half and the southern peninsula; except for Portugal, which had been established as a separate kingdom in the 11th century.

Meanwhile, the monarchs of Aragón had become supreme on the east side of the peninsula (as well as in Sicily and Naples) and, when united with Catalonia, ruled from southern France to Valencia. The scene was now set for the transcendental step that would lead to the creation of the modern Spanish nation: the marriage of the heir to the Aragonese throne, Ferdinand V, to the heir to the throne of Castile, Isabella I, thenceforth known as *Los Reyes Católicos* (The Catholic Monarchs).

MODERN PERIOD: Ferdinand (who was a model prince in Machiavelli's famous work of that name) and Isabella spent most of their reign strengthening the monarchy and expanding their dominions, including financing the expedition of Columbus. Their daughter, Juana (the Mad), was too handicapped to rule and so her son Charles was elevated to the throne when Ferdinand died. Charles' father was Phillip the Fair of the Hapsburgs, the family who were in control of the Holy Roman Empire which included half of Europe and most of the western hemisphere, so Charles also gained the title of Emperor Charles V. His son, Phillip, to whom he abdicated the crown in 1556, soon added Portugal to his domain. Portugal held an empire of its own, including Brazil in the New World and Mozambique in Africa, as well as several high-powered trading enclaves in Asia. By the end of the 16th century, Spain's dominions literally ringed the world.

The 17th century saw, however, a serious decline in the monarchy first with Phillip III, then Phillip IV, and then Charles II, all exhibiting decreasing capacity to rule wisely and increasing desire to live licentiously on the vast income from their New World mineral riches. During this century, Portugal and many of the European territories were lost. When Charles II died in 1700 without an heir, the Bourbons of France took the throne because Charles' sister had married into that royal family. (The current king, Juan Carlos, is a Bourbon.) The series of Bourbons who ruled during the 18th century—Phillip V,

Charles III, Charles IV, and Ferdinand VII—proved to be only marginally better than the Hapsburgs who preceded them, so Spain's holdings continued to dwindle, culminating in the loss of all the American possessions by 1825 (except the Caribbean islands and the Philippines). In 1808, Napoleon seduced the decadent Ferdinand VII with the good life in France, meanwhile installing his own brother on the Spanish throne. The Spaniards reacted swiftly, starting on the *dos de mayo* (the second of May) of the same year and, with the help of the British (for the first and only time in history), soon regained the crown for Ferdinand. The scene was set for continuing conflict when Ferdinand's brother, Don Carlos, at the head of Basque and Navarrese extremists, disputed Ferdinand's claim to the throne.

The 19th century was thus characterized by three so-called "Carlist Wars" of succession and, in 1898, the Spanish-American War. The Bourbons did manage to hold the throne, but lost the remaining territory of the Empire (Cuba, Puerto Rico, Santo Domingo, and the Philippines). This loss gave rise to widespread intellectual speculation on the causes of Spain's decline by the so-called Generation of 1898.

The early years of the 20th century saw the rise of new populist ideas and continuing labor unrest. In 1923, General Miguel Primo de Rivera established a dictatorship with Alfonso XIII's support. The unrest continued, however, especially in Catalonia. In 1931, the King was forced to abdicate and go into exile by the Republican (essentially socialist) party, which, in the same year, proclaimed the government to be Republican. In 1936, the elections were won by the socialist forces and José Antonio Primo de Rivera (Miguel's son) was head of a rightist revolutionary party. In the same year, the revolutionaries began an all-out civil war in the south under the direction of General Francisco Franco. Soon afterward, Germany supported the rebels (Hitler was planning to conquer Europe and used Spain as a testing ground for his weapons), and the Republicans were supported by the Soviet Union (allegedly in exchange for some 50 metric tons of gold reserves) and the International Brigade (American volunteers served in the Abraham Lincoln Brigade). Ernest Hemingway covered the war as a journalist and later immortalized the brutality of it in *For Whom The Bell Tolls*. By 1939, the Franco forces had won the war, over a million Spaniards had died and another half-million were in exile.

As a means of gaining Hitler's support, Spain had promised to remain neutral in any wars he engaged in, and was thus not directly involved in World War II. After the war, Spain found itself somewhat of an outcast in international circles because of its neutrality and generally perceived sympathy to Germany. It finally became a member of the United Nations in 1955 and returned to active diplomatic involvement, but with limited success due to the authoritarian regime headed by *El Caudillo* (The Chief), Generalissimo Francisco Franco.

In providing for his succession, Franco proclaimed that Spain was a monarchy and Juan Carlos (born in 1938), grandson of Alfonso XIII, would be the future king. When Franco died in 1975, the young king was installed and the process of creating a constitution began. The document was approved in 1978 and orderly elections have occurred since that time. The death of Franco did not signify the disappearance of rightist sentiment, however, and, as late as 1981, the right-wing military attempted a coup. Juan Carlos reacted swiftly to put it down and thus reassured the world that he was firmly a democratic ruler.

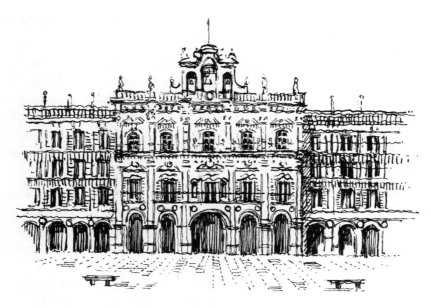

*Plaza Mayor, Salamanca*

## PLAZAS

It may be helpful to understand the general layout of most of the cities and towns of Spain. The "heart" of most of them is the main plaza, often referred to as the *Plaza Mayor*. Some larger cities, like Madrid, have a central plaza in the old quarter plus others in the more recently constructed sections of town. Small towns usually have just one main plaza in the center of the old quarter, the vicinity you probably most want to visit. The main plaza is frequently the liveliest area of the city and is often surrounded by shops and outdoor cafés. This will typically be the site of the cathedral and other historic buildings and the area where the ancient custom of the *paseo* (evening stroll) takes place. Plazas serve as excellent orientation points. There is usually parking either in the plaza itself or in a nearby garage, which makes for a good place to park your car since it will be easy to find and you are in the heart of the sightseeing area.

## REGIONS AND PROVINCES

Spain is divided into regions, each of which has its own distinct personality and flavor. The landscape changes constantly and as you move from one region to another, you feel as if you are visiting totally different countries. The regions are further divided into provinces. At the bottom of each hotel's description, we indicate the region where it is located, while the province is shown in the hotel's address. The provinces are extremely important since there are many towns with identical names, so you need to know in which province your hotel is located in order not to get lost.

## SIESTA

Except for restaurants, almost every place of business closes for two to three hours in the day, sometime between 1 and 5 pm. This includes all but the largest tourist attractions (e.g. the Prado), most stores (El Corte Inglés department store is an exception), and offices. (Banks don't reopen to the public in the afternoon.) So, about the only activities in which to engage during the siesta are dining, drowsing, walking, or driving. You will most likely find "Spanish time" easy to adapt to.

## TELEPHONES

Telephone calls made from your hotel room can be exceedingly expensive if you charge the call to your hotel bill. The easiest and least expensive way to call the USA is to use your cellphone.

## TIPPING

As everywhere, tipping is not a simple matter on which to give advice. Most restaurants and hotels include *servicio* in the bill, but a small tip is appropriate when the service is good, especially in restaurants frequented by tourists. "Small" means different things to different people, but certainly should not exceed 5%. In informal bars and cafeterias, no tip is expected.

# TOURIST OFFICES OF SPAIN

The Spanish tourist offices are a rich source of information about Spain. You can visit their website at *www.okspain.org* or *www.spain.info,* or write in advance of your holiday for information. Their contacts are as follows:

USA: Tourist Office of Spain, 845 North Michigan Avenue, Suite 915-East, Chicago, IL 60611, tel: (312) 642-1992, fax: (312) 642-9817, email: *chicago@Tourspain.es.*

Tourist Office of Spain, San Vicente Plaza Building, 8383 Wilshire Boulevard, Suite 960, Beverly Hills, CA 90211, tel: (323) 658-7188, fax: (323) 658-1061, email: *losangeles@Tourspain.es.*

Tourist Office of Spain, 1221 Brickell·Avenue, Miami, FL 33131, tel: (305) 358-1992, fax: (305) 358-8223, email: *miami@Tourspain.es.*

Tourist Office of Spain, 666 Fifth Avenue, 35th Floor, New York, NY 10103, tel: (212) 265-8822, fax: (212) 265-8864, email: *nuevayork@Tourspain.es.*

CANADA: Tourist Office of Spain, 2 Bloor Street West, Suite 3402, Toronto, Ontario, M4W 3E2, tel: (416) 961-3131, fax: (416) 961-1992, email: *toronto@Tourspain.es.*

ENGLAND: Spanish National Tourist Office, 22–23 Manchester Square, London W1M 5AP, tel: (020) 7486-8077, fax: (020) 7486-8034, email: *info.londres@Tourspain.es.*

SPAIN: Tourist Office of Spain, Plaza Mayor 3, 28012 Madrid, tel: 91-588-1636, fax: 91-366-5477, email: *infotur.spain@Tourspain.es.*

The Tourist Offices of Spain can provide you with general information or, at your request, specific information about towns, regions, and festivals. Local tourist offices (*oficina de turismo*) are found in most small towns throughout the country—they are well marked and usually located in the heart of the town or city. They offer an incomparable on-site resource, furnishing town maps and details on local and regional highlights that you might otherwise miss. Those in the regional capitals are especially well equipped to provide you with colorful and informative brochures on the surrounding area. Make the local *oficina de turismo* your first stop at each destination.

## TRAINS

The Spanish National Railways (called RENFE) has an extensive network of trains throughout the country with various rail passes, round-trip fares, and special rates available for children and seniors. Trains connect almost every city in Spain. In addition to the normal trains, there are others that offer exceptionally fast, convenient service. One of these is a bullet train called the *AVE*, which runs several times a day between Madrid and Seville with one stop en route in Córdoba. This once-cumbersome journey now takes a mere two and a half hours. The *AVE* is air conditioned, offers a choice of first- or second-class seating, and has cafeteria service. The *Talgo 200* high-speed trains connect Madrid and Málaga in four and a half hours and Madrid and Cadiz in five, and offer amenities such as personal audio/video systems. Tickets for both the *AVE* and the *Talgo 200* can be purchased in the USA through Rail Europe.

Also available are the *Estrella,* night trains with first- and second-class accommodation, sleeping compartments (berths or couchettes), and sometimes a restaurant or cafeteria service (depending upon the route and time of departure). For long-distance routes, the *Train-Hotel* offers a new dimension in train travel, providing top quality and comfort. These "traveling hotels" cover routes from Barcelona to Milan, Zurich, Paris, and Seville, and from Madrid to Paris, offering *Gran Clase* accommodation, superb restaurant service, and often such extras as individual videos in the carriages, private telephones, and personal attendants.

Rail tickets and passes can be purchased in the USA through Rail Europe, which you can access for information on schedules and the best possible fares. You can book tickets online through our website, *www.karenbrown.com.*

ANDALUSIAN EXPRESS: Spain's answer to the famous Orient Express is called the Andalusian Express (*Al-Andalus Expreso*). From the beginning of April to the end of

October, this luxurious *belle-époque* train travels weekly on a six-night package. Starting in Madrid or Seville, passengers spend five nights aboard the train, which travels through a landscape of olive groves and white towns, ending the trip in Seville or Madrid. A night in Madrid or Seville before the journey completes the package. This meticulously restored train from the 1920s has thirteen cars including two sumptuous dining cars, two bars (one resembles a London club, the other a chic European bistro), five richly paneled sleeping cars (each with six deluxe, double cabins and two luxury suites), and two shower cars (with twenty showers, each with its own private dressing room). All of the cabins have their own washbasin (suites also have private toilet and shower). This train is expensive, but offers a nostalgic journey that combines sightseeing excursions along with your meals and accommodations. Reservations for the Andalusian Express can be made in the United States through Marketing Ahead—tel: (212) 686-9213, toll free: (800) 223-1356, fax: (212) 686-0271, email: *mahrep@aol.com*. Identify yourself as a "Karen Brown traveler" using the code number KBG2006MA to get 5% discount (individuals only, please—this offer is not available through your travel agent). In Europe, reservations can be made through Iberrail in Madrid: tel: 91-571-5815, fax: 91-571-6056, email: *ibermad@iberrail.es*.

*Introduction–About Spain*

# About Itineraries

This section features itineraries covering most of Spain. They may be taken in whole or in part, or strung together for a longer journey. Each of the itineraries highlights a different region of the country, and they are of different lengths, enabling you to find one or more to suit your individual taste and schedule. At the beginning of each itinerary we suggest our recommended pacing to help you decide the amount of time to allocate to each region. You will enjoy yourself much more if you concentrate on a smaller number of destinations and stay for at least a couple of nights in each, rather than spending most of your precious vacation rushing from place to place. Each itinerary map shows all of the towns and villages in which we have a recommended place to stay.

We have intentionally not specified how many nights to stay at each destination—your personality and time restraints will dictate what is best for you. We strongly suggest concentrating your time in fewer locations in order to relax, unpack, and savor the atmosphere and novelty of the spot. We recommend choosing a few hotels that most appeal to you and using them as hubs from which to explore the surrounding regions.

If you're new to Spain and planning a trip there, we hope that upon reading through the itineraries and hotel descriptions, you'll get a feel for which places merit the most time and which can be done justice with an overnight stay. In other words, this guide should be a reference and not a prescription for your personalized trip.

# HOW TO FIND YOUR WAY

ITINERARY MAPS: Accompanying each itinerary is a map showing the routing and places of interest along the way. These are an artist's renderings and are not meant to replace a good commercial map. Before departure, it is truly vital to purchase detailed maps showing highway numbers, expressways, alternate routes, and distances. There are many maps you can buy covering the whole of Spain, but these are not precise enough. Michelin has seven regional maps of Spain that are exceptionally reliable. We also use the Michelin Motoring Atlas of Spain and Portugal with the same scale as the regional maps, where 1 cm = 4 km. We sell Michelin maps in our website store at *www.karenbrown.com*.

# FAVORITE PLACES

As you read through our itineraries, you might become muddled as to choices. All of Spain is enchanting—filled with towns that brim with the romance of yesteryear. To assist you, we have described some of our favorite places. Many of these are so well known that they are probably already on your schedule to see, but others are gems that we were surprised to discover. The following list of "favorites" is very subjective—destinations that we think outstanding. Most of these are also featured in our individual itineraries. In the back of the guide you can find hotel accommodations in all of the following places:

ARCOS DE LA FRONTERA (Andalusia): Arcos de la Frontera is one of the many charming towns dotting the hills that rise from the Costa del Sol. Its setting is very special—the indisputably beautiful town is set on a rocky promontory with cliffs dropping down to the Guadalete River. The town has narrow, sloping streets lined by whitewashed houses, a magnificent cathedral, and several charming places to stay.

ÁVILA (Castilla y León): Ávila cannot help being on every list of special places. Located conveniently close to Madrid, the town is one of the best-preserved in Spain. Try to approach from the west where you get the most impressive first impact of the town—

you will be astounded by the perfection of the 12th-century crenelated walls punctuated by mighty stone towers surrounding the city. These medieval fortifications are without a doubt some of the finest remaining in Europe. Within the town are a maze of narrow streets and a splendid cathedral that must not be missed.

BARCELONA (Catalonia): Barcelona, the second largest city in Spain, is on the Mediterranean coast, not far from the French border. We have a complete chapter devoted to this delightful city (see *Barcelona Highlights*).

CARMONA (Andalusia): Carmona is located just a short drive east of Seville and makes a delightful day's excursion, or overnight. The walled city crowns a small hill that rises out of the vast plains of the Guadalquivir. The main entrance is on the lower level through the old Moorish gates, leading to a maze of narrow streets that twist up the hill. Although there are several churches to peek into, the main attraction is the town itself. In its former glory, Carmona was obviously a town of great wealth—the streets are lined with 17th- and 18th-century palaces built by nobility.

CHINCHÓN (Madrid): Chinchón is just a tiny town, about an hour's drive south of Madrid. Being close to a major city makes Chinchón even more special—it's a surprise to find such a quaint, unspoiled town nearby. The fascinating feature of Chinchón is its Plaza Mayor, a real gem. The vast plaza is enclosed on all sides by picturesque three-storied, whitewashed houses with rustic red-tiled roofs. A double row of wooden balconies stretch out from the upper two stories, forming a perfect perch for watching the bullfights. Yes, bullfights: during the season, the plaza is completely sealed and transforms into a picturesque bullring.

CUENCA (Castilla-La Mancha): Cuenca is only about a two-hour drive southeast of Madrid, yet is not as well-known as many of Spain's towns that, in our estimation, are not nearly as spectacular. If time allows, definitely include Cuenca—and plan to stay for several days because there is so much to see in the area: the dramatic castle at Belmonte, the Romanesque church in Arcas, the fanciful rock formations in *La Ciudad Encantada* (The Enchanted City), and the Roman amphitheater at Segóbriga. But Cuenca, itself, is the highlight. The town is perched high on the top of a rock formation that drops straight down to the River Huécar. Clinging impossibly to the cliffs are the *casas colgadas* (hanging houses) whose wooden balconies stretch out over open air. Narrow streets and steep stairways make walking an adventure. Spanning the deep gorge carved by the river, a narrow, walking bridge connects the old town with the cathedral (now housing a parador) on the other side of the chasm.

GRANADA (Andalusia): Granada is instantly a favorite of all who visit. When you see the mountain setting, it is easy to understand why this was the last stronghold of the Moors. From its lofty perch, the Alhambra, a fairy tale of palaces built around courtyards filled with flowers, fruit trees, tranquil pools, and beautiful fountains, dominates the newer city. The interior walls are covered with tiny, colorful tiles creating intricate patterns that are enhanced by slender columns, graceful arches, and fancy plasterwork. Obviously, the Moors were great romantics—all the senses are rewarded from the fragrance of the gardens to the soothing melody of the fountains. You must not rush your time here.

GUADALUPE (Extremadura): Guadalupe was a marvelous surprise to us. We knew about its Franciscan monastery, where pilgrims have come since the 14th century to worship the Black Virgin of Guadalupe, but we did not expect to find a town of such utter charm. Many of Spain's medieval towns are stunning in their central core, but modern civilization has crept right to their periphery. Not so with Guadalupe: the town exemplifies great architectural purity and there is nothing new to jar the senses.

HONDARRIBIA (Pays Basque): Hondarribia—on some maps named Fuenterrabía—is a picturesque coastal town in northern Spain almost on the border of France. Our preference always gravitates towards towns that are unspoiled and Hondarribia certainly fits the bill. Although close to traffic-congested San Sebastián, Hondarribia maintains the quiet ambiance of a small medieval town. It is located on a gentle hill overlooking a sparkling blue bay lined with modern holiday condominiums and dotted with colorful yachts. Yet within the walled town itself, time stops still. Starting at the lower gates, the streets lead up the hill, terminating in a large plaza with one side opening to a belvedere overlooking the bay. Another side of the plaza is faced by one of Spain's most special paradors, Parador de Hondarribia, while brilliantly colored houses with wooden balconies line the other two.

LEÓN (Castilla y León): León—once the capital of Castilla y León—is a fascinating city dating back to the 10th century, just begging to be explored. Narrow streets spread like a maze in every direction, leading to quaint squares accented by colorful fountains. León's most outstanding sight is its gorgeous, 13th-century Gothic-style cathedral with 125 splendid, stained-glass windows that must not be missed. Another superb edifice is the *Antiguo Convento de San Marcos* (Monastery of St. Mark), one part of which unbelievably houses one of Spain's most spectacular paradors. If overnighting in León, you must stay here, where you have the chance to step into living history.

*Antiguo Convento de San Marcos*

MADRID (Madrid): Madrid needs no introduction. Spain's capital, located right in the center of the country, is usually the first stop for every tourist coming to Spain. Although a large city, it is a beautiful one, filled with parks and fountains and some of the finest museums in the world. Definitely not to be missed. We have a complete chapter devoted to this wonderful city (see *Madrid and More*).

MÉRIDA (Extremadura): Mérida is a must if you have even the slightest interest in archaeology. The Roman ruins here are astounding and conveniently grouped together so you can wander from one to the other. Especially awesome is the theater built by Agrippa, the son-in-law of the Emperor Augustus. A semi-circle of tiered-stone bleachers faces onto a huge stage backed by a two-storied gallery held up by slender columns interspersed with marble statues. Just across the street from the park where the ruins are located is a stunning museum—a modern edifice of admirable design with a massive, arched, brick ceiling pierced by skylights that set off to perfection the many Roman artifacts displayed within.

PEDRAZA DE LA SIERRA (Castilla y León): Pedraza de la Sierra became an instant favorite. Obviously it is popular with Madridians who flock here on weekends to escape the heat of the city, dine in Pedraza's charming restaurants, and overnight in her pretty hotels. Weekends are busy, but if you go midweek, you will find a quiet, enchanting, walled village built upon a small knoll with views out over the countryside in every direction. Walls encircle the lower part of the hill and a castle crowns the summit. The Plaza Mayor is a gem—almost like a stage setting with picturesque houses with wide balconies facing the square. The narrow side streets are lined with medieval houses, many with family crests above the stone doorways.

PICOS DE EUROPA (Asturias): Picos de Europa is a range of mountains just before you reach the coast going north from Madrid. What most people relate to when they think of Spain's mountains is the Pyrenees, but for sheer drama, in our estimation they don't compare with the Picos de Europa. A national park has been set aside to protect these magnificent peaks and provide a paradise for those who want to enjoy nature at its finest. The jagged limestone mountains thrust straight up into the sky, a majestic spectacle reminiscent of the mighty Dolomites in Italy. Lush meadows enhanced by sparkling mountain streams complete the picture of perfection. This is a paradise for those who love hiking, mountain climbing, horseback riding, or fishing.

RONDA (Andalusia): Ronda is tucked high in the hills up a winding road from the Costa del Sol. A rich Arabic and Christian heritage has left its mark on the town that is filled with palatial houses. It was in Ronda that bullfighting first began, and even today bullfights are still held in the colorful bullring. However, it is the setting that makes Ronda stand out from many of the other white villages of Andalusia—the town is split by a deep gorge spanned by an incredibly high, 18th-century arched stone bridge.

SALAMANCA (Castilla y León): The Tormes River flows below the city with roads leading up from the riverbanks to meet at the top of the hill in the bustling Plaza Mayor. And what a plaza this is! The plaza is an architectural masterpiece built in the 18th century by Philip V. It is enclosed by three-storied buildings constructed with a pastel, ochre-colored stone whose ground levels are fronted by a series of identical arches that form a dazzling arcade all around the square. Along with all of this come crowds and lots of souvenir shops.

SANTIAGO DE COMPOSTELA (Galicia): Santiago de Compostela is a highlight of Spain and well worth a detour if you are anywhere in the northwestern part of the country. According to legend, Saint James's grave was found by simple shepherds guided to the site by a field of stars, and his remains reside in a shrine in Santiago's magnificent cathedral. Since the 11th century, the city has been the destination of millions of pilgrims who have made the perilous journey by foot across Europe to worship at the shrine. The first travel guide ever written was printed to help these pilgrims along their way. To ease their journey, hospices sprang up along the route, several of which are now paradors featured in this book. Santiago's cathedral faces onto a stunning plaza, still bustling with pilgrims. Facing onto the same plaza is one of the original hospices, now housing one of Spain's most deluxe hotels, Parador Hotel Dos Reis Católicos.

SANTILLANA DEL MAR (Cantabria): Santillana del Mar is a charming small town in the north of Spain. There are no magnificent cathedrals or museums. Rather, it is the town itself that is the magnet. It is amazing that it could remain so untouched—the whole town is like a living museum and as you wander along the charming streets. It is as if you have stepped back in time. There are no modern buildings, no hint of the 20th century. Stone mansions, many with the noble owner's crest above the door, line the narrow lanes. Just 2 kilometers away are the famous Altamira Caves with their incredible prehistoric drawings.

SEGOVIA (Castilla y León): Without a doubt Segovia has the most dramatic location: it is set high on a rocky promontory surrounded by the Rio Eresma and Rio Clamores. At the city's western end is the Alcázar, with its multitude of gabled roofs and turrets rising from tall crags—the quintessential fairytale castle. The cathedral is a magnificent Gothic affair dating from 1525. The aqueduct, begun in the 1st century A.D., carried water to the town until the 19th century. It's an excellent town for walking, shopping, and people watching from a restaurant on the Plaza Mayor.

SEVILLE (Andalusia): Hands down, Seville is our favorite major city in Spain. It really has all the ingredients to make it special: a lovely setting, a manageable size for walking, a romantic old quarter, beautiful buildings, many parks, friendly people, good shopping, great restaurants, and excellent hotels. For more in-depth information on Seville, see our itinerary *Seville Highlights*.

SIGÜENZA (Castilla-La Mancha): Sigüenza is a small village northeast of Madrid, tucked into the barren, rocky landscape. This picture-perfect town of pretty, pastel-colored houses roofed with thick, rustic tiles seems a world away from modern civilization, yet it is less than a two-hour drive from Madrid. As always, there is the Plaza Mayor in the center of town and also a lovely, 12th-century cathedral, which is well worth a visit (be sure to see the exquisite statue of Martín Vázquez de Arce, squire to Isabella the Catholic). The houses in Sigüenza climb in tiers up the hillside to an imposing castle that has been converted into a parador.

SOS DEL REY CATÓLICO (Aragón): Sos del Rey Católico is one of the most picturesque towns in Aragón. This is an area of many desolate, windswept, rocky hills, often crowned by a tiny town piercing the sky. For many years, these walled towns were deserted, but a few have survived, including Sos del Rey Católico. The town has more an air of a museum that a vibrant lived in town. It was named for the Ferdinand the Catholic, who was born here in 1452 and went on to unite Spain. Be sure to wear sturdy walking shoes, for the town is built on a hill that is laced with cobbled streets and walkways that always seem to go straight up or down.

TOLEDO (Castilla-La Mancha): Toledo is justifiably popular: hardly any tourist visits Madrid without taking a side trip to Toledo. Most come for the day; but to enjoy the town to its fullest, try to spend the night so that you can settle in after the busloads of tourists have left. The site itself is worth a journey—Toledo huddles on a plateau that rises steeply above the River Tagus, which forms a steep ravine looping around the city. Within its mighty walls, Toledo is a virtual museum. Don't miss the spectacular Gothic cathedral with paintings by El Greco, Van Dyck, and Goya; or the Iglesia de Santo Tomé where El Greco's best work, the *Burial of Count Orgaz*, is displayed. Also, see the Alcázar, a huge 13th-century fortress converted by Charles V into a royal palace.

TRUJILLO (Extremadura): Trujillo is closely linked with the conquest of America, since many of the explorers who ventured to the New World were born here. Most famous of these is Francisco Pizarro, the conqueror of Peru, whose impressive statue stands in the Plaza Mayor—there is an identical statue in Lima. The Plaza Mayor is especially interesting, with a distinct personality distinguishing it from those in many other towns. Its shape is irregular and the ground slopes so that the buildings border it on various levels. Be sure to take the trail up the hill to the 10th-century fortress, which hovers above the town. Although the fortress is mostly in ruins, the vistas are lovely.

# Itinerary Overview

Santiago de
Compostela

Old Castile and The
Cantabrian Coast

Costa Brava
and Beyond

Pilgrimage
to Santiago

Treasures Off
The Beaten Track

Barcelona

Madrid
and More

Madrid

Cradle of the
Conquistadors

Moorish
Memories

Andalusian
Adventures

Málaga

# About Hotels

There still exist in Spain numerous places where you may find yourselves the only English-speaking guests in the castle. Yes, *castle!* Private proprietors, as well as the government, have created some of the most romantic hotels in all of Europe in historical sites such as castles, palaces, convents, and monasteries—many found in locations boasting some of the most spectacular sights in all of Europe.

In *Places to Stay* at the back of this guide is a selection of hotels that we consider to be the most delightful in Spain. A detailed description, an illustration, and pertinent information are provided on each one. Some are large and posh, offering every amenity and a price to match; others small and cozy (often with correspondingly smaller prices), providing only the important amenities, such as private baths, personality, and gracious personnel. Our choices were not governed by room rate, but rather by romantic ambiance, location, and warmth of welcome. We have visited every hotel that appears in the book, and our selection covers a wide price range—tailored to fit every budget.

Sometimes we could not find an ideal hotel in an important sightseeing location where we felt we needed to have a place to recommend. In such situations, we have chosen for you what we consider to be the best place to stay in the area. We try to be consistently candid and honest in our appraisals. We feel that if you know what to expect, you won't be disappointed.

## HANDICAP FACILITIES

If there is *at least* one guestroom that is accessible by wheelchair, it is noted with the symbol &. This is not the same as saying it meets full disability standards. In reality, it can be anything from a basic ground-floor room to a fully equipped facility. Please discuss your requirements when you call your chosen place to stay to see if they have accommodation that is suitable for you.

# HOW TO FIND YOUR HOTEL

In the Maps section, at the front of the book, there is a key map of the whole of Spain, plus 6 maps showing each recommended hotel's location. The pertinent map number is shown on the *top line* of each hotel's description.

Our maps give you only a broad concept of where the hotels are located. You *must* buy detailed regional maps before leaving home. Because they are exceptionally accurate, have excellent indexes, and are readily available, we use Michelin maps as a cross-reference. On the second-to-last line of each hotel's description, we also indicate the number of the Michelin map on which the town where your hotel is located can be found. We sell Michelin maps in our website store at *www.karenbrown.com*.

# ICONS

We have these icons in the guidebooks and more on our website, *www.karenbrown.com*. ❄ Air conditioning in bedrooms, ☕ Breakfast included in room rate, 🧒 Children welcome (age given on website), ♨ Cooking classes offered, 💳 Credit cards accepted, ☎ Direct-dial telephone in room, ⛰ Dinner served upon request, 🐕 Dogs by special request, 🛗 Elevator, 🏋 Exercise room, @ Internet or Wireless access available for guests ⊘ Some non-smoking rooms, P Parking available (free or paid), 🍴 Restaurant, 🛎 Room Service, 🌿 Spa, 🏊 Swimming pool, 🎾 Tennis, 📺 TV with English channels in bedrooms, 💍 Wedding facilities, ♿ Wheelchair friendly bedrooms, ⚓ Beach nearby, 🏌 Golf course nearby, 🚶 Hiking trails nearby, 🐎 Horseback riding nearby, ⛷ Skiing nearby, 🏄 Water sports nearby. Icons allow us to provide additional information about our recommended properties. When using our website to supplement the guides, positioning the cursor over an icon will give you further details.

# PARADORS

The Spanish government operates a system of hotels called *paradors* (literally "stopping places"), which are widely acknowledged to constitute the most outstanding bargain in the country for quality received. The first paradors were created in 1928 in an effort to encourage tourists to those areas of Spain lacking adequate hotel facilities. Over the years, the number of paradors has grown tremendously as new ones have been added (periodically others are taken temporarily "off the market" while closed for renovation). A few of the paradors are situated in starkly modern buildings with no concession to an old-world theme; others are of new construction, but built in a creative regional style. However, the great majority of paradors are imaginatively installed in remodeled historic buildings. Numerous paradors are simply stunning and in breathtaking locations, such as the Parador de Granada in Granada—imagine staying in a 15th-century convent literally *within* the Alhambra grounds, just steps from its fabulous palaces and gardens!

The paradors are not privately owned so do not expect the proprietor to be at the front desk to greet you warmly. The management is very professional and the quality of service dependable. The mood of each parador seems to reflect the talents of the individual in charge. The excellence of some of the paradors shows that there are indeed some extremely capable managers in the group—some of the best are women. Also, the amenities vary between the paradors: almost all that we visited had hairdryers, many had small refrigerators in the room, and some even had bathrobes and turndown service.

While you could travel throughout Spain staying practically only in paradors, we also recommend a variety of other charming hotel accommodations. We give in-depth descriptions of our favorite paradors, along with many other choices of exceptional places to stay. We have not included every parador in Spain in this book, although we have visited almost all of them.

All paradors have good to excellent dining rooms serving regional culinary specialties from a set menu or *à la carte*. Local wines are also featured. They do not specialize in light fare, however, so be prepared to eat substantially. If you follow the Spanish tradition of taking your big meal at midday, paradors provide good stopping places en route. If you don't feel up to two large meals a day, at most paradors (and hotels) you can frequently purchase a sandwich or snack at the bar. The set menu for lunch or dinner usually features a three-course meal. Food-wise, another bonus is that all of the paradors serve a generous buffet breakfast with an attractively displayed assortment of meats, cheeses, breads, fruits, juices, yogurts, and even sometimes egg dishes. Breakfast is not included in the tariff.

Another advantage to staying at a parador is that there are almost always signs that lead you from the edge of the town (sometimes even from the freeway) to the parador. This may sound like a minor advantage, but it can save time and frustration.

Not only are there stunning contemporary paradors, such as the sensational Parador de Ronda, but the "old timers" are radically improving. As each parador takes its turn for renovation, the most talented interior designers in the country are being hired to plan the decor. The refurbished properties are emerging as real beauties—rivaling the finest private hotels in Spain.

In addition to being an overall good value, paradors offer some extremely appealing rates for travel off-season. These special rates (which are not available at every parador) are most frequently offered mid-week and usually begin the first of November and last until the end of June. The exact dates and qualifications vary at each parador. Another terrific value (if you are over 60 years old) is the senior rates that give a whopping discount—35% discount for the first and second nights and 50% discount for the third night on. These senior rates are offered only off-season, and at some hotels are valid only mid-week—the rules vary with each parador. So, if you are traveling off-season (frequently the nicest time to travel anyway), be *sure* to ask if there are any discounts available.

PARADOR RESERVATIONS—MARKETING AHEAD: Reservations for all of the paradors (and many of the other hotels featured in this guide) can be made with Marketing Ahead, the Paradores de Turismo's representative in New York. You can call, fax, email, or use the hot link from our website to make reservations. Identify yourself as a Karen Brown traveler using the code number KBG2006MA to get 5% discount (individuals only please—this offer is not available through your travel agent). Reservations are confirmed within 48 hours and require a $50 deposit (per hotel). Reservations must be prepaid 30 days prior to departure from the USA and cover the room, tax, and breakfast. Vouchers showing proof of payment will be mailed to you. The price in dollars is guaranteed upon prepayment (prices displayed locally in euros may fluctuate with the exchange rate). For further information contact Marketing Ahead, 381 Park Avenue South, Suite 718, New York, NY 10016, tel: (212) 686-9213, toll free: (800) 223-1356, fax: (212) 686-0271, email: *mahrep@aol.com.*

# PAYMENT BY CREDIT CARDS

Whether or not an establishment accepts credit cards is indicated in the list of icons at the bottom of each description by the symbol ▭. We have also specified in the bottom details which cards are accepted as follows: none, AX–American Express, MC–MasterCard, VS–Visa, or simply, all major.

# RATES

Rates for paradors are their published 2007 rates. All other properties are those quoted to us, either verbally or by correspondence, for 2008. The rates given generally cover the least expensive to the most expensive double room (two people), not including the 7% tax (IVA). *Please always check prices and terms when making a reservation.*

The rates hotels charge are regulated by the Spanish government, with inflation causing periodic upward adjustments in prices (usually at the beginning of the year). Most hotels have an intricate system of rates, which vary according to season, local special events, and additional features such as sitting rooms, balconies, and views. We give the price of breakfast where it is not included. May through June and September through October are lovely times to travel and frequently offer slightly lower rates than July and August, which are the two hottest months in most of Spain. If you can travel in early spring, late fall, or winter, you can often realize substantial savings. Many hotels also have rates for *media pensión* or *pensión completa*, which mean breakfast and an additional one or two meals. These are often an excellent value and should be investigated where convenient. Children are welcome virtually everywhere in Spain, and frequently there are special rates for those under 14 years old.

Breakfast in all the paradors (and at many of the hotels) is a bountiful buffet where you can have all you want to eat. If you decline breakfast, be sure it can be broken down separately on your bill—in a few places it must be included.

# RESERVATIONS

It is important to understand that once reservations for accommodation are confirmed, whether verbally, by phone, or in writing, you are under contract. This means that the proprietor is obligated to provide the accommodation that was promised and that you are obligated to pay for it. If you cannot, you are liable for a portion of the accommodation charges plus your deposit. Although some proprietors do not strictly enforce a cancellation policy, many—particularly the smaller properties in our book—simply cannot afford not to do so. Similarly, many airline tickets cannot be changed or refunded without penalty. We recommend insurance to cover these types of additional expenses arising from cancellation due to unforeseen circumstances. A link on our website (*www.karenbrown.com*) will connect you to a variety of insurance policies that can be purchased online.

Whether or not to reserve ahead is not a question with a simple answer: it depends upon the flexibility in your timetable and the season in which you are traveling. In peak season, all hotel space is at a premium and a super star (such as the Parador de Granada in Granada) frequently mandates reservations six to eight months in advance. Other popular hotels with limited rooms are similarly booked, especially those located in towns of particular tourist interest.

For those who prefer the comfort of knowing where you are going to lay your head each night, the following are various ways of making reservations:

EMAIL: This is our preferred way of making a reservation. All hotels featured on the Karen Brown website that have email addresses also have those addresses listed on their web page (This information is constantly kept updated.). You can link directly to a property from its page on our website using its email link. *Always spell out the month as Spaniards reverse the American month/day numbering system.*

FAX: Faxing is a quick way to make a reservation (remember to send your fax number for response). Dial the international access code (011), followed by the country code for Spain (34), then the local telephone number. Following below is a reservation request letter written in Spanish with an English translation. You can photocopy this to use for either your faxes or letters to Spain. (See "EMAIL" about dates.)

LETTER: If you plan early, you can write to the hotels directly for your reservations. Because the mail between the United States and Spain tends to be slow outside the large cities, allow six weeks for a reply. (See "EMAIL" about dates, and "FAX" for letter in Spanish.)

RESERVATION SERVICE: Most of the hotels in this guide can be booked through Marketing Ahead, who will make reservations and prepayments on your behalf. Further information can be found at the back of this book.

TELEPHONE: A convenient method of making reservations is to call, although you might not always find someone at the other end of the phone who speaks English. The advantage is you can have your answer immediately. Remember that Spain is six hours ahead of New York for most of the year. (See "FAX" for dialing instructions.)

# Reservation Request

*Muy señores nuestros*:

Dear Sirs:

*Rogamos reserven para* _____ *noche(s)*

We are writing to request (number of) night(s) at your hotel

*a partir del día* _____ *de* _____ año _____ *hasta el día* _____ *de* _____ año _____

Arriving   (day)       (month)   (year)       departing (day)   (month)         (year)

_____ *habitacion(es) sencilla(s)*

      number of single rooms

_____ *abitacion(es) doble(s)*

      number of double rooms

*con cama adicional* ____       *con vista al mar* ____       *con terraza* ____

with an extra bed           with a sea view          with a terrace

*con vista al patio* ____         *con vista a la plaza* ____      *en la parte Antigua* ____

facing the patio             facing the plaza           in the old part

*Somos* _____ *personas.*

We are (number of) persons in our party.

*Les rogamos nos informen sobre la disponibilidad de habitacion(es), el precio de la(s) misma(s), y el depósito requerido. En espera de su respuesta les saludamos, atentamente,*

Please advise availability, rate, and deposit needed. Awaiting your reply, we remain, sincerely,

YOUR NAME, ADDRESS, AND CONTACT INFORMATION.

44

# *Moorish Memories*

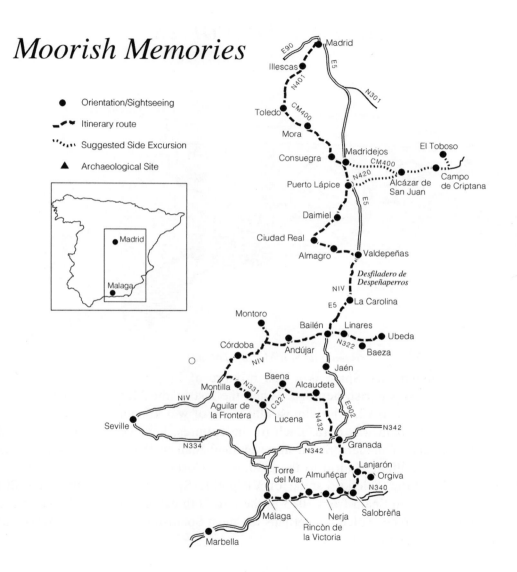

● Orientation/Sightseeing

▬ ▬ Itinerary route

''''''' Suggested Side Excursion

▲ Archaeological Site

Madrid

Malaga

Madrid

Illescas

Toledo

Mora

Consuegra

Puerto Lápice

Daimiel

Ciudad Real

Almagro

Valdepeñas

*Desfiladero de
Despeñaperros*

La Carolina

Montoro

Bailén

Linares

Ubeda

Córdoba

Andújar

Baeza

Jaén

Baena

Alcaudete

Montilla

Aguilar de
la Frontera

Lucena

Seville

Granada

Lanjarón

Orgiva

Torre
del Mar

Almuñécar

Salobreña

Málaga

Nerja

Rincòn de
la Victoria

Marbella

Madridejos

El Toboso

Campo
de Criptana

Alcázar de
San Juan

E90

E5

N401

CM400

N301

CM400

N420

E5

NIV

E5

N322

NIV

N331

C327

N432

E902

NIV

N342

N334

N342

N340

# Moorish Memories

*Puente de San Martin, Toledo*

The culture of contemporary Spain is a rich mixture of its prehistoric Celtic-Iberian, Roman, Visigothic, and Moorish heritage. When the last of the Moors (Moslems) were expelled from Granada in 1492, after almost 800 years of war known as the Reconquest, the modern nation of Spain was born. Each of the cultures, however, left its mark and nowhere is the variety of modern Spain more evident than in the area covered by this itinerary: from cosmopolitan Madrid to the glamorous Costa del Sol, playground of the jet set. You visit historic Toledo, capital of Visigothic Spain from the 6th to the 8th centuries and of Christian Spain from 1085 to the mid-16th century. Chosen home of the renowned painter, El Greco, Toledo is perhaps the most Spanish of all Spanish towns and a veritable open-air museum of history.

If you are an ardent Cervantes (or a *Man of La Mancha*) fan we offer a side trip across the plains of La Mancha to visit the home of Dulcinea. Then on to Córdoba—capital of Moorish Spain and, in the 10th century, second in wealth and luxury only to Baghdad. Córdoba still recalls the glory of the Moslem empire on the peninsula. After that, you visit the Moors' last stronghold, Granada, where the most spectacular architectural monument of the culture, the Alhambra, towers majestically over the city. This itinerary ends on the sunny beaches of the Costa del Sol (Coast of the Sun), where European royalty and Hollywood stars moor their yachts.

Your route passes many kilometers of olive groves and vineyards and winds through small towns spilling down mountainsides under the remains of ancient castles. Be sure to sample the regional wines, the delicious cold gazpacho soup (there is nothing so refreshing on a hot day), and the varied seafood specialties.

PACING: When you leave Madrid, plan on an overnight stay in Toledo or Almagro and spending two nights in both Córdoba and Granada before heading for a sojourn on the coast.

Whether before or after your stay in Spain's capital city, a journey to her southern cities, steeped in Moorish heritage and graced with Mudéjar mementos, should not be missed. So, when you are ready to leave the hustle and bustle of **Madrid**, head south to follow in the footsteps of Don Quixote and the warriors who reclaimed Spain for the Christians.

Take N401 south from Madrid to **Toledo**, passing through the medieval town of **Illescas**. Fortified Toledo is lovely to come upon, and you may wish to take a turn around the walled city (bear right just before entering the Bisagra gate) when you first arrive. When you witness the incredible views of the city from the hillside across the River Tagus, you understand what inspired El Greco's famous painting, *View of Toledo* (now in the Prado).

Be prepared for wall-to-wall tourists as you tour the abundance of sights in Toledo. When the capital was moved to Madrid in the 16th century, Toledo remained the center of the Catholic hierarchy in Spain, and the **cathedral** (13th to 15th centuries) is one of the largest in the world. Highlights include the decorative high altar, the ornate choir stalls, and the sacristy with its paintings by El Greco, Titian and Goya. In **Iglesia de Santo Tomé** church, you can view El Greco's famous *Burial of the Count of Orgaz* in its original setting (the sixth figure from the left is said to be a self-portrait of the artist) and the **El Greco House and Museum,** which lends an idea of how he lived. Also noteworthy is the startling Mudéjar decoration of the **El Tránsito** and **Santa María la Blanca synagogues**. The **Museo de Santa Cruz Museum**, with its fine 16th- and 17th-century art, includes paintings by El Greco.

Toledo is loaded with souvenir shops and is famous for its swords and knives—you find both decorative and real ones in all shapes, sizes, and prices—and for its Damascene ware: gold, silver, and copper filigree inlaid in black steel. There is an abundance of sightseeing but, above all, walking the ancient, winding streets of the city, pausing for refreshment at one of the many cafes in the **Plaza de Zocodover**, and soaking up the essence of Spanish history are the highlights of Toledo's offerings.

*Moorish Memories*

Leave Toledo on CM400. You are soon in **La Mancha** (from *manxa*, an Arabic word meaning parched earth), the land of Cervantes' Don Quixote, famous for its wine, cheese (*queso manchego*), windmills, saffron, olive trees, and ceramics. Above **Consuegra**, you pass the ruined 12th-century castle surrounded by 13 windmills. (The best picture-taking spot is after you leave the town to the east.)

If you are an ardent Cervantes (or a *Man of La Mancha*) fan take a side trip to El Toboso to visit a reproduction of the home of the peerless Dulcinea, reluctant recipient of the knight-errant's undying love (closed Mondays, open March to October). It's about 50 fairly fast kilometers each way. Head east from Madridejos on CM400 around the wine-trade town of **Alcázar de San Juan** continuing east on N420 to reach **Campo de Criptana** where, it is claimed, Don Quixote had his tryst with the windmills. A few kilometers farther east you see the **Ermita Santisma Virgin de Criptana** church on a knoll. Turn beside it for the 15 kilometers drive through sky-wide countryside to the village of **El Toboso** which comes into view several kilometers before you reach it. Just southeast of the church in the center of the village is Dulcinea's home. The house supposedly belonged to Ana Martínez whom Cervantes renamed Dulcinea (*dulce* = sweet + Ana). Tour the house with its 17th-century furniture and intriguing antique olive oil press on the patio in the back. Across the street from the church is a collection of over 300 editions of the novel in everything from Japanese to Gaelic. A number of interesting facsimiles and signed and illuminated editions are housed there, too. Return to Alcázar de San Juan and from there head for **Puerto Lápice**, where you can follow the signs to the delightful **Venta del Quijote**—a well-restored example of the type of inn where Don Quixote was dubbed knight. The Venta has a charming restaurant and bar, as well as some cute little shops.

Back on the main itinerary route you pass through the fertile plains of the Campo de Calatrava as you pass **Daimiel** and **Ciudad Real** on the way to the interesting town of **Almagro**, once the main stronghold of the knights of the military Order of Calatrava who battled the Moors during the Reconquest. Almagro's unique, oblong **Plaza Mayor** is surrounded by wooden houses—many of which are cafes and restaurants—and the restored 16th-century **Corral de Comedias** (in the southeast corner) where the plays of the Spanish Golden Age were performed. It is similar in style and epoch (as were the plays) to the Elizabethan theaters of Shakespeare's time. You will enjoy exploring the town's cobbled streets and alleyways with their marvelous whitewashed houses, sculptured doorways, and shops selling the renowned, locally tatted lace. A number of historic buildings are in the process of restoration.

Leave Almagro heading for **Valdepeñas**, a short drive to the east. Join the NIV and head south, climbing gradually into the pine-forested Sierra Morena until, at the **Despeñaperros Gorge** (*despeña perros* means throwing off of the dogs, i.e., Moors), you officially enter Andalusia. The Andalusians are fond of saying that this is where Europe ends and Africa begins. This is not a total exaggeration—Andalusia has a markedly different culture and a much stronger Moorish tradition than the rest of Spain.

You pass through La Carolina before coming to Bailén, where you head east on N322 through Linares to **Úbeda**. Recaptured from the Moors in 1234, it once served as an important base in the Reconquest campaign. The heart of all Spanish towns is the plaza, and Úbeda's striking oblong **Plaza Vázquez de Molina** was designed for lingering, lined with palaces and mansions with classic Renaissance façades, grills, and balconies and the beautiful El Salvador chapel. You can also spot the remains of old town walls and towers around town. Úbeda's elegant parador (on the plaza in a 16th-century palace) offers an imaginative lunch menu, if the time is appropriate.

From Úbeda it's a short drive to captivating **Baeza**, the seat of a bishop during the Visigothic period and a prominent border town between Andalusia and La Mancha during the Reconquest. Golden seignorial mansions testify to its importance as a Moorish capital before 1227, when it became the first Andalusian town to be reconquered. Make time to drop by the tourist office in the enchanting **Plaza de los Leones**, pick up a town map, and wander on foot from there to visit this open-air museum of architecture, from Romanesque through Renaissance.

Return to Bailén, then head west toward Córdoba. You pass **Andújar**, with a pretty little plaza dominated by an ochre-colored Gothic church and an arched Roman bridge across the Guadalquivir. You are in the major olive-producing region of Spain now, and drive by continuous symmetrical rows of olive trees (*olivos*). After passing Villa del Rio, on the left bank of the river, you see the fortified town of **Montoro**. This was an important stronghold during the Moorish period, and today is a center for olive oil production. The remaining kilometers to Córdoba pass through seemingly endless olive groves.

**Córdoba** was the most opulent of the Moorish cities in Spain and is today a vast vibrant city. Córdoba is such a popular destination that it sometimes seems that every person who comes to Spain stops here. Park by the river and walk into historic heart of Córdoba, the old **Barrio de la Judería** or Jewish quarter. The old city boasted a university to which scholars from all over Europe came to study in the 11th and 12th centuries, when it was the largest city in Europe. Just a small portion of the historic metropolis remains as a virtual maze of twisting streets, modern and ancient shops, and colorful bars and cafés. Even on foot, it is very easy to lose your sense of direction in the tiny streets as each one begins to look like the rest. This is especially true if you allow darkness to catch you— which you should let happen if possible, since the area takes on a very different, magical aspect when lit by its quaint lanterns.

Bounded by the Barrio de la Juderia, the **Mosque (*Mezquita*)** is the highlight of a visit to Córdoba. Begun in 785 and added onto over the centuries, it appears as a vast square of apparently endless red-and-white-striped arches, with a second level above the first to providing a feeling of openness. Hakam II added the elaborate prayer niche (*mihrab*) and the lavish caliph's enclosure (*maqsura*). In the 16th-century part of the mosque was destroyed and a cathedral was built. Even though the Emperor Charles V had approved the idea, he is said to have lamented "the destruction of something unique to build something commonplace" when he saw the result. Hire an audio guide in the courtyard— adjacent to where you purchase your admission tickets.

Search out the **Alcázar de los Reyes Cristianos**, just a couple of blocks from the mosque. Its gardens with their water terraces built in the 14<sup>th</sup> century are a sight to behold.

*Córdoba Mosque (Mezquita)*

Head south out of town on NIV to follow the Wine Road (*Ruta del Vino*) on a journey to Granada at the foot of the Sierra Nevada. At Cuesta del Espino, bear southeast on N331 through **Fernán Nuñez** and Montemayor—with 18th- and 14th-century castles—to **Montilla**, an ancient town perched on two hills. A short time later **Aguilar de la Frontera** appears, an old hilltop town whose whitewashed, octagonal plaza of San José is particularly charming. Before turning northeast to **Cabra,** you see **Monturque**, with fragments of its ancient town walls; and **Lucena**, a center of the Andalusian wine trade (in whose ruined Alcázar the last Moorish king in Spain, Boabdil, was once held prisoner). Near Cabra are the ruins of the **Castillo de los Condes** and **San Juan Bautista church**, one of the oldest in Andalusia.

Continue northeast on a beautifully scenic stretch of road to **Baena**, tiered gracefully on a hillside. In the upper, walled part of town are some wonderful Renaissance mansions. From here you can look forward to a lovely, if not speedy, drive on N432 through **Alcaudete** dominated by a ruined castle, and **Alcalá La Real** overseen by the **Fort of La Mota**, before reaching Granada. As you arrive near the town, it is vital that you do not follow signs for Granada Centro. Take exit (km) 133 off the N323 signed for Alhambra, which (following signposts) takes you for the 6-km drive to the Alhambra complex.

**Granada** fell to the Moors in 711. After Córdoba was recaptured by the Christians in the 13th century, Granada provided refuge for its Moslem residents under whom it flourished until 1492 when the city was recaptured by Ferdinand and Isabella, marking the official end to almost eight centuries of Moorish presence in Spain.

The **Alhambra** with its **Generalife Gardens** takes a complete day to visit. The ticket booths open at 9 am and it is handy to be there a few minutes early to avoid lines. Alhambra comes from the Arabic name "Red Fort" and, although it is red, its somewhat plain exterior belies the richness and elegance of its interior. After your visit to this magical place, we are sure you will agree with the poet Francisco de Icaza who, after experiencing the Alhambra and then seeing a blind beggar, wrote: *Dale limosna, mujer, que no hay en la vida nada como la pena de ser ciego en Granada;* meaning "Give him alms, woman, for there is no greater tragedy in life than to be blind in Granada." Look carefully to see a plaque with this inscription set into the Torre de la Vela on the palace grounds.

Most of the Moorish part (the **Alcázar**) dates from the 14th century. The palace of the Emperor Charles V, one of the finest Renaissance structures in Spain, was designed and begun in the 16th century. It now houses a museum of pieces from the Alcázar and a fine-arts collection of religious painting and sculpture.

The magnificent tile-and-plaster geometric decoration is an expression of Moslem art at its zenith. The stunning patios and gardens with their perfectly symmetrical design will dazzle you as you stroll through the various halls and chambers. Equally appealing are the cool, green gardens of the Generalife, the summer palace. Countless fountains—now, as then, moved by gravity only and surrounded by sumptuous flower gardens, orange trees, and cypresses—testify to a desert culture's appreciation of water.

Several spots on the north side of the grounds offer splendid views of the old Moorish quarter (the Albaicín) across the River Darro, as well as of the city of Granada. The same is true of the towers of the **Alcazaba** (fortress), which is the oldest part of the complex.

Try to schedule a nocturnal visit to the Alhambra grounds. Some nights it is totally illuminated and others only partially (ask at the hotel for the current schedule). Either way, the experience is unforgettable and dramatically different from a daytime visit. Also, inside the grounds are two good dining spots located in hotels: the Parador de Granada and the Hotel America.

*Lion's Court, Alhambra, Granada*

*Moorish Memories*

But your visit to Granada should not end here. The **cathedral**, in the center of town, with its adjoining Royal Chapel (*Capilla Real*) was ordered built by the Catholic monarchs Ferdinand and Isabella for their final resting place and their tombs have been there since it was finished in 1521. Subsequently, their daughter, Juana the Mad, and her husband, Phillip the Fair, plus Juana's son, Prince Miguel, were buried here. Juana's other son was Emperor Charles V of the Holy Roman Empire and King of Spain in the 16th century.

The **Alcaicería** (the old silk market) around the cathedral is now a tourist area full of souvenir shops. At its west end is Granada's most attractive plaza, **Bibarrambla**. It is a marvelous place to sit with a cold Spanish beer and watch the Granadinos (including the gypsies who live nearby) go about their daily business. For the Granadinos and for all Spaniards, this includes plaza-sitting; and for the gypsies, it includes begging from the plaza-sitters.

The old **Albaicín** quarter retains much of its former flavor. For an unbelievable view of the Alhambra and Generalife, try the terrace of the **Iglesia de Santo Nicholas** in the Albaicín at sunset, and do not forget your camera. Though it is something of a walk, we do not recommend that you try to drive into the Albaicín's maze of tiny streets (although an experienced Granadino cabbie can manage it). Beyond the Albaicín to the east is the gypsy cave-dwelling area called **Sacromonte**, famous for its gypsy dancing and infamous as a tourist trap.

If time permits and you like mountain scenery, you should definitely take the 60-kilometer round trip to the peaks of the **Sierra Nevada** southeast of the city. An excellent road (at its highest levels, the highest in Europe) winds its way to the winter-sports area of Solynieve (sun and snow) in the shadow of the two highest mountains on the Iberian Peninsula, the **Cerro de Mulhacen** (3,480 meters) and the **Pico de Veleta** (3,428 meters). There is a 37-kilometer road that ascends to the summit of Mulhacen and down the other side to Prado Llano, but it is open only in early fall.

Leave Granada on N323, which runs south to the coast through the wild terrain of the **Alpujarras**—the mountains to which the Moors fled, and from which they launched their futile attempts to retake Granada. After about 15 kilometers, you pass over the **Puerto del Suspiro del Moro** (Pass of the Moor's Sigh) where, it is said, Boabdil, the last of Granada's Moorish kings, wept as he turned to take a last look at his beloved Granada upon his leave-taking. The contrast in scenery on the Motril road is breathtaking: green valleys, rows of olive and almond trees, and the towering, snow-capped peaks of the Sierra Nevada.

If you get an early start, this scenic detour is well worth the hour or so it adds to the journey: About 40 kilometers from Granada, turn left on A348 and continue to **Lanjarón**, a lovely small spa with mineral springs in a gorgeous mountain setting, with a ruined castle perched on a shelf above it. The water is supposed to cure various ailments and is bottled and distributed nationally—if you order mineral water with your meals, you have probably tried it already. Continue on A348 to **Orgiva** at the edge of the Alpujarras. This is the area the Moors occupied for more than a century after Granada fell to the Catholic monarchs. In this picturesque, little mountain village you find fine views of the Alpujarras, the Sierra Nevada, and the smaller Sierra de la Contraviesa to the south. Leave Orgiva on A348 toward the south and turn right after 3 kilometers on A346. Thirteen scenic kilometers later, you arrive back at N323, which you follow to the coastal highway N340.

Turn right and you soon have the pleasure of coming upon **Salobrèña**, a picturesque, white-walled village crowning a rocky promontory surrounded by a waving sea of green sugar cane. These *pueblos blancos* (white towns) are typical of the warmer areas of Andalusia and you see several as you drive along. Park at the edge of the town and stroll up to its partially restored Alcázar to enjoy the splendid view of the surrounding countryside and the Mediterranean.

As you head west from Salobreña, there are numerous lookout points with fabulous views of the sea and the beautiful coastline. The road winds along the coast through the small seaside resort of **Almuñécar**, with its ruined Castillo de San Miguel. A bit farther on, near the village of Maro, are the impressive **Nerja Caves** (*Cuevas de Nerja*), definitely worth a visit—vast stalactitic caves with prehistoric paintings and evidence of habitation since Paleolithic times. Its archaeological revelations (including parts of Cro-Magnon human skulls) can be seen at the small museum nearby. The caves are efficiently run and offer a cool break from driving. Continuing west, you reach the resort and fishing port of **Nerja**, known for the Balcón (balcony) de Europa, a terrace-promenade with wonderful views rising high above the sea near the center of the charming little town.

You pass through the seaside port of **Torre del Mar**, with its pretty lighthouse, and the village of **Rincon de la Victoria**, where another, smaller cave (*Cueva del Tesoro*) with prehistoric drawings can be visited in a park above town. Unlike the Nerja caves, this one was formed by underground water and presents a quite different impression. The area is popular with local Malagueños for weekend beach excursions.

Follow the coast road and you arrive in **Málaga**, the birthplace of Pablo Picasso, the provincial capital, and one of the oldest Mediterranean ports.

*Toledo*

*Moorish Memories*

# Andalusian Adventures

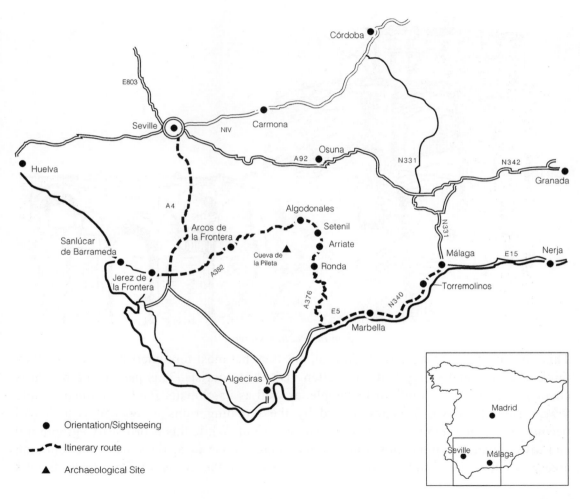

Orientation/Sightseeing

- - - Itinerary route

▲ Archaeological Site

# *Andalusian Adventures*

*Ronda, Puente Nuevo*

This itinerary features western Andalusia, the area that most foreigners picture when they think of Spain, and surely that most often visited by tourists. This part of the region is characterized by the warmth of its people, as well as its climate. *Pueblos blancos,* white towns, stepping down hillsides topped by the brooding ruins of ancient castles will become a common, though never commonplace, sight. While this is primarily agricultural and cattle-raising country, this itinerary also includes one of Spain's major metropolitan areas: Seville—the country's fourth-largest city and the scene of Don Juan, Bizet's

*Carmen*, Mozart's *Figaro,* and glorious 16th-century adventures to and from the exotic New World. It also includes the most tourist-intensive area in the country—the Costa del Sol from Málaga to San Pedro de Alcántara.

This is the part of Spain that extends to within about 15 kilometers of the northern tip of Africa and was the first area conquered by the Moors in 711. Except for the relatively small group of Moslems in Granada, Seville was also the last area reconquered by the Christians in the 13th century, making it the area that retains the strongest traces of Moorish culture—not necessarily just architecture—to the present day.

The culinary specialties of the area include gazpacho and fried seafood dishes. Due to the warm climate, sangría is also delightfully ubiquitous. And, of course, this is the home of sherry, whose name comes from the English pronunciation of the wine-producing center of Jerez (formerly spelled Xerez, with the *x* pronounced *sh*).

PACING: Skip the Costa del Sol if you are not one for crowds and opt instead to spend several days in the hinterland before heading up for a stay in Ronda or Arcos de la Frontera before exploring Seville.

**Málaga** had seen occupation by the Romans, Visigoths, and Moors, before being recaptured by the Catholic monarchs in 1487. Today, Málaga lies prey to a new onslaught, as tourists flock from Northern Europe to soak up the sun—an invasion that has somewhat dimmed its old-world charm. However, this seaside town still has much to offer. It is famous for its Málaga dessert and aperitif wines (sweet Pedro Ximenes, and Dulce and Lágrimas muscatel). Early works of Picasso can be found in the **Museo de Bellas Artes** on the Calle San Agustín. Explore the cobbled side streets off the main plaza where you can relax at outdoor cafés, and check out the bustling shopping street, Marqués de Larios. From the 14th-century ramparts on the nearby **Gibralfaro** (lighthouse hill) are gorgeous gardens with magnificent views of the town and harbor, and just down from there is the 11th-century **Alcazaba** (Moorish fortress).

It's only an hour's drive from Málaga to Ronda. Leave Málaga on A7-E15 along the coast (following signs for Cadiz, among various other destinations) past touristy

**Torremolinos** (which Michener's characters from *The Drifters* would no longer recognize) and **Fuengirola** before reaching **Marbella**, the most aristocratic of the **Costa del Sol** resorts, with its hidden villas, lavish hotels, long, pebbly beach, and the inevitable remains of a Moorish castle. If you like shopping, you will enjoy the many elegant international shops in the city, where strolling along the main street and side streets is a pleasure. Numerous restaurants of all types and categories are available here, including La Fonda, with a Michelin star, on the Plaza de Santo Cristo. From Marbella, take the N340 and continue west for a few kilometers to **Puerto Banus**, where the marina is home to enough yachts to rival Monaco or the French Riviera. Unless your yacht is moored there, you will have to park in the lot just outside the harbor area proper and walk in. Inside are numerous chic shops, bars, and restaurants. This is the center of Spain's jet-set scene.

From Puerto Banus, return to the freeway for just a few kilometers and turn north on A376 towards **Ronda**. For sheer dramatic setting, Ronda takes the prize. Ronda is perched on the edge of the Serranía de Ronda, slashed by 153-meter gorges and cut in two (the old *Ciudad* through which you enter from the south, and the new *Mercadillo*) by the Tajo ravine carved by the Guadalevín River (which explains why every other sentence describing the site must necessarily include the word "view").

On your stroll through the town, be sure to include the **bullring** with its wrought-iron balconies. One of Spain's oldest (1785), it inspired several works by Goya. Francisco Romero, the father of modern bullfighting (he introduced the cape and numerous so-called classical rules), was born here in 1698. His descendants continued what is still known as the Ronda school of bullfighting. Farther on you discover the spectacular **Puente Nuevo** (the 18th-century bridge that connects the two parts of town and which you crossed on your way in) with its incredible view of the ravine. When you cross it, you are in the Ciudad section with its winding streets and old stone palaces. Visit the Plaza de la Ciudad and its church, **Santa María la Mayor**, whose tower (a former mosque) affords still more picture-perfect views. Some dramatic walking excursions (30 minutes each) can be taken on footpaths leading off the Plaza del Campanillo down to ruined Moorish mills; or look for the footpath to the upper mills that offer spectacular views of a waterfall and the Puente Nuevo. To the left of the Puente Nuevo (near the Puente Romano, or Roman Bridge) is the **Casa del Rey Moro** (note the Moorish azulejo plaque in the façade), a lavishly furnished old mansion with terraced gardens and a flight of 365 stairs cut into the living rock leading to the river and the Moorish baths. The ancient ambiance is hard to beat and invites you to take your time strolling around the lovely streets and plazas. In the newer Mercadillo section of town, Carrera de Espinel is a picturesque, pedestrian-only shopping street. You find it running east from near the bullring.

Though Ronda encourages you to linger, take comfort in the fact that you are headed to another impressive town, Arcos de la Frontera, following the signs to **Arriate** and **Setenil**. The latter is a classic, little white town with one very interesting aspect—at the bottom of the town, in the ravine, the houses are actually built into the cliff itself. All along this route, you enjoy numerous spectacular views of the mountainous countryside. Leave Setenil in a westerly direction and follow MA486, then MA449, which seem to be taking you back to Ronda. However, on reaching A376, take a right and you'll be back on the road to Arcos de la Frontera.

Back on A376, after about 6 kilometers, you see a road (MA505) to the left indicating the way to the **Cueva de la Pileta**. Upon arrival in this desolate place, park your car and climb the steep path to the small entrance to the cave, almost hidden among the rocks. You need to join a group of other tourists and follow a guide to visit the caves. (Before leaving Ronda, check with the tourist office or at your hotel to verify what hours the caves are open.) If there are only a small number of tourists when you visit, you may be allowed to see some of the ancient black-and-red animal drawings found here. The paintings are said to predate those in the famous Altamira Caves and, apparently, indicate that the caves were inhabited 25,000 years ago. The ceramic remains from the caves are claimed to be the oldest known pottery specimens in Europe.

Wind your way back to A376 and continue northwest, then west on the A382. You are on a road called the **Ruta de los Pueblos Blancos**, or white-town route, and you soon see why as you pass several very picturesque little towns with their whitewashed buildings and red-tile roofs. On the right, you'll see **Montecorto** and have a splendid view of the mountains in front of you. A bit farther, the town of **Zahara**, with a ruined castle and Arab bridge, rises to your left. Built on a ridge, it was a stronghold against the kingdom of Granada during the Moorish occupation.

You notice on this itinerary several towns with the "de la Frontera" tag on their names. This means "on the border" and alludes to their status during the Reconquest of Spain from the Moors. As you approach Arcos, you have several marvelous opportunities to capture its incredible setting on film.

*Santa María de la Asunción church, Arcosde la Frontera*

*Andalusian Adventures*

**Arcos de la Frontera** clings impossibly to an outcropping of rock with the Guadalete River at its foot. Navigate carefully up its maze of narrow, one-way alleys or you may (as we did once) find yourself backing down those steep, twisty streets in the face of a big truck with traffic being expertly (sort of) directed by amused locals. Since you are approaching from the north, the route up the hill to the Plaza de España at the heart of the old town on top is fairly easy. Although the view here is the main attraction, you will also want to see (and perhaps climb the tower of) the **Santa María de la Asunción** church on the plaza and wander through the ancient, romantic, winding streets of the old town, where you get a real feeling that you have stepped into life as it was in the Middle Ages.

The next destination, Seville, is the centerpiece of romantic Spain and, appropriately, has retained its beauty and ambiance even in this modern age. We hope you have managed to leave enough time to enjoy its unsurpassable attractions. Leave Arcos heading west, still on the white-town route, and you pass rolling hillsides resplendent with sunflowers (if it is summer), numerous typical Andalusian *cortijos,* or ranches, and more dazzling white villages. Then the terrain becomes flatter, and the roadside towns less impressive, as you approach the famous town of **Jerez de la Frontera**.

Jerez's main attraction is visiting the bodegas where sherry is made. The traffic in and out of Jerez is exasperating. Most of the bodegas are open for visitors from 9 am to 1 pm only, so plan your time accordingly. Unfortunately, due to the ever-increasing number of interested visitors, some bodegas have instituted a reservation policy. To be on the safe side, call ahead as soon as you know when you plan to be in Jerez (ask for assistance from your hotel desk staff). English seamen in the 18th century found sherry wine an agreeable alternative to French wine. The varieties commonly produced here are *fino* (extra dry, light in color and body), *amontillado* (dry, darker in color and fuller-bodied), *oloroso* (medium, full bodied, and golden), and *dulce* (sweet dessert wine).

The Jerez region is also renowned for quality horse breeding. The famous Lippizaner horses originally came from this area and are trained at the **Real Escuela Andaluza de Arte Ecuestre**. Dressage displays are given on Thursdays.

When you are ready to call it a day and discover what **Seville** has in store for you, make your way to the A4 toll road, which takes you there in no time. From the outskirts, follow the signs indicating *centro ciudad*, while keeping your eye on the skyline's most outstanding landmark—the towering golden spire of the Giralda, attached to the magnificent cathedral, which is the largest in the world.

In order to fully appreciate the many marvels of Seville, turn to the itinerary *Seville Highlights*.

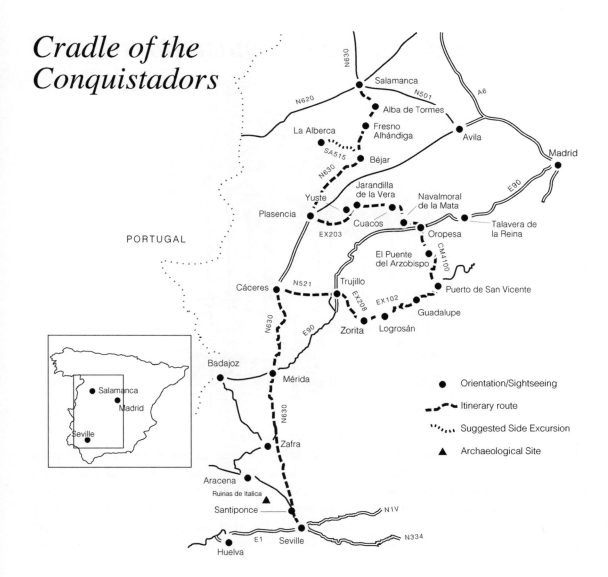

# Cradle of the Conquistadors

PORTUGAL

N630
Salamanca
N501
A6
N620
Alba de Tormes
La Alberca
Fresno Alhándiga
Avila
Madrid
SA515
Béjar
N630
Jarandilla de la Vera
Yuste
Navalmoral de la Mata
Plasencia
Cuacos
E90
EX203
Oropesa
Talavera de la Reina
El Puente del Arzobispo
CM4100
Cáceres
N521
Trujillo
Puerto de San Vicente
EX208
EX102
N630
E90
Guadalupe
Zorita
Logrosán
Badajoz
Mérida
N630
Zafra
Aracena
Ruinas de Italica
Santiponce
N1V
Seville
E1
N334
Huelva

Salamanca
Madrid
Seville

● Orientation/Sightseeing

▬ ▬ Itinerary route

⋯⋯ Suggested Side Excursion

▲ Archaeological Site

# *Cradle of the Conquistadors*

*Roman Theater, Mérida*

Most of this itinerary finds you in Extremadura—an area of Spain less frequented by tourists, which is part of its appeal. The name *Extremadura* originated during the Reconquest period and translates as "land beyond the River Duero" (which runs across the country from Soria to Valladolid to Zamora). Historically somewhat at the periphery of national life, and less privileged economically, the area was rich in young men eager to seek their fortunes in the New World, as the name of this itinerary suggests. Some famous Extremadurans you may recognize are Hernán Cortés, conqueror of Mexico; Francisco Pizarro, conqueror of Peru; Orellano, explorer of the Amazon; and Balboa, discoverer of the Pacific Ocean. Indeed, since the explorations were sponsored by Queen Isabella of Castile, which included Extremadura, only Castilians were given the opportunity to make the journey to the New World during the 16th century. The area is still resplendent with fine old mansions built with treasures found in Mexico and Peru.

Typical cuisine of Extremadura includes one of our favorite Spanish specialties: raw-cured ham (*jamón serrano*); as well as lamb stew (*caldereta de cordero*), fried breadcrumbs with bacon (*migas*); and numerous game dishes such as pheasant (*faisán*) and partridge (*perdiz*). The major local wine is a simple white called Almendralejo.

The last destination brings you into Old Castile and the enchanting medieval university city of Salamanca.

PACING: If you are especially interested in Roman remains, plan on spending the night in Mérida, then choose a hub in the center of the itinerary and spend three nights there to really enjoy this lovely area before heading north to Salamanca.

It is never easy to leave Seville, Spain's most romantic city; but, if you fall under its spell, you will be back. However, Spain offers many additional enchantments and much more of it remains to be seen, so set your sights north. Note: For more in-depth suggestions on sightseeing in Seville, see our chapter titled *Seville Highlights.*

Leave Seville heading west across the bridge and turn north toward Mérida on the N630 to **Zafra**. Zafra preserves one of the most impressive fortified palaces in the region, now the **Parador de Zafra,** on one of the prettiest little plazas in the area. Actually the former palace of the Duke of Feria, it was the residence of Hernán Cortés just before he embarked for the New World. Its conversion to a parador has not spoiled it in the least, and it's worth a short visit to see the fabulous chapel and the other faithfully restored public rooms. Leave Zafra on N435 and join the N630, which takes you to **Mérida**, repository of the richest Roman remains in Spain—all in a modern, sprawling city.

Founded in 25 B.C., the Roman town of Emerita Augusta, now Mérida, was so well situated at the junction of major Roman roads that it was soon made the capital of Lusitania. Outstanding Roman remains dot the city: bridges, temples, a racecourse, two aqueducts, an arena, and a theater—all attesting to Mérida's historical importance under Roman occupation. If your time is limited, you must not miss the **Roman Arena** (built in the 1st century B.C. with a seating capacity of 14,000) and next to it, the **Roman Theater** (built by Agrippa in the 1st century B.C. with a seating capacity of over 5,000). The astounding theater alone, with its double-columned stage, is worth a detour to Mérida. (If you are here in late June or early July, see if the Classical Theater Festival is offering live performances.) Just across the road from the arena and theater is a stunning modern museum that you must not miss, **Museo Nacional de Arte Romano**. In this spectacular brick-vaulted, skylit building many Roman artifacts and panels of mosaics are displayed. Be sure to also see the **Casa Romana del Anfiteatro** (1st century A.D. with mosaics and water pipes) and the **Alcazaba** at the city end of the Roman bridge (built by the Moors in the 9th century). Near the Alcazaba you find the **Plaza de España**, Mérida's main center of activity. It is a wonderful place to sit with a drink at one of the outdoor cafés and watch the world go by.

Head north out of Mérida to **Cáceres,** the second-largest city in Extremadura and a national monument. Although surrounded by a congested, modern city, the old city is totally walled-in. Called **Barrio Monumental** it has abundant medieval atmosphere though it appears more as a museum because few people live there. Cáceres was hotly disputed during civil wars between Castile, León, and Extremadura, which explains its extraordinary fortifications. Incredibly well preserved, the walls are mostly of Moorish construction, although they were built on, and incorporated bits of, previous Roman walls. Tradition has it that the most glorious of the military orders in Spain, the Knights of Saint James (Santiago) was founded here, and for centuries, Cáceres was renowned for the number of knights in residence. Many of the mansions were built in the 16th century with money brought back by the conquistadors from the American colonies.

A few hours of wandering along the winding, stepped streets and visiting a museum or two richly reward the effort. You can park in the **Plaza del General Mola** (also known as the Plaza Mayor) where the main entrance gate sits. To the right of the largest of the dozen remaining wall towers, **Bujaco tower**, you enter through the **Arco de la Estrella** (Star Arch) into the **Plaza de Santa María** where you find the **Iglesia de Santa María** with its lovely ornamental wooden screen behind the altar and a 15th century crucifix the Cristo Negro (Black Christ). Nearby the **Museo Provincial** contains contemporary art and archeology from the region. Behind the museum you find the Barrio de San Antonio, the old Jewish quarter, full of small whitewashed cottages. Throughout the town the many, handsome family mansions testify to the austere mood of the 15th and 16th centuries. None has much decoration, save the family escutcheons that are mounted above the doors—silent testimony to the nobility of the residents. As you walk along the narrow streets do not forget to look up at the church towers, where you often see storks nesting precariously above the rooftops.

When you are ready to move on, head east on N521 to the most famous cradle of conquistadors, **Trujillo**, a charming city, still pure in its medieval atmosphere, which is uncontaminated by modern construction. Its most famous sons were the Pizarro brothers, ingenious and tumultuous conquerors of the Inca Empire in Peru in the middle of the 16th century. The quantities of gold and silver mined there and shipped home in just 50 years created chaos in the economy of all of Europe.

Trujillo boasts a number of splendid mansions constructed with the booty of the travelers to the Americas. Most of the old quarter centers around the spectacularly beautiful **Plaza Mayor**, where there is a large statue of Francisco Pizarro who conquered Peru. The irregular shape and different levels of the plaza make it one of the most charming and appealing in the country. On the plaza, among the many monumental buildings, is the grand home built by his brother, Hernando Pizarro, the Palacio del Marqués de la Conquista. Nearby is another example of a grand home built with New World wealth the **Palacio de Ornella-Pizarro** built by Francisco de Orellana who explored the Amazon and Equador. The mansions here were built a bit later than those of Cáceres, and thus, are not quite so austere. The **Iglesia de Santa María la Mayor**, a block off the plaza, contains a pantheon of several of Trujillo's illustrious sons. The winding, stone streets around the plaza impart an unusual degree of charm and tranquility, inviting you to linger and wander around town.

Before leaving Trujillo, stroll up the hill to see the partially ruined castle, which towers over the town. There is a pretty little chapel, lovely views, and always a refreshing breeze.

From Trujillo, take EX208 south through beautiful countryside, which in spring displays a carpet of green laced with flowers and dotted with cork trees. Turn in left at the tidy little town of Zorita toward Logrosán, and soon begin to climb into the gray ridges of the Guadalupe mountains. A drive of 20 kilometers, through mountainous landscape changing from gray to green, takes you over Puerto Llano pass (unmarked) and exposes some fabulous panoramas of the fertile valleys below. Be on the lookout for the town of **Guadalupe**, because your first glimpse of the tiny white village will take your breath away. Crowned by a golden fortified monastery it nestles in the shadow of its ancient ramparts.

*Guadalupe*

*Cradle of the Conquistadors*

The Virgin Mary is supposed to have appeared to a humble herder in this vicinity in 1300 and to have indicated where he should dig to unearth her image. When the pastor arrived home, he discovered his son had died, so he immediately invoked the aid of the Virgin and the boy revived. He and his friends dug where she had indicated and discovered the famous black image in a cave. They then built a small sanctuary for her on the spot. In the 14th century, Alfonso XI had a Hieronymite monastery built there after his victory over the Moors at the Battle of Salado, which he attributed to the **Virgin of Guadalupe**. The monastery has been a popular pilgrimage destination ever since, and the Virgin of Guadalupe has come to be one of the most important religious figures in Spain and Spanish America. Columbus named one of the islands in the Caribbean (now French) after her because he had signed the agreement authorizing his expedition in Guadalupe. When he returned from his voyage with six American Indians, they were baptized here. A short time later, the Virgin appeared again, in Mexico, to a peasant and she became the patron saint of Mexico.

When you tour the **monastery**, be sure to see the Camarín with the image of the Virgin and her 30,000-jewel headdress, the Moorish Cloister with its two stories of graceful arches, and the church with its Zurbarán paintings and many other art objects. The positively charming main plaza in Guadalupe has an ancient stone fountain at its center and old mansions huddled around it. Take time to just sit and watch the world go by from this vantage point. As for shopping, this is an area known for ceramics, and Guadalupe is no exception. Worked copper and brass are also local specialties.

If you enjoy ceramics and embroidery, note that this region is the national font for their manufacture (it used to be that you knew where tiles had been made by the colors used), so you might want to do a little shopping along your route today. Return to EX102 and turn left toward Puerto de San Vicente pass (follow the signs to Talavera de La Reina). The rocky crests of the Sierra de Guadalupe become sharply pronounced on the approach to the pass. Bear left (CM4100) to **La Estrella** and **El Puente del Arzobispo**, a traditional ceramics center with many shops. The graceful, old humpback bridge that takes you across the River Tagus (Tajo) dates from the 14th century. You see a beautiful hermitage on your right as you leave town. From here it is a quick hop to **Oropesa** a quiet town spilling down the hillside below the castle. It is noted for its embroidery, and has retained a captivating, medieval flavor and numbers of handsome noble homes. You find many opportunities to buy local products both here and in nearby Lagartera. You are treated to some panoramic views of the valley of the Tagus and the Gredos mountain range.

When you are ready to depart from Oropesa, go west on NV E90 to Navalmoral de la Mata where you turn north on EX119 for a pretty drive through rich, green tobacco fields dotted with drying sheds to **Jarandilla de la Vera**, overlooking the Vera plain, whose castle (now a parador) was once owned by the Count of Oropesa, and is also where Emperor Charles V resided in 1556 while waiting for his apartments to be completed at the monastery of Yuste, just west of town on EX203. **Yuste** is famous as the last retreat of Charles V. Mentally and physically burned out after more than three decades at the head of the world's greatest empire, this is where he died in 1558. You can visit his small palace and share the view he loved of the surrounding countryside. It is easy to imagine the serenity he must have found in this solitude near the end of his otherwise stormy life.

Go on to Plasencia from Yuste, turning north on N630. If you have time, we heartily recommend a detour (you need to have a detailed map and be prepared to drive winding roads) to **La Alberca**, northwest on SA515 beyond Bejar. This tiny, isolated town has preserved its historic charm to an unusual degree, and the sight of its picturesque, stone houses overhung with timbered balconies richly rewards the effort.

Back on N630, bear right at Fresno Alhandiga onto SA120 to **Alba de Tormes**, dominated by the 16th-century Torre de la Armería, the only remnant of a former castle of the Dukes of Alba—among the greatest land barons of their time. This small town is one of the most popular pilgrimage destinations in Spain because Santa Teresa of Ávila, important church reformist and mystic, founded a convent and died here over 400 years ago. In the **Carmelite Convent,** you can visit the cell where she died and view her relics in a coffer beneath the altar. Her small, ornate coffin is in a place of honor above the high altar. And before leaving town, you should peek into the beautiful Mudéjar-Romanesque **Church of Saint John** on the central plaza.

Cross the River Tormes and head northwest to **Salamanca**, a Castilian town so rich in history that it is now a national monument. The **Plaza Mayor**, is exquisite largely because it was built as a whole in the 18th century and is, thus, highly integrated in design.

Next pay a visit to the 12th-century **Saint Martin's Church**. Not far from here, down the Rua Mayor, you find the **Casa de las Conchas** (conch shells), a 15th-century mansion whose entire façade is covered with carved stone shells, with the motif repeated in the grillwork and elsewhere. At the next corner is the Plaza de Anaya, and beyond on the left are the **"new" cathedral** (16th century) and the **"old" cathedral** (12th century). The former is Gothic, the latter Romanesque with an apparently Byzantine dome—quite unusual in Western Europe. Both are good examples of their periods and contain many worthy treasures.

Across from the Plaza de Anaya and the cathedrals is the back of the university. Go around to the opposite side to discover the **Patio de las Escuelas** (Patio of the Schools). Salamanca's major claim to fame is its **University**, the first in Spain, founded in 1218 by Alfonso IX de León. By 1254, when Alfonso X "the Wise" established the law school, Salamanca was declared one of the world's four great universities (along with Paris, Bologna, and Oxford). Columbus lectured here, as did San Juan de la Cruz and Antonio de Nebrija. Fray Luis de León, one of Spain's greatest lyric poets, was a faculty member here when he was imprisoned for heresy by the Spanish Inquisition. After five years in prison, he was released and returned to his classroom (which you can still visit). His first words when he was back were, *"Dicebamus hesterna dia . . ."* ("As we were saying yesterday . . ."). In the 20th century, Miguel de Unamuno taught here and served as rector. Not to be missed is the patio itself with the statue of Fray Luis, and the entrance to the university, perhaps the premier example of Plateresque art in Spain. Finished in 1529, it serves as an elaborate façade for the basic Gothic edifice. If you look carefully, you can find a small frog carved into the doorway. A student pointed it out to us on our last visit, and neither she nor we have the slightest idea why it is there, nor what the artist must have had in mind when he included this incongruous item.

As you continue back down to the river, you see the **Puente Romano** with its 26 arches: the nearest half are actually from the 1st century, the others are later constructions. On the bridge, you discover the stone bull that played a devilish part in the original picaresque novel, *Lazarillo de Tormes*.

*Bell Tower of San Martin, Trujillo*

*Cradle of the Conquistadors*

# Old Castile and the Cantabrian Coast

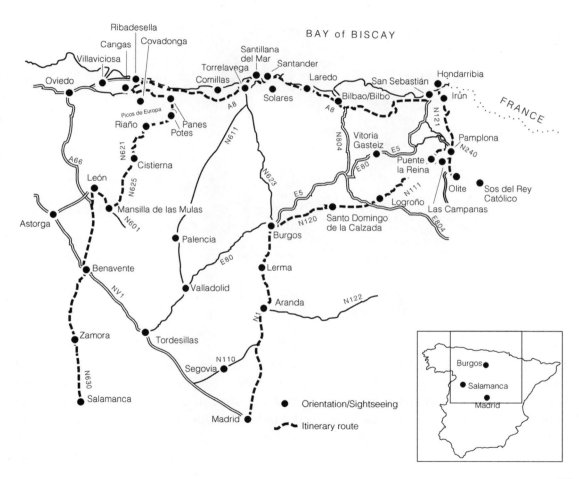

BAY of BISCAY

Ribadesella
Cangas  Covadonga
Villaviciosa
Santillana
del Mar
Torrelavega  Santander
Oviedo  Comillas
Laredo  San Sebastián  Hondarribia
Solares  Bilbao/Bilbo  Irún
FRANCE
Picos de Europa  A8  A8
Riaño  Panes  N611  Vitoria
Potes  N804  Gasteiz  Pamplona
N621  N623  E5  Puente  N240
Cistierna  E80  la Reina
León  N625  Logroño  Olite  Sos del Rey
N111  Católico
Mansilla de las Mulas  E5  Las Campanas
Astorga  N601  Santo Domingo
de la Calzada  E804
Palencia  N120
Benavente  Burgos
NV1  E80  Lerma
Valladolid  N122
Zamora  Aranda
N630  Tordesillas  N1
N110
Segovia
Salamanca
Madrid

● Orientation/Sightseeing

┄ Itinerary route

Burgos
Salamanca
Madrid

77

# Old Castile and the Cantabrian Coast

*Picos de Europa*

This itinerary takes you through the north-central section of Spain. Beginning in Old Castile, it includes Asturias, the Basque region, then Navarre (originally Basque, but later "Romanized"), and back to Castile. It features some of the best-preserved medieval villages in the country, gives you an authentic taste of Spain in the 11th through the 15th centuries, and will amaze you with some of the most spectacular natural landscape on the continent. This is an area filled with ancient cities, even more ancient caves, seaside

*Old Castile and the Cantabrian Coast*

resorts (which are favorites of Spaniards on their summer vacations because of the cooler climate), and, in the Basque region, Spain's premier cuisine. (The Costa Brava runs a close second.) Along the way, you will enjoy some of Europe's best hotels and some of Spain's finest scenery.

The coastal areas of Asturias and the Basque provinces were the only areas to escape Moorish occupation, and it was from there that the Reconquest (led by the legendary Pelayo) began in 718. The region similarly resisted Roman domination and thus retains the most remarkable prehistoric sites to be found in Spain. Castile traces its beginnings to the 9th century when the Christians built fortress-castles to establish and hold their frontier against the Moslems. Soon it was joined with the kingdom of León, became the major power in the Reconquest, and, ultimately, in the creation of the modern nation. The Spanish language is still called *Castellano*, after Castile. Geographically, the itinerary includes the high central *meseta*, or large mesa, the spectacular Cantabrian mountain range, and the coast along the Cantabrian Sea.

PACING: After overnighting in Salamanca, drive north to the Picos de Europa to spend time soaking in the scenery before heading off for a couple of nights along the busy northern coast. Conclude this itinerary with at stay in Olite or Sos del Rey Católico before going to Madrid.

This itinerary begins in the old university town of **Salamanca**. The Tormes River flows below the city with pedestrian roads leading up from the riverbanks to meet at the top of the hill in the bustling **Plaza Mayor,** an architectural masterpiece built in the 18th century by Philip V. It is enclosed by three-storied buildings constructed with a pastel ochre-colored stone, whose ground levels are fronted by a series of identical arches that form a dazzling arcade all around the square. Along with all of this come crowds and lots of souvenir shops. To explore the city, start at the river and follow San Pablo up to the Plaza Mayor, then loop back down to the river by the Rua Mayor. Be sure to include the characterful buildings of the **university** (*universidad*), the *catedral nueva* (**new cathedral**), the *catedral vieja* (**old cathedral**), and the *Casa de las Conchas* (House of Shells). Be sure to find the "frog on a skull" on the façade of the University of

Salamanca, a delightful old university city. From here, the N630 takes you north into the older part of Old Castile: the traditional Spain of castles and earth-colored towns in the vast meseta.

If you have time, detour into **Zamora,** which sits on the bank of the Duero River. Visit the **cathedral** on the main plaza and take a peek inside the **Parador de Zamora** across the square. It is magnificently installed in the 15th-century palace of the Counts of Alba and Aliste, and the public rooms are decorated with beautiful tapestries, coats of arms, and suits of armor.

Continue north, following the signs for León as you bypass Benavente, and follow the N630 into **León**. Leon, now a large provincial capital, was the heart of the ancient kingdom of the same name and the center of Christian Spain in the early days of the Reconquest. As the Christians drove the Moors ever farther south, León was united with Castile, and thereafter, began to lose its power and importance. It's is a great pedestrian town, so procure a map of the city and head for the **Cathedral Santa María de la Regla**, one of the country's outstanding Gothic edifices and an important stop on the Way of Saint James pilgrimage route. It features some of the most fabulous stained-glass windows in all of Europe (hope for a sunny day), which should not be missed. There are 125 windows of every period since the 13th century, said to total some 1,800 square meters of glass. If you are lucky enough to be there when the choir is practicing, you will have a thrilling experience. North of the cathedral are portions of the old city walls. To the south is the medieval quarter of the city and the small, colorful Plaza Mayor, overhung by ancient buildings and mixed with new shops. Down by the river, the **Hostal de San Marcos** a huge elaborate building was begun in 1513 and completed in the 18th century. It houses a parador and a museum in the cloisters.

Leaving León, take N601 in the direction of Valladolid. In the middle of the little town of Mansilla de las Mulas, follow the sign pointing to the left to Villomar and the Picos de Europa, and you find yourself on a flat, straight road paralleling the Esla River through numerous, quaint little villages. The first glimpse of the sharp, gray **Picos de Europa**

(European Peaks), into which you will soon be climbing, appears and beckons as you leave the town of Cubillas de Rueda.

The Picos de Europa are indeed spectacular. They rise to almost 2,743 meters within 25 kilometers of the coast and provide stark, desert-like landscapes that contrast vividly with the humid, lowland zone. Sheer cliffs, broken only by huge slabs of jutting granite, pierce the sky. The Torre de Cerredo is the highest peak at 2,648 meters. The entire range, rivaling the Dolomites in dramatic mountain splendor, occupies some 1,330 square kilometers of northern Spain. This region is a haven for mountain climbing and has very controlled policies on hunting and fishing. Inquire in any of the numerous guide centers in the towns for information about these activities.

*Horreos, Picos de Europa*

In Cistierna, take the N621 following signs to Riaño, and start your ascent into one of the most scenic, natural landscapes in Europe. From Riaño, continue on the N621 for about 50 kilometers to Potes and continue north on N621 to **Panes**; then turn left and follow AS114 west in the direction of Cangas de Onís. This scenic drive follows the crystal-clear Cares River. Along this stretch of road are numerous picturesque mountain villages. No apartment blocks around here—the architecture is strictly local—old stone houses with red-tile roofs and wooden balconies, usually hung with drying garlic, are the typical sight. About 23 kilometers after leaving Panes, you come to **Arenas de Cabrales**, noted for its blue cheese. Cabrales cheese is made in these mountains from a mixture of cow's, goat's, and ewe's milk. If you want to sample some, watch for the signs found all along here for *queso de Cabrales*. The cheese can also be found in other towns of the area.

In this region, you will also notice many *horreos*, or grain-storage sheds, raised above the ground outside the farmhouses. These *horreos*, supported on pillars of rock, are especially colorful when viewed with the Picos de Europa in the background.

Leaving Arenas de Cabrales, continue west for about 26 kilometers until you see a road heading south to **Covadonga**. On the approach into town is a breathtaking view to the right of the Romanesque-style **Basilica of Our Lady of the Battles**, built in the late 19th century. This tiny town is touristy, but its setting is spectacular. Tourists also come to visit the **Santa Cueva**, a shrine tucked into a cave in the mountain, dedicated to the Virgin of Battles. It is the legendary place where Pelayo initiated the Reconquest of Spain from the Moslems in 718. The religious war raged on and off until 1492. Inside is the famous image of the Virgin of Covadonga, patron saint of Asturias, along with the sarcophagi of Pelayo and several of his relatives. In the treasury are the many gifts presented to the Virgin. Beneath the cave is a small pool, with a spring on one side, where you see visitors to the shrine collecting "holy" water.

If you are faint of heart, read no further. The area's main attraction is reached by a very steep, incredibly narrow road uphill from Covadonga (Los Lagos). About 7 kilometers further is the **Mirador de la Reina** (overlook) with views of the **Sierra de Covalierda** and the sea. If you persevere about 5 kilometers farther, you come to **Lago Enol** and

**Lago Ercina**, crystal-blue mountain lakes in a spellbinding setting in the **Montana de Covadonga** nature reserve. Though the road is tortuous, it is worth every twist and turn. You pass through green fields strewn with boulders before you reach the icy lakes. At a point called, logically enough, **Entre Dos Lagos** (Between Two Lakes), both lakes are visible from the top of a hill.

From Covadonga, return by the same road and rejoin the AS114, where you turn left to skirt Cangas de Onís and follow signposts for Santander onto the N634. (**Cangas de Onís** is a most attractive town, well worth a detour—it has a picture-perfect, 13th-century, humpbacked bridge adjacent to the modern road bridge.) You soon come to the N634, where you turn right in the direction of Santander joining the autopista A6, which whisks you along through some very pretty countryside, to the exit for Santillana del Mar.

In **Santillana del Mar,** the major attraction is atmosphere. It could fairly be called the most picturesque village in Spain and has retained its harmonious old-world feeling to an uncommon degree. The pure Romanesque architecture, from the Collegiate Church to the houses along Calle de las Lindas, will delight and amaze you. Just walk around and soak it in, there are some delightful shops and museums. One of the joys of the town is that it is completely pedestrian, though you are allowed to take your car in if you are staying here.

Another attraction of this area is its rich archaeological heritage. The **Altamira Cave** with its 14,000-year-old paintings of bison and other animals became so famous that visitors were damaging the ancient paintings with the large quantities of carbon dioxide they exhaled in the caves every day. To solve the problem, a full-scale reproduction has been made at the Altamira museum. Information on this and other caves that are open to the public is available at the Santallina del Mar tourist office just adjacent to the town car park.

When you have finished sampling the unforgettable atmosphere of Santillana, head east on the autopista (A6 which becomes A8) around **Santander**, a mostly modern provincial capital whose old city was destroyed in 1941 by a tornado and the resulting fires. The road turns south to skirt the bay and continues inland through cultivated farmland around **Colindres**, where you regain sight of the sea. Shortly afterward, you bypass Laredo, a popular seaside resort with a beautiful, large beach on Santona Bay. The freeway moves away from the coast, for a bit, through green rolling hills.

As you continue east on the A8, enter the **Basque Region** (*Vizcaya*), where you notice many of the town names indicated in both Basque and Spanish. Unlike the other languages in Spain, Basque is not a "Romance" or "Neo-Latin" language. Indeed, no one is sure where it comes from.

An hour's drive from Santander brings you to **Bilbao**, a huge city whose most outstanding tourist attraction is the **Guggenheim Museum** with its prime location along the bank of the Nervión River, with the Puente de La Salve, one of the city's main bridges, above it. Designed by Los Angeles architect Frank Gehry, it makes a statement for Bilbao, as the Opera House makes for Sydney. It is an extraordinary melding of interconnecting shapes with soaring blocks of limestone, gigantic curved forms of titanium, and massive curtains of curving glass—resulting in an enormous sculpture said to resemble a ship. The Guggenheim collection includes a broad range of modern and contemporary art—much of which is displayed in an ongoing series of contemporary exhibits. Be aware that a detailed map of Bilbao is needed to find the Guggenheim—the Bilbao *oueste* exit avoids the maze of downtown streets and brings you out on the riverbank opposite the Guggenheim.

Heading east from Bilbao (following signs for Irun and Francia), the A8 traverses over more attractive countryside of rolling hills, farms, and fields. Take exit 2 for **Hondarribia** (called *Fuenterrabía* in Spanish) and the airport (*aeropuerto*). Continue for several kilometers and enter under the narrow stone gate into the cobbled streets of old-town Hondarribia. On the main square is the **Parador de Hondarribia** located in a 10th-century castle that was considerably remodeled in the 16th century by the Holy Roman Emperor, Charles V. It has served as host (while a palace) to numerous monarchs in its long history. Hondarribia was often coveted by the French because of its strategic position. The castle was constructed with stone walls many meters thick. The small plaza

*Old Castile and the Cantabrian Coast*

in front of the parador overlooks a marina filled with colorful sailboats. On the other sides of the square are colorfully painted houses with iron or wood balconies. Stroll the narrow, cobblestone streets of town and walk down to the newer part of Hondarribia by the harbor, with its shops and cafes.

Leave Hondarribia towards France and take the N121A to Pamplona. It's a very scenic drive where the road goes from narrow, as it traces the River Bidasoa along the French border, to a major road, as it travels through tunnels and around picturesque villages of red-roofed houses surrounded by verdant fields, with the Pyrenees as a backdrop. After traversing the summit via the Puerto de Velate tunnel, the scenery quickly becomes more urban as you approach Pamplona.

**Pamplona** was the capital of the ancient kingdom of Navarre from the 10th to the 16th centuries, and is now best known for the "running of the bulls" festival of San Fermín (July 6–20), made famous by Ernest Hemingway in *The Sun Also Rises* (published in Britain as *Fiesta*). If you are not a fan of big cities, simply follow the ring road in the direction of Zaragosa, bringing you onto the autopista A15, and exit at Olite.

**Olite**, surrounded by agricultural lands and vineyards, is known as the "Gothic city," and you see why as the massive 15th-century fortress of Charles III, the **Palacio Real de Olite**, dominates the town. It has been restored to a semblance of its former glory. Visit royal bedchambers, grand halls, and climb the battlements for excellent views of the delightful old streets of the town. Part of the castle is the magnificent **Parador de Olite**. Just beside the parador is the 13th century former royal chapel, **Iglesia de Santa Maria la Real**, with its carved Gothic portal. Among the town's old streets you'll find several wine bodegas.

If you want to visit the birthplace of Spain's most famous monarchs, Ferdinand of Aragón, head east to **Sos del Rey Católico** perched atop a hill in the middle of the large flat plain. It seems as though it might blend into the brown mountain, if it were not for the square tower that juts up above the town. Sos is more museum than lived-in town and has undergone lots of restoration. Park beyond the walls and head for the **Sada Palace ,**a museum where you can visit the very bedroom (so it is claimed) where Ferdinand of Aragón was born. He was a model for Machiavelli in his classic study of governing in the days of monarchy. He was also the husband of Isabella, and the two were known as "The Catholic Monarchs" (*Los Reyes Católicos*) because of their strong support of the Church during the time of the Protestant Reformation Plan. There are splendid views of the fertile countryside from the castle and church at the top of the hill.

*Sos del Rey Católico*

You might also want to make a trip to **Javier** to visit **Javier Castle** via Sanguesa (bear right). It is an 18th-century castle built on the site of the birthplace of Saint Francis Xavier (1506), one of the early members of the Jesuit order and a very effective missionary to Japan in the service of the Portuguese. If you happen to be there on a Saturday night in the summer, you can see a sound and light show.

Return to Pamplona and continue west on N111, which was the Way of Saint James, to **Estella** where, in the Middle Ages, pilgrims stopped to venerate a statue of the Virgin reportedly found in 1085 by shepherds guided by falling stars. The Kings of Navarre

*Old Castile and the Cantabrian Coast*

chose this as their place of residence in the Middle Ages. Be sure to see the **Plaza San Martín** with, among many beautiful historic edifices, the 12th-century palace of the Kings of Navarre, one of the oldest non-religious buildings in Spain.

Rejoin the N111 and travel around the modern city of **Logroño**. Between Logroño and Burgos is the rampart-encircled **Santo Domingo de la Calzada**, whose most impressive 12th-century **cathedral** has a live rooster and hen in residence—in commemoration of a miracle which supposedly occurred when a young pilgrim's innocence was proved by the crowing of an already roasted cock. (They are replaced each year on May 12th.) On signs leading into town, you see the brief poem summing up the legend, which says, *Santo Domingo de la Calzada/ cantó la gallina/ después de asada.* Although the legend says a cock, the poem says a hen was his salvation. Maybe it just rhymed better. In any case, there is one of each in the cathedral. Its 18th-century belfry is famed as the prettiest in La Rioja.

From Santo Domingo, continue on the N120 through undulating wheat and potato fields (still following the Way of Saint James) to **Burgos**. Burgos is a large, not particularly charming city, but of historical interest. The capital of Old Castile from 951 to 1492 (when it lost its position to Valladolid), Burgos, has strong associations with the victorious Reconquest. Spain's epic hero, El Cid Campeador (champion), was born Rodrigo Díaz in nearby Vivar in 1026. His exploits in regaining Spain from the Moslems were immortalized in the first Spanish epic poem in 1180 and subsequent literary works. He and his wife, Ximena, are interred in the transept crossing of the cathedral.

The **cathedral** is, without doubt, the leading attraction of Burgos. Surpassed in size only by the cathedrals of Seville and Toledo, the flamboyant Gothic structure was begun in 1221 by Ferdinand III (the Saint) and completed in the 16th century. The artworks in the many chapels inside constitute a veritable museum. The two-story cloister contains much stone sculpture of the Spanish Gothic school. Do not fail to walk around the outside to see the marvelous decoration of the various portals. On the south side of the cathedral, if you walk toward the river, you pass through the highly ornate city gate called the Santa María arch. After crossing the river, you continue down Calle Miranda to the **Casa de**

**Miranda**, an archaeological museum. North of the cathedral, you can ascend the hill that harbors castle ruins and affords excellent city views. Enjoy the pretty pedestrian street along the riverfront, with its shops, lively bars, and cafés.

When it is time to leave Burgos, head south on the N1 to **Madrid**. For details of what to see and do in and around Madrid, refer to our itinerary *Madrid and More*.

# The Costa Brava and Beyond

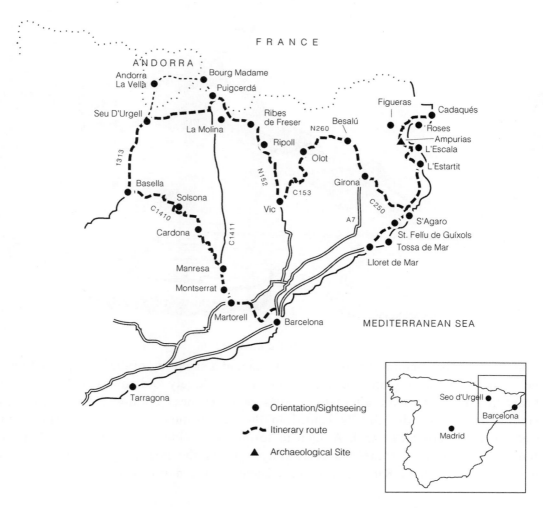

FRANCE

ANDORRA

Andorra
La Vella
Seu D'Urgell
1313
Basella
Solsona
C1410
Cardona
C1411
Manresa
Montserrat
Martorell

Bourg Madame
Puigcerdá
La Molina

Ribes
de Freser
Ripoll
N152

Vic

N260
Olot
C153

Besalú

Girona

Barcelona

Figueras
Cadaqués
Roses
Ampurias
L'Escala
L'Estartit

A7
C250
S'Agaro
St. Felíu de Guíxols
Tossa de Mar
Lloret de Mar

MEDITERRANEAN SEA

Tarragona

● Orientation/Sightseeing

▬ ▬ Itinerary route

▲ Archaeological Site

Seo d'Urgell
Barcelona
Madrid

# The Costa Brava and Beyond

*Tossa de Mar*

This itinerary is essentially a tour of Catalonia and a sampling of the multiple delights to be savored in this region: spectacular mountains, lovely old towns and castles, and beautiful seacoasts with alternating cliffs and beaches. Catalonia has been settled continuously since the Greeks landed in the 6th century B.C. In the 15th century, Catalonia was combined with Aragón to form a vast kingdom extending to Naples in Italy, and it became, somewhat reluctantly, part of the new kingdom created by the marriage of Ferdinand, King of Aragón, to Isabella, Queen of Castile.

Catalonia has fiercely defended its autonomy during its entire history. As a Republican stronghold in the Civil War of 1936–1939, the region experienced a great deal of the bloodshed. When the Nationalists (under Francisco Franco) won, regional autonomy was suppressed. Only after the adoption of the new constitution of 1978 were the various regions allowed to regain a measure of autonomy, and Catalonia was the first to do so.

In addition to Spanish, the regional language of Catalan is widely used. As in Galicia and the Basque country, you often see things spelled in the regional dialect and, since 1978, most official signs have been replaced with bilingual ones. Cuisine in Catalonia vies with that of the Basque region for the title of best in the country. It includes many seafood and meat dishes with a variety of sauces. In Catalonia, the mixture of sandy beaches, rugged coastlines, gorgeous mountain scenery, and fine food offers something for everyone.

PACING: Depending on how far you want to go on your first night out of Barcelona, choose between Cardona or Seu d'Urgell for your first overnight. Allow at least two nights in the Pyrenees and two nights at the beach before returning to Barcelona. Begin this itinerary with a stay in Barcelona, an impressive and prosperous city with much to see and do. For suggestions on sightseeing in Barcelona, see *Barcelona Highlights*.

Leave Barcelona by going south on the A2 freeway to exit 25 just outside of town. Turn right on NII to **Martorell**, an ancient town where the Llobregat River is spanned by the Puente (bridge) del Diablo, said to have been built by the Carthaginian general, Hannibal, in 218 B.C. He erected the triumphal arch in honor of his father, Hamilcar Barca. Continue on NII to Abrera and bear right on C1411 to reach **Montserrat**, whose ragged, stark-gray silhouette makes you see instantly why it is called "serrated mountain." After entering the village of **Monistrol**, follow the signs to the monastery on top of the hill— about 7 kilometers, along a zigzagging road offering increasingly magnificent views. You can opt for the *funicular* (cable car ) from a clearly marked point just before Monistrol, if you would rather avoid the mountain driving and the sometimes severe parking problem up top. Taking the cable car certainly makes the trip more enjoyable for the driver.

The golden-brown **monastery** at the crown of Montserrat contrasts strikingly with the jutting, gray peaks of the mountain. The setting is ultra-dramatic, and it is claimed that on a clear day you can see the Balearic Islands in the Mediterranean. The monastery church is home to the famed Moreneta, or **Black Madonna**. The figure, reportedly made by Saint Luke and brought to Barcelona by Saint Peter, was hidden in the Santa Cueva (holy cave) at the time of the Moorish invasions, then found by shepherds in the 9th century. This is the patron saint of Catalonia, and is venerated by thousands of pilgrims annually. Numerous marked paths and cable cars take you to various viewpoints, as well as the monastery, along the 22-kilometer massif.

After you have visited this marvelous mountain, one of the most famous in the world for its unusual appearance (the inspiration for Montsalvat in Wagner's *Parsifal),* return to Monistrol and turn left to **Manresa**. Visit the elaborate 14th-century collegiate **Church of Santa María de la Seo** on a rocky cliff above the town. Follow the signs for Solsona and, as you leave town, do not fail to look back to catch a spectacular view of Montserrat in the distance. Follow the Rio Cardoner through red, pine-covered ridges, punctuated with little farming towns, to **Cardona**, beautifully situated and crowned by an outstanding fortress/castle, which just happens to be the **Parador de Cardona**. This magnificent parador retains much of its 10th- and 11th-century construction, and the purely Romanesque Collegiate Church of Saint Vincent is in the center.

Cardona's earliest significance was as a source of salt for the Romans. The conical mountain of salt to the south of town has been mined for centuries. The town itself is very quiet unless you happen to be there on Sunday, market day, when things are considerably busier. If you time your visit for the first half of September, you can experience the annual festival with a "running of the bulls," similar to that of Pamplona.

A lovely side trip is to the ancient brown-and-red village of **Solsona**, about 15 minutes away, which is entered through a stone gate in the old town wall. It has a salt and craft museum, and a quaint old quarter for wandering. The parador in Cardona is wonderful, but Solsona is a more interesting town.

Head northwest out of Cardona following a lovely stretch of road through rugged hillsides, dotted with ruins of castles and monasteries, through Solsona (worth a stop if you did not make the side trip above).

Continue to **Basella**, then turn north, following the Segre River for the 50-kilometer drive to Seu d'Urgell. At this point, the **Pyrenees** begin to show their brooding presence in the distance ahead. Cross the Segre to reach the aquamarine Oliana reservoir. From the banks of the reservoir, you get splendid views of the lake surrounded by its gray-green sheer cliffs, which occasionally seem almost man-made, giant, stone edifices. At the other end of the reservoir is **Coll de Nargo**, a village stacked on the hillside like a layer cake. Beyond **Organya**, the cliffs become steeper and closer as you traverse the deep Organya gorge. The gray cliffs rise to 610 meters here and make an impressive backdrop before you come out into the fertile valley where Seu d'Urgell is located.

**Seu d'Urgell** is handily located at the confluence of two rivers; one flows from France, the other from Andora. It has a small, historic center with a 12th-century **cathedral** and a **Museo Diocesa** full of medieval manuscripts and works of art, located near the parador. Be sure to head for the **Olympic park** to enjoy canoeing and rafting. Another park contains a reconstruction of the ancient cloisters with a fun twist—all the gargoyles are heads of famous persons (we spotted Marilyn Monroe). The town makes an excellent base for walking in the summer, cross-country skiing in the winter, and visiting Pyrenean Mountain villages.

If you want a daytrip that combines scenery with shopping, shopping, shopping, you can take a daytrip from Seu d'Urgell to **Andorra**, cross into **France**, and return to Seu. Just 9 kilometers north of Seu, you reach the border of the tiny principality of Andorra, which is under the joint administration of the Bishop of Urgell and the French government. Recognized throughout history for the fierce independence of its residents, Andorra is now known mostly as a duty free zone, and thus a shopper's paradise. You see an infinite number of duty free stores selling goods lining the streets both in and around the capital, **Andorra La Vella**. Besides shopping, Andorra offers mountain scenery *sans pareil*. You ascend through pine forests crowned by the barren, blue-gray, snow-dotted peaks of the

Pyrenees. It is truly a breathtaking drive. You see numerous ski areas as you cross the Envalira Pass and descend the mountainside to the French border. From here, it is a short drive through the French Pyrenees to **Bourg Madame**. Just outside of town, you cross back into Spain at **Puigcerdá**, a small, fortified border town. From here, head west through the pretty valley of the Segre River back to Seu.

On the first part of today's drive the signposting is tricky, so follow carefully within this paragraph. Leave Seu following signposts to Barcelona and the Cadi tunnel (neither of which you are going to but this gets you well on the way) to your first destination the ski resort of La Molina. Follow the Segre gorge to Bellver de Cardanya, after which you take a right turn (Cadi Tunnel) and the road brings you through verdant meadows in a high valley. Now ignore signs for Cadi and follow signs for Puigcerdá, until you see a right turn down to the ski resort of La Molina (on an unnumbered rural road).

**La Molina** is one of Catalonia's most important ski resorts. From here, the road climbs up to the N152, a mountain road that clings to the hillside high above the valley and winds you down through **Ribes de Freser**, a village of pastel-colored buildings along the River Ribes. Follow the valley down skirting the town of **Ripoli** with its extensive suburbs. There's a **Benedictine monastery** founded by Visigothic Count Wilfred "the Hairy" in the heart of town, but parking is very difficult. Wilfred was responsible for freeing Catalonia from the domination of Charlemagne.

Leaving Ripoli, follow the N260 almost to Vic, turning left through Manlleu onto the B522; which brings you to Sant Marti Senscorts, where you follow the C153 in the direction of Olot. The higher you drive, the more the scenery improves. You must make the short detour to the quaint, little town of **Rupit**, where gray stone houses snuggle against cliffs alongside the river. Walk across the footbridge into town; stroll through the age-old cobblestone streets and plazas with their stone houses and iron balconies hung with colorful flowers. It is a perfect place for pictures and an old-world atmosphere pervades.

Skirt **Olot** and, just after the long tunnel, glance back to see **Castellfollit de la Roca** poised on a rocky outcrop at the very edge of a deep ravine.

**Besalú** is well worth a visit. Skirt the town until you pass the old bridge on your right (park and walk into town). Stroll the streets with its shops and restaurants. Sit for a while and soak up the atmosphere of the town's colorful square. The tourist office by the bridge will supply you with a map of the town.

*Besalú*

Leaving Besalú, the C150 brings you quickly to Girona a bustling, historic city whose traffic-clogged streets deter you from heading for its historic center. The Roman walls (*Passeig Arquelògic*) provide a walkway around the city. Downtown there are several rows of old houses crowded beside the river. Behind them is the Ramblar de Libertat with its shops and cafes.

From Girona, it's a short drive to the **Costa Brava** (Wild Coast)—which runs south from the French border to Blanes. It's a lot less "brava" than it used to be, with the appearance every few kilometers of another hotel or resort filled with white cottages with red-tile roofs and all the support and entertainment services that go with them. But the sea and the rugged coastline are as beautiful as ever. The water is a clear, deep blue and dotted with sailboats and motor cruisers. Choose a base with a suitable hotel and set out to explore.

Villages from north to south:

**Cadaques** is a whitewashed and picturesque fishing town/artist colony that surrounds the harbor.

**Roses** lies at the head of a sheltered bay, its sandy beach is the longest in the Costa Brava—a mecca for watersports.

**L'Escala** is a smaller resort with fine beaches and a small fishing harbor protected by two inlets.

**Begur** is a hilltop town just inland of the coast. Its castle ruins offer a nice view of the town and its maze of streets. From Begur, you have excellent views of the coast.

**Agua Blava** is a rocky cove dotted with recreational boats. There are several lovely hotels overlooking the blue cove.

**Llafranc** is a very attractive resort with a curve of white sand and a harbor of boats. A promenade leads from here to the adjacent town of **Calella**, a pretty resort town with an impressive botanical garden on a cliff overlooking the sea.

**La Platja d'Aro** has a long, sandy beach lined with high rise hotels

**S'Agaró** is an elegant resort with a large, public beach and magnificent homes in a private, gated community.

**Tossa de Mar** is magnificent in a beautiful setting with a pretty, little beach curving to the cobbled streets of the old town, crowned by a lighthouse, surrounded by 13th-century walls, and impressive round towers. From here, the road follows a spectacular, cliff top route to **Lloret de Mar** (whose natural beauty is somewhat tempered by high-rise apartments and hotels). It has a long, golden beach, which makes it exceedingly popular, especially in the summer months when its population more than triples.

# Pilgrimage to Santiago

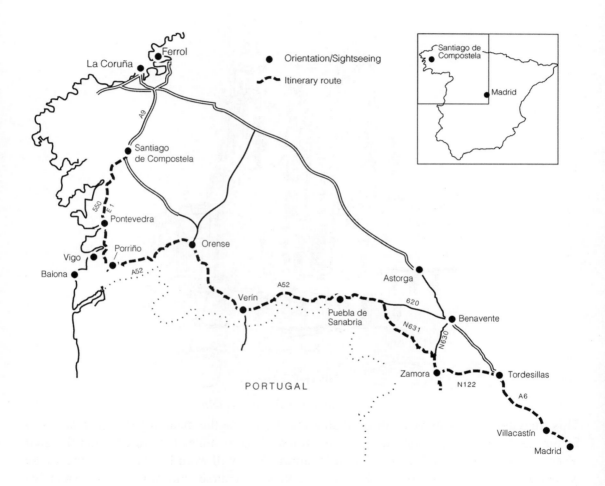

Orientation/Sightseeing

Itinerary route

# Pilgrimage to Santiago

*Cathedral, Santiago de Compestela*

This itinerary takes you to a hallowed spot that was once the most popular destination in Spain: Santiago de Compostela, site of the tomb of Saint James the Apostle and the goal of countless, religious pilgrims for a millennium. You will even be staying in one of the places they stayed in (modernized a bit since then, of course, and rather more expensive now). Most of the destinations described are in the region of Galicia, which is basically, that part of Spain directly north of Portugal: the provinces of Lugo, Pontevedra, La Coruña, and Orense. It was at one time part of Portugal, but (as a result of some royal intrigues) was separated from that kingdom in 1128. Although everyone speaks Spanish, Galicia has its own special language (somewhat a mixture of Portuguese and Spanish). Because of this, you will notice some spelling variations in town names, depending on whether the Galician or the Castilian spelling is used. The area is separated from the rest of the country by several mountain ranges. Perhaps for that reason, Galicia seems to have kept its face turned to the sea and has developed a strong, seafaring tradition and economy. It is also the region that has maintained the strongest Celtic influence since the Celts invaded the peninsula around 3,000 years ago. Galician folk music still has the sound of bagpipes (called here the *gaita*), and the name Galicia is from the same root as Gaul and Wales. Galician cuisine, like that of Portugal, puts a lot of emphasis on cod (*bacalao*) prepared in many ways. *Empanadas* (folded meat or fish pies) are a typical dish, as is *lacón con grelos*, consisting of smoked pork shoulder and turnip greens. Shellfish are also commonly available. Be sure to try *vieira* (scallops), a regional specialty prepared in many delicious ways.

PACING: This itinerary is our suggested route for those who prefer to drive between two of Spain's spectacular destinations—Madrid and Santiago de Compostela. Leaving Madrid, make Zamora your first overnight. The sights of this characterful walled town can easily be seen in a few hours. The next suggested stop, Verín, is chosen not for its charm, but for its convenience in breaking the journey, so one night is all you need. When you reach Baiona, one night will suffice. Allow at least two nights in Santiago de Compostela.

This itinerary begins in **Madrid**, a most convenient starting point, and a city worthy of more visits, time and again. Be sure to spend a few days enjoying the many museums (exhibits are constantly changing) and taking advantage of fine dining before heading off to northwestern Spain. For more in-depth suggestions on sightseeing in and around Madrid, see *Madrid and More*. This part of the country is all too often foregone by the traveler (considering it relatively inaccessible and with time only for the better-known tourist attractions), but this region has its share of the best sights in the country and a flavor all its own.

Leave Madrid, heading northwest on the A6 freeway until it turns into NVI and continue north towards Zamora. After a few kilometers, you pass **Arevalo**, one of the oldest towns in Castile; where, in a 14th-century castle, Isabella spent her early years. She was born in nearby **Madrigal de Las Altas Torres,** whose lovely Plaza de la Villa is typical of Spain and is dominated by the Church of Saint Martin's two Mudéjar towers. The **Convent of Saint Francis** was founded by the saint himself in 1214. If church architecture is your interest, you should see the beautiful **Our Lady of the Lugareta Nunnery**, 2 kilometers south of town. It constitutes one of the major Romanesque structures in Spain.

Next you come to **Medina del Campo**, historically a very important Castilian market town, but now not really worth a stop. However, the historic market town of **Tordesillas**, where you cross the Duero, one of Spain's major rivers, does make an interesting stop. Juana the Mad (Ferdinand and Isabella's daughter) locked herself away in the **Santa Clara Convent** here for 44 years after the death of her husband, Phillip the Fair in 1506. The convent has a beautiful patio, and the nearby church has a fabulous *artesonado* ceiling, which you should not miss. This is also the place where the Spanish and Portuguese signed a treaty in 1494 that divided the world between them. Setting a line some 1,620 kilometers west of the Cape Verde Islands, it resulted in Spain's ownership of all of South America except Brazil.

From Tordesillas, turn west through the small fortified town of **Toro**, picturesquely situated above the Duero and well known for its wines; and then to **Zamora**, which figured prominently in *El Cid* and has been a point of contention between various warring factions since the time of the Visigoths. Castile and Portugal battled for possession of the strategic town. It was occupied first by one and then by the other in a chaotic point of the struggle. The fortified town seems to be wall-to-wall churches; but if you can see only one, visit the impressive 12th-century **cathedral**, whose tower dome ringed by arched windows should not be missed. Its museum has a stunning collection of

15th- and 16th-century Flemish tapestries. The town, with its many beautifully preserved Romanesque monuments, is a great place for simply strolling and poking down narrow streets and alleyways. Its wealth of beautiful mansions and quaint little plazas add greatly to the charm and atmosphere.

When you are ready to continue the pilgrimage, head north from Zamora on the N630 then bear left after onto the N631, which takes you through the **Sierra de la Culebra** (snake) National Reserve. At **Mombuey**, watch for the lovely 13th-century church—now a national monument. Several mountain ranges converge in the area you pass through, forming a gloriously scenic setting. Rustic, stone houses with slate roofs and iron or wood balconies are characteristic of this region.

The landscape grows increasingly rugged as you near **Puebla de Sanabria**. If time allows, stop to see this fine example of a small, Castilian hill town that dominates the countryside. Visit the plaza at the tiptop of town, ranking among the most remarkable we have seen. It perfectly preserves a medieval atmosphere, flanked by hunkering whitewashed houses, the old city hall with its wooden gallery, and a reddish 12th-century granite church. The plaza can be reached by car by crossing the river and bearing left, or, for the hardier among you, on foot from the east side. Either way, you will love the atmosphere and panoramic views from the top.

Join the A52 freeway heading west. Unless you are staying at the parador, bypass Verín (a modern metropolis), passing over numerous viaducts with views of the surrounding countryside. You officially enter Galicia, characterized by rocky landscape and equally rocky buildings constructed from the native stone. Continue on toward Orense, passing between green hillsides dotted with stone houses.

The provincial capital of **Orense**, a large town spread along the river, is famed for its sulfur springs. Beyond its large urban area, it has an enchanting old quarter with twisting, stepped streets overhung by old houses, delightfully punctuated with picturesque plazas. This was an important capital of the pre-Visigoth Suevi in the 6th and 7th centuries. An old bridge (near newer ones), across the Miño, was constructed on the foundations of a

13<sup>th</sup>-century Roman bridge. Take time out to stop here to see the Plaza Mayor and its Romanesque Bishop's palace. Park in one of the plazas and walk around the old quarter to visit the shops.

*Baiona*

Continue in the direction of Vigo. The A52 freeway whisks you through the beautiful **Miño Valley**. (Legend has it that gold existed here, thus the name of Orense from the Spanish *oro*, meaning gold.) The highway borders a landscape carpeted with vineyards, and parallels the River Miño as far as Ventosela. Then the landscape turns into scrubby green hills with the occasional isolated farm. Take the A52 almost to Vigo, where the AP9 freeway leads you to **Baiona**, whose former inhabitants were the first to hear the news of the discovery of the New World when the *Pinta* moored here in 1493 (the *Santa María* sought refuge in Lisbon after a storm). Subsequently, it continued to be a major port for the many gold- and silver-laden ships that followed thereafter from America. Thoughts similar to these will likely come to mind as you stroll the perfectly preserved seaside battlements encircling the **Parador de Baiona**, the premier tourist attraction in town (non-guests of the parador pay for visiting privileges). The castle ramparts are 3 kilometers long and some parts date from the 2nd century B.C. (other parts are as recent as the 17th century). The walk around them affords bird's-eye views of the crashing sea, the port, and the coastline stretching into the horizon. If you crave more, you can visit Baiona's 12th-century collegiate church or drive the 30 kilometers down the coast to the Portuguese border. About halfway, you pass the little fishing village of **Oya**. At the end of the road is the port of **La Guardia**.

From Baiona, follow the AP9, around Vigo and Pontevedra**,** to **Santiago de Compostela**. According to legend, Saint James (in Spanish, Santiago or Sant Yago) the Apostle came to Galicia and spent seven years preaching there. After he was beheaded in Jerusalem, his disciples brought his remains back to Spain by boat, mooring in Padrón, and (after some difficulty), he was finally buried. Seven centuries later, in the year 813, mysterious stars appeared in the sky above his grave and led the Bishop Teodomiro to the spot. The traditional explanation for the name Compostela is that it comes from the Latin *Campus Stellae* or field of stars. The city that grew up around the area was named Santiago de Compostela, and Saint James became the patron saint of all Spain. From that time, pilgrimages began and continue (although not quite so numerous as in those times) to the present day. Most pilgrims from Europe took the Way of Saint James through modern-day Vitoria, Burgos, and León. Another route, considered dangerous because of highwaymen, ran closer to the northern coast. As many as two million pilgrims per year made the exhausting journey in the Middle Ages.

Santiago de Compostela is justifiably one of Spain's most famous cities. Begin your sightseeing at the magnificent **Plaza de España**, bordered on the north side by the **Parador Hotel Dos Reis Católicos**, built (at the order of Ferdinand and Isabella as a hospice for the pilgrims) on the east by the baroque cathedral, on the south by the Romanesque College of San Jerónimo, and on the west by the neoclassical city hall.

The **cathedral** dates from the 11th to 13th centuries and was built on the site of Saint James's tomb (and several earlier churches). An unusual feature of the building is the existence of plazas on all sides, which allow encompassing views of the cathedral from the plazas and vice versa. Be sure to take a stroll around the cathedral through the Plaza

Inmaculada on the north, the Plaza de la Quintana on the east, and the beautiful Plaza de las Platerías (Silversmiths) on the south side. Probably the most impressive artistic element of the cathedral is the Pórtico de la Gloria (sculptured doorway). As millions of pilgrims have before you, touch the central pillar Santos dos Croques (Saint of Bumps), said to impart luck and wisdom. The high altar is magnificent, and there's often a line of devout pilgrims waiting to go behind the altar to embrace the mantle of the 13th-century statue of Saint James.

You will also see modern-day pilgrims throughout Spain, walking to Santiago along the Way of Saint James, following the same roads that have been trod by millions before them. As might be imagined, the journey used to be a treacherous one with bandits and various fiefdoms at war along the route. Pilgrims wore a hat adorned with three scallop shells and carried a tall staff. These symbols identified them as pilgrims on a religious journey and were supposed to guarantee them safe passage through dangerous lands. The pilgrims today usually carry a tall staff and frequently wear a badge of scallop shells.

As for the rest of Santiago, most of it can be seen by walking across the plaza and on Calle del Franco in the streets to the south. These narrow, cobbled, pedestrian streets are full of old, stone buildings, many small plazas, shops of all kinds. Numerous restaurants and cafés line the narrow streets, which should be explored at leisure for a taste of northern-Spanish atmosphere. Be sure to include a morning walk round the colorful market (every day but Sunday).

SIDE TRIPS: If you need an excuse to extend your stay in the area there are some interesting side trips. If quaint, fishing villages and gorgeous scenery appeal, get some bread, some smooth Galician San Simön cheese, and slightly sparkling, white *ribeiro* wine and head west on C543 to **Noya**, turning north on C550 to explore the coastal road along the *rías*. If more history of the Way of Saint James intrigues you, drive east on N547 to **Arzúa**, then on to **Melide**—both stops on the medieval pilgrims' route. If large cities attract you, the major city in Galicia, **La Coruña**, is only an hour away via the A9 freeway. This was Generalissimo Franco's hometown, which (understandably) became an important industrial center during his regime.

*Pilgrimage to Santiago*

# Treasures off the Beaten Track

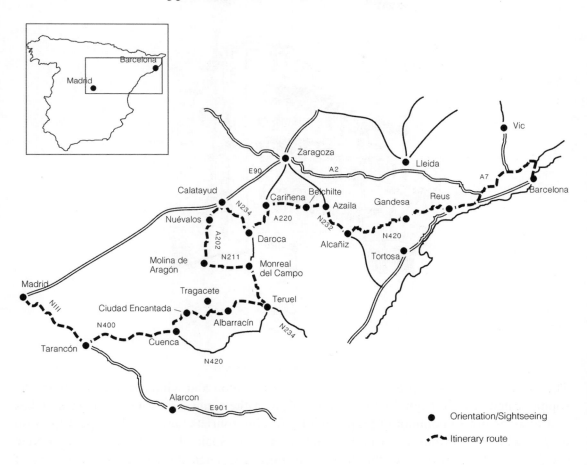

# Treasures off the Beaten Track

*Hanging Houses, Cuenca*

This itinerary starts off in New Castile, traverses Aragón and winds up in Barcelona, the sophisticated seaside capital of Catalonia. Most of the route, as its name suggests, takes you to areas not so commonly frequented by foreign tourists, and should appeal to those of you who are anxious for a more intimate taste of Spain. It heads east through New Castile, which holds in store the beautifully rugged Cuenca Range; and Cuenca, one of Spain's most enchanting medieval towns, famous for its "hanging houses." Then the route continues on to Aragón with its small, earth-colored, hidden villages nestled in gorgeous, scenic mountain valleys or in the midst of olive groves and vineyards. It is easy to understand why these are considered some of the most ancient settlements in the country: the medieval and Moorish past is evident at every turn.

Starting in the 11th century, Aragón began to expand its dominions. Within three centuries, it included parts of southern France, Catalonia, Navarre, and all of southeastern Spain, Sicily, and Naples. Thus, when Ferdinand II of Aragón married Isabella I of Castile (which included the eastern half of Spain) in 1464, the modern nation-state was born. No longer so extensive, the old kingdom is now characterized mostly by agricultural activity. The final stop, Barcelona, provides considerable contrast: it is Spain's second largest city and one as glamorous and worldly as any in Europe.

Almost all tourists fly into or out of Madrid when visiting Spain. After a few days enjoying this lovely city, many then drive on to Barcelona, another of Spain's jewels. It is possible to take a freeway most of the way from Madrid to Barcelona—possible but not very interesting. This itinerary outlines a much more engaging way to make the journey from Spain's largest to its second-largest city. By following this route, you enjoy some fabulous sights that are truly "off the beaten track." For more in-depth suggestions on sightseeing in and around Madrid see *Madrid and More*.

PACING: This itinerary links Madrid and Barcelona. Cuenca, a fascinating cliff-top town, merits an overnight stay. Plan on spending one night in Teruel. If you want to linger to explore the Monasterio de Piedra Park, stay for a night in Nuévalos. One night is suggested for Alcañiz before heading to Barcelona.

Make your way to the southeast side of Madrid and head out of town on the A3 freeway (which becomes NIII when you leave the city). Continue through Arganda del Rey, then wind through lovely scenery to **Tarancón**, a little country town with a Gothic church and a mansion built by Queen María Cristina. As you drive, you get a strong feel for one of Spain's major geographical features, the central meseta, or plateau. The drive east between here and Cuenca is one of the loveliest in Spain—through pretty rolling hills of wheat and sunflowers contrasting with pale, golden hay fields.

**Cuenca** was originally constructed on the top of the cliff. This is the part known today as the old town, the area of most interest to the visitor. The best way to reach this district is to turn sharply right just after you cross the river as you head into town following the pink signs for *Casco Antiguo*. The road climbs steeply and enters a small plaza through a massive stone gate. Park here and explore this engaging town by foot.

Once you are in the old town ask for directions to the hanging houses *(casas colgadas)*, seemingly perched in midair at the edge of the cliff. Inside one of these ancient structures, in impressive and tasteful surroundings, is Spain's most important **Museo de Arte Abstracto** (abstract art). The extensive collection of Spanish masters is a must to visit. Also situated in one of the old, cliff-top houses is the restaurant **Meson Casas Colgadas**. If it is not mealtime, you still might want to stop for a cool drink and to savor the views over the ravine. The very best place to photograph these old houses is from the middle of the footbridge that leads to the parador.

The Gothic **cathedral**, parts of which date from the 13th century, is a highlight of the town: be sure to go in to see the elaborate interior. The treasury, **Museo Diocesano**, is also worth a visit—among other works of art, there are two paintings by El Greco. Sit in the lively **Plaza Mayor** to soak up the typical Spanish flavor of the town and save some time for a leisurely walk through the picturesque streets and alleys of this old quarter.

When you are ready to leave Cuenca head north on CM2105 into the **Serranía de Cuenca** a vast mountainous area dissected by two gorges. After 23 km you come to the viewpoint **Ventana del Diablo** which gives you a fabulous view of the gorge. A few kilometers further on, turn right for the 5-kilometer side trip to the **Ciudad Encantada** (Enchanted City) where the limestone has been eroded into shapes that resemble (with a bit of imagination) buildings, animals, and monsters. You buy your ticket from the booth and follow a well-marked footpath for about an hour through the interesting rock formations.

*Treasures off the Beaten Track*

Join up again with the CM2105 going east through **Una,** a village beneath towering cliffs, and **La Toba**, at the end of a lovely turquoise reservoir that sits beneath the cliffs. Follow the meandering Júcar River and watch carefully for the right-hand turn signpost for Teruel. This narrow road climbs up the **Puerto de El Cubillo Pass** into the **Montes Universales**. This scenery is wonderful, with pine trees lining the narrow road and the sharp gray mountain crests in the distance.

Cresting the pass, watch for a monument in the meadow to your left. It marks where the Tagus River begins its long journey to the Atlantic through Toledo and Lisbon in Portugal. It is amazing to see that this important river's origin is a tiny spring flowing out from under a pile of rocks. Continue winding amidst marvelous scenery with expansive views of the valley. Skirt the little town of **Royuelo** and the river gorge to the spectacularly situated little mountain town of **Albarracín**. Designated a historical monument by the national government, this whimsical town looks as if it were carved into the living rock below the ruined castle whose towers reach toward the sky.

Albarracín is a medieval gem with narrow, twisting, cobblestone streets (almost exclusively pedestrian) and ancient brick, stone, and wooden houses whose roofs practically touch each other over the tiniest alleyways. The atmosphere cannot have changed much over the past several hundred years. The handsome **cathedral**, with its collection of 16th-century Brussels tapestries, is interesting to visit, and it is fun to explore the numerous ceramics shops selling their locally made wares.

A half-hour drive finds you in the industrial city of **Teruel**. Surrounded by the gorges of the Río Turia, it is rich in Mudéjar monuments. Mudéjar is the style created by the Moors who continued to live in Christian-dominated areas even after they were reconquered. The Moors remained in Teruel a particularly long time, hence the prevalence of the style here. Five Mudéjar towers, detached belfries with obviously Oriental ornamentation, are spread around the old town. The 13th-century **cathedral** has a coffered ceiling painted with scenes of medieval life. One of the five towers is the belfry for the cathedral.

Next to **Iglesia de San Pedro** (which has another of the towers as a belfry) is the funerary chapel of the "**Lovers of Teruel**." The legend of Isabel and Juan Diego, who lived in the 13th century and who died of grief at being unable to marry because of her father's disapproval. They were buried in a single grave and their remains are on display here in a glass coffin topped by an alabaster relief of the lovers reaching out to touch hands. To visit the chapel, ring at a nearby door (indicated by a sign) and someone will come down to open it for you. (Tip a couple of euros.)

Just east is the triangular Plaza del Torico (baby bull), a popular gathering place with a tiny statue of, logically enough, a baby bull in the center.

When you are ready to move on, travel north on what must be one of Spain's best country roads (N234) towards the tidy farming center of **Monreal del Campo**, at the foot of the Sierra Menera, and bear left by the impressive, tiny fortified town of **Pozuel del Campo** with its crumbling walls and huge, imposing church. Continue to **Molina de Aragón**, an ancient, pre-Moorish village, once a hotly disputed strong point between warring Aragón and Castile. Perched above the town is a dramatic, red-tinged fortress surrounded by extensive crumbling walls and several restored towers, of which one, the 11th-century Torre de Aragón, is a national monument. This fortress was one of several, including Sigüenza and Alarcón, which served as a second line of Christian defense during the Reconquest.

Turn north in Molina de Aragón, first along a flat road through farmland, then on a more scenic drive through rugged countryside toward Nuévalos, and the **Monasterio de Piedra,** a monastery founded in 1195 that was by the 18th century a vast monastic establishment. You can tour the older portion of the buildings: the chapter house, the refectory, the Cistercian monks' cellars and the kitchen that was allegedly the first place in Europe where drinking chocolate, from Mexico, was prepared. A hotel is located within the monastic buildings—see listing. Surrounding the monastery is a lush park watered by the river that flows through the grounds in capricious ways, forming waterfalls and pools of great beauty. Be sure to visit the series of waterfalls La Caprichosa (the whimsical lady) and the 52-meter Cola de Caballo (horse's tail)—you can see both from a vista point and from underneath in the Iris Grotto. In contrast to the rushing cascades, the lake properly carries the name of Mirror Lake, a truly spectacular natural sight. Buy a ticket at the entrance and follow the arrows for an unforgettable stroll.

Nearby the pretty little town of **Nuévalos** sits in a valley at the head of a vast reservoir surrounded by the deep-red hills. (Scenery lovers should take a side trip to the spa of **Jaraba**, reached by going south to the tiny village of Campillo de Aragón and turning right. You have a 12-kilometer drive through a red, green, and gold patchwork quilt of fields as you go over the Campillo Pass, then you descend into steep canyons lined with dark-red cliffs. This is a dramatic excursion.)

Leave this gorgeous setting by heading northeast to Calatayud. Drive through alternately dusty gray plateaus and deep-red earth planted with fruit trees, vines, and olives, along with occasional hay and wheat fields. **Calatayud** is built up against a hillside, crowned by the minaret of an old mosque and the ruins of the Moorish **Kalat-Ayub** (Castle of Ayub). You might want to stop for a closer inspection of the Mudéjar tower sitting impressively atop its rocky ridge above the hillside covered with tiny houses. You can see the castle on the mountain well before you reach the town, but it blends in so well with the stone ridge that you may not notice unless you are watching for it.

From here drive southeast on the N234, passing the dramatic ruins of a castle above the little village of **Maluenda**, then drive through **Velilla**, **Fuentes de Jiloca**, and **Montón**, all picturesque villages hugging the hillside above the lush Jiloca River valley. As you leave Montón, notice that the vines begin to be replaced by fruit trees on the red landscape.

Turn right on N330 to reach the town of **Daroca**. This beautifully situated medieval town is still enclosed by crumbling 13th-century walls with 114 towers. Park near the first gate you come to and take time to stroll along the Calle Mayor, visit the church of **Santa María** church, and the **Plaza Mayor**.

Back on N330, drive northeast over the winding **Puerto de Paniza Pass**. As you descend from the pass, you come to **Cariñena**, a little town famous for its wine.

Head east on the A220, driving through seemingly endless vineyards on the gently undulating, reddish-brown hills. A short drive brings you to **Fuendetodos**, the birthplace of Francisco de Goya y Lucientes, one of Spain's greatest artists. The **Casa Museo de Goya** is definitely worth a short stop to see the simple house where he lived. The house is furnished with 18th-century pieces in an effort to re-create the way it must have looked when Goya lived there. You can even see the room where he was born. An admission ticket also gives you access to the engraving museum just up the street. (Closed Mondays.)

Continue east, through scrubby hills occasionally alternating with lush green vineyards, to **Belchite**, which was extensively destroyed during the Civil War (1936–39). The rebuilt town stands next to the ruins of the former one, a grim monument to the horror of that conflict. The old town soon appears on the right as you leave: an eerie moonscape of bombed-out buildings, houses, and church.

A short drive farther, after a stretch of pancake flat pastureland, lies **Azaila** sitting atop its rocky cliff. Turn right on the N232 winding up through the town for the drive to **Híjar**, another beautiful, small hilltop town overlooking the Martin River from behind its ruined walls. The terrain around the town changes to reflect the ravines carved by the river. From Híjar it is a short drive to **Alcañiz**.

As you enter town, you see the **Parador de Alcañiz** sitting high above the town. Part of the 12th-century castle was converted to a palace in the 18th century, and that part now houses the parador. Behind the palace the 12<sup>th</sup>-century keep, with its 14<sup>th</sup>-century frescoes, is open as a museum.

Wander down into town to the **Plaza de España** flanked by the **town hall** (*ayuntamiento*) with a Renaissance façade, the arcaded 15th-century **Lonja** (trade hall) with its gothic arches, and the highly elaborate, baroque façade of the colossal **Colegiata de Santa María** (Saint Mary's collegiate church).

Head southeast on N232, then take N420 east towards Tarragona. As you leave Alcañiz, you see terraces of olive trees on the rolling hillsides. About 8 kilometers past **Calaceite**, at **Caseres**, you officially enter Catalonia. Since Catalonians speak (in addition to Spanish) their own language, Catalan, you find a number of words spelled differently from the way you may be used to (e.g., river is *riu* instead of *río*).

Nearing **Gandesa,** olive groves give way to vineyards. The town has been rebuilt since it suffered severe destruction during the Civil War and thus is a relatively modern town, at the end of a pretty drive. After crossing one of Spain's most important rivers, the Ebro, at Móra de Ebro, you arrive at the new town from where the best view of the old quarter, built right up to the river's edge on the opposite bank, is presented.

Now the grape dominates completely as you enter the rich wine-growing valley around **Falset**. The vast vine-clad hills are dotted with tiny villages that seem to float above the vineyards on their little hillocks. Look back as you leave Falset, for there is an enchanting view of the town.

The highway follows a winding downward course through a number of passes to Reus, the birthplace of architect Antonio Gaudí and also known for its wool weaving. The town is now mostly industrial and not particularly appealing to tourists. Just past Reus, join the A7 freeway for a short drive into **Barcelona**. For sightseeing suggestions, see *Barcelona Highlights*.

# *Barcelona Highlights*

*Barcelona*

Barcelona is Spain's second-largest city, but its distinct history and regional culture make it anything but a small-scale Madrid. Its personality, architecture, customs, proximity to France, and long-term importance as a Mediterranean seaport make it a sophisticated and cosmopolitan city. The whole region of Catalonia, especially its capital city of Barcelona, has long resisted absorption by Castile-dominated central authority. Catalans pride themselves on their industriousness and prosperity, both immediately evident to the visitor. Barcelona is a fascinating, bustling, and charming city that will enchant you.

PACING: Barcelona is a vivacious city that blends the historic structures of the old town with the scores of buildings left by the upsurge of modernism. Plan on staying three nights to explore fully the delights the city has to offer.

As in most large and unfamiliar cities, a good way to start your visit is by taking advantage of an organized bus tour, which will orient you and give you a more enlightened idea of how and where to concentrate your time. There are a variety of tours available in English—ask the hotel concierge to arrange one for you.

Street signs (and maps) are often in the Catalan language. In Barcelona, you see *carrer* instead of *calle* for street, *passeig* instead of *paseo* for passage, *avinguda* instead of *avenida* for avenue, and *placa* instead of *plaza* for town square. The nerve center of the city is the large Plaza de Catalonia on the border between the old city and the new. It is singularly impressive, with many fine monuments and sculptures. Beneath it is the hub of the subway system and the shopping arcades along the underground Avenida de las Luces (lights).

All of the downtown sights are within walking distance of the plaza, including the festive **Ramblas**. Ramblas (a cosmopolitan, stone-paved promenade running generally south from the plaza to the waterfront) comes from the Arabic word for riverbed, which is what this once was. Now it is a chic and shady street, lined with shops and hotels and frequented by anyone and everyone visiting Barcelona. At the plaza end are kiosks selling newspapers and books in many languages. From there, a bird market takes over and the street is adorned with cages full of colorful birds. Next are lovely flower stalls, then a series of tree-shaded cafés, perfect for people watching. On the right side of the street (as you walk toward the waterfront) and just before you reach the flower stalls, you find a busy public market where it is fun to stroll, enjoying the amazing variety of produce and fresh fish that Barcelonans have to choose from.

At the waterfront end of Ramblas is a monument to Christopher Columbus and a re-creation of his famous ship, the *Santa María*. King Ferdinand and Queen Isabella were holding court here when Columbus returned from his first voyage and announced the incredible news of his discovery of a route to the Orient (he still thought this is what he had found). Visit the *Santa María* and try to imagine what it would be like to set out into unknown waters on a two-month voyage, as Columbus did in this tiny ship in 1492. You can also take boat rides around the harbor from here.

A few blocks east of the Ramblas is the colorful Gothic Quarter (*Barrio Gótico*), a virtual maze of old buildings, streets, and alleyways. A marvelous 15th-century cathedral dominates the area, which also contains the city hall (*ayuntamiento*) with its lovely sculptures, paintings, and beautifully decorated chambers and halls. There is a rich selection of atmospheric *tapa* bars and chic shops, including some interesting antique stores, in this lively area.

Still farther east is the famed Calle Montcada, lined with handsome, old mansions. Two of these contain the **Picasso Museum** with an impressive display of virtually every period of the famous painter's work. Although born in Málaga, Picasso spent much of his life (especially during his formative years) in Barcelona. His most famous paintings are not housed here, but the museum does contain many examples of his early work.

Even more intriguing are the works of another famous Barcelona artist, Antonio Gaudí (1852–1926), the avant-garde architect. His **Holy Family (Sagrada Familia) Church** is the city's most famous landmark, its perforated spires visible from various points around the city. You'll certainly want to take a closer look at this marvelous, unfinished building with its intricately carved façades and molten-rock textures (best reached by subway). Many of Gaudí's imaginative creations resemble life-size gingerbread houses. Numerous examples of his work can be found in the city: the **Casa Batlló**, **Casa Mila**, and the **Pedrera** are on the Paseo de Gracia, and the **Palacio Guell** is just off the Ramblas. They all attest to the apparent rejection of the straight line as a design element in the highly individualistic style of this innovative artist. Because they cannot be moved from Barcelona, they are more an integral part of the city's personality than the paintings of Picasso or Miró, which can be seen in art museums all over the world.

*Holy Family Church, Barcelona*

An area not to be missed is **Montjuich**, occupying a tree-shaded hill in the south of the city and best reached by the metro (Plaça d' Espanya). It's an excellent vantage point and was originally the site of a 17th-century defensive fort (which now contains a military museum). A number of interesting public buildings were erected here for the 1929 exposition. The **Museum of Catalan Art** is in the **Palacio Nacional** and contains fine Gothic and Romanesque sections, featuring wonderful examples of religious art that have been rescued from abandoned churches all over the region. These are magnificently displayed, often as complete church interiors.

Also in Montjuich is the **Pueblo Español** (Spanish town) which is an entire little village constructed for the 1929 exposition, utilizing the varied architectural styles of Spain. Some of the structures are re-creations of actual buildings, and some simply imitate regional styles. The entrance, for example, is a reconstruction of the towers of the city wall of Ávila. It is an impressive achievement and is now essentially a shopping area featuring *artesanía* (arts and crafts) from the different regions. If you have been to other areas of Spain, you will be struck by the unique juxtaposition of the various architectural styles.

Montjuich is also the setting of one of the most wonderful of all the sights in Barcelona—the beautiful **dancing fountains** (*fuentes*). For a truly unforgettable experience, ask at your hotel for the days of the week and the time at night they are augmented with lights and music. Music from classical to contemporary accompanies the multicolored, ever-changing water sprays in a symphonic, sensory experience. If you go an hour early and are prepared to wile away the time watching the Barcelonans stroll around the park, you should be able to secure a seat in front of the palace.

Be sure to visit the **Fundación Joan Miró**, with several hundred examples of this native son's bold and colorful paintings, along with works by other contemporary artists—definitely worth a visit if you are a modern art devotee.

There is ample nightlife in Barcelona. The best approach is to ask your hotel concierge, since shows change constantly. One permanent offering, however, is the **Scala**, an international, Las Vegas-style review, which is very professionally presented and is enjoyable even if you do not have an understanding of the Spanish language. There is a dinner show (the food is only passable) and a later show at midnight without dinner. You need to ask your hotel concierge to make reservations for the Scala, since it is highly popular both with locals and tourists.

# *Madrid and More*

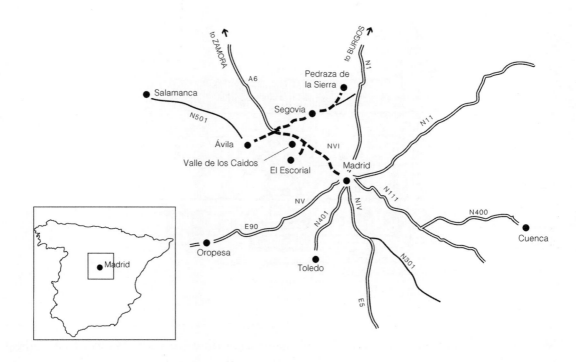

# Madrid and More

*Plaza Mayor, Madrid*

We rediscover Madrid with increasing pleasure each time we visit. Madrid (the highest capital in Europe) is a big, vigorous city—comparable in size to other western European capitals—but yet a comfortable one for the first-time visitor. Madrid's attractions will not overwhelm you if you have only a few days to devote to the city, but offer more than enough diversity and stimulation for a longer stay. If you are experiencing Madrid for the first time, a popular method of familiarization is to take a double-decker bus tour (ask at the front desk of your hotel). You will get an idea of the city layout, and can return at your convenience to spend more time in places that pique your interest. Or you may prefer to strike out on your own from the start, armed with a detailed sightseeing guide, a good city map (available at your hotel), and your sense of adventure.

PACING: Allow at least two nights for Madrid sightseeing, more if you are an avid art-gallery person.

A car is more trouble than it is worth in Madrid, which shares the traffic problems common to all large cities. If your visit here is at the outset of your trip, we suggest that you not pick up your rental car until you are ready to leave and, if Madrid is your last stop, that you turn your car in the day you get here. Otherwise, leave your car in a protected parking lot for the duration of your stay.

The major things to do and see are often within walking distance of downtown hotels, or readily accessible by "metro," the easily understood and extensive subway system that transports you swiftly and inexpensively to every important intersection in the city. Cabs are also reasonable for trips around town. But walk when you can, because downtown Madrid is made for wandering, with wide, bustling boulevards lined with gracious, old-world buildings, lively outdoor cafés, and narrow, old streets winding through colorful neighborhoods and picturesque plazas. Below we mention a few of our favorite sights.

Probably the greatest attraction in the city is the world-class **Prado Museum**, housed in a splendid 18th-century building. Its facilities are constantly being expanded and upgraded, and it boasts one of the finest permanent art collections in Europe, as well as popular and well-presented special exhibitions. Most of the private collections of the Spanish monarchs are here. As with the Louvre in Paris or the Uffizi in Florence, you could spend days here and still not do justice to its treasures. Depending on your knowledge of and interest in the arts, we suggest you either take a tour of the museum's highlights (private if possible), or purchase a guidebook, study the directory, and set out in search of your particular favorites. The best of Goya, Velázquez, El Greco, and Murillo are here and should be seen, if nothing else.

Just across the street from the Prado is another rare prize, the **Thyssen Bornemisza Museum**. Here you find a stunning collection of over 800 paintings that span the range of great masters from the 13th century to the present day. Much of this art was the collection of Baron Hans Heinrich Thyssen Bornemisza who sold it to the nation in 1993. It is an outstanding collection of western art from Italian and Flemish primitives to modern and pop. You'll delight in seeing masterpieces by Holbein, Rubens, Hockney, Constable, Winslow, Picasso, Hopper, Sisley, Degas, Titian, Canaletto, Degas, Van Gogh, and Constable, to name but a few.

A few minutes' walk away down Paseo del Prado is **Reina Sofia,** a museum of 20th-century art, housed in an 18th-century hospital. Exterior glass elevators were added in 1990 when the building was converted to the National Museum. Highlights include works by Miró, Picasso, and Dali.

For a stroll in the park, head for **Parque del Buen Retiro** behind the Prado, an enormous Central Park-like haven where *madrileños* stroll, bike, boat, and relax at all hours. The park also hosts outdoor concerts and theater.

A short distance south of the Retiro Park, near the Atocha train station on Calle Fuenterrabía, is the fascinating **Royal Tapestry Factory** (Real Fábrica de Tapices) where tapestries are being made as they have been since the 18th century. There are also some original tapestry drawings by Goya.

The neo-classic **Royal Palace**, at the west end of downtown, was conceived by Phillip V, but first occupied by Charles III. Napoleon proclaimed it the equal of Versailles, and it is definitely worth a visit. The extensive grounds and rooms, each a veritable art museum, provide a glimpse of how the Bourbons lived during their heyday in Spain. The beautiful **Plaza de Oriente** (so named because it lies on the east side of the palace) is downtown's largest and is adorned with over 40 statues of Spanish and Visigothic royalty, with an equestrian statue of Phillip IV at its center.

For archaeology buffs, the **Museo Arqueológico** emphasizes Iberian and classical material and includes the famous Dama de Elche.

*Parque del Buen Retiro, Madrid*

If you are traveling with children, don't miss a visit to the huge **Casa de Campo** where there is a zoo, an amusement park, and a lake. The area used to be the royal hunting grounds.

Just southeast of the Royal Palace is the heart of the old city and one of the most monumental squares in the country, the 17th-century **Plaza Mayor**. An excellent place to people watch from an outdoor café, the old plaza is completely enclosed by tall historic buildings and has a statue of Phillip III in the middle. If you leave the plaza through the Arco de los Cuchilleros (on the south side), you will discover many typical bars and restaurants, tucked on streets that take you back in time.

There is a colorful Sunday flea market, called **El Rastro**, a few blocks south of the Plaza Mayor on Calle Ribera de Curtidores. Absolutely everything is sold here, both in permanent shops and temporary booths, and *madrileños* and tourists alike shop here in droves. You may even find some genuine antiques at bargain prices, but "buyer beware" is the rule here. Haggling over prices (*regateando*) is appropriate at El Rastro, unlike most other places in Spain.

About halfway between the Royal Palace and the Prado Museum is the huge plaza called **Puerta del Sol**. This is the center of activity in downtown Madrid and, in a sense, the center of Spain because all of the main highways (those designated with an "N") radiate from here. Inlaid into the sidewalk on one side of the plaza you find a plaque marking *Kilometro 0*. Some of the city's best shopping is to be found in the immediate vicinity, including a bustling pedestrian street lined with boutiques.

Shopping for antiques can be fun in Madrid. The largest concentration of antique shops is in the area southeast of the Puerta del Sol, especially on Calle del Prado between the Plaza de Santa Ana and the Plaza de las Cortes.

Madrid's night scene has something for everyone—from elegant dining and highbrow cultural events to colorful hole-in-the-wall *tapas* bars and pulsating, new-wave discotheques. Your best sources for information about what is going on in Madrid are the complimentary *What's on Madrid*, readily available from tourist offices and your hotel. The concierge at your hotel can make arrangements for you, too—from dinner to bullfights to flamenco shows.

SIDE TRIPS: **El Escorial**, **Ávila**, **Segovia**, and **Pedraza de la Sierra** may be visited in several ways. There are organized bus tours leaving from the Plaza de Oriente early every morning that include visits to El Escorial, Ávila, and Segovia (but not Pedraza) in one day. Your hotel can make the arrangements for you: the price is reasonable and the guides speak English. This method, however, is necessarily a rather quick tour of these wonderful towns and gives you very little flexibility. But if all you want (or have time for) is a quick look, this is probably your best bet.

A better way to go, in our opinion, is to drive yourself. This allows you to allocate your time as you please. These towns are all close to Madrid and close to each other. If you leave very early in the morning and plan just a short time in each, you could see El Escorial, Ávila, and Segovia then drive on to Pedraza, where you could have dinner. But if you decide you do not want to rush, choose whichever town seems most interesting and stay overnight en route.

Head northwest on A6 from Madrid for about 30 kilometers to exit 47, where you take the M600 to reach the **Monastery of Saint Lawrence the Royal of El Escorial** (Monasterio de San Lorenzo el Real de El Escorial), better known as just **El Escorial** and one of Spain's most impressive edifices. Built by King Phillip II in the late 16th century, the building was designed to house a church, a monastery, a mausoleum, and the palace for the royal family. One of Phillip's main motivations was a promise he had made to dedicate a church to Saint Lawrence on the occasion of an important Spanish victory over France that occurred on the feast day of that saint. A second motive was that his father, Charles V, emperor of the largest empire the world had ever known, had expressed the wish that a proper tomb be erected for him. So when Phillip II moved the capital from Toledo to Madrid in 1559 in order to put the capital in the center of the country, he began construction of El Escorial on the site of the slag heap (*escorial*) of some abandoned iron mines. The construction took place from 1563 to 1584 and resulted in a huge complex that measures 206 x 161 meters and has approximately 1,200 doors and 2,600 windows. Perhaps no other building more faithfully reflects the personality of its owner than this.

Phillip II was a deeply religious man, obsessively so in the opinion of many. (It is perhaps understandable, since he spent most of his life in mourning. Seventeen of his close relatives died during his lifetime, including all of his sons but one, and his four wives.) He thus lavished great sums of money on the decoration of the religious parts of the building, while the palace itself was a simple, even austere affair from which Phillip ruled half the world. Subsequent monarchs added some decorative touches to the apartments or installed additional ones, as in the case of the Bourbon apartments. The Pantheon of the Kings, directly below the high altar of the church, contains the remains of almost all the Spanish monarchs from Charles V on (with the kings on the left, queens on the right). The lavishly decorated library contains some 40,000 volumes, and there and elsewhere in the building you discover examples of the works of all the great painters of the 16th century. El Escorial elicits varied reactions from visitors, some seeing it as a morose pile of rock with 2,600 too-small windows, others as a totally unique royal monument built by a unique monarch. There is certainly no denying its interest as a symbol of some important aspects of 16th-century Spain.

Head back toward A6 via M600 and watch for a turnoff to the left leading to the **Valle de los Caidos** (Valley of the Fallen). If you are a Spanish Civil War buff, you might enjoy visiting this grandiose memorial to the country's Civil-War dead found at the end of a wooded valley and visible from far away—a 120-meter-high by 46-meter-wide cross (which has an elevator on the north side). This is the final resting place of Generalísimo Francisco Franco, who ruled Spain from 1939 to 1975.

Return to the A6 freeway and continue northwest to Villacastin, leaving at exit 81 where you take the A51 for the fast drive to **Ávila.** Approached from any direction, Ávila is a dramatic sight, but the most stunning view is when you arrive from the west. Enclosed by stone walls, it stands today as it must have appeared to potential aggressors in the Middle Ages. The 11th-century fortifications (the oldest and best preserved in Spain) are over 2 kilometers long, 3 meters thick, and average 10 meters in height. They have 9 gates and 88 towers. Circle the walls to find parking, for it's a town easily explored on foot. A stroll along the sentry path atop the walls gives you a close-up view of the many storks' nests perched in the towers and rooftops of the city.

Within the medieval city, the fortress-like **cathedral** is a particularly fine one: mostly early Gothic in form, it contains some beautiful stained glass and ironwork. The **Convento de Santa Teresa**, a few blocks southwest of the cathedral, is built on the birthplace of the famous 16th-century mystic writer, who is generally credited with defeating the Reformation in Spain by carrying out reforms of her own. Inside there are relics related to the saint and some fine altars. In the immediate vicinity are some lovely, picturesque 15th-century houses. You will enjoy strolling around this ancient town with its tiny plazas and cobbled streets.

Just outside the walls on the northeast corner is **St. Vincent's Church**, founded in 1307. Noteworthy are the Tomb of the Patron Saints (12th century), a crypt with the stone where Saint Vincent and his sisters were martyred (in the 4th century), and the west entrance with its rich Romanesque sculpture.

Also outside the walls, via the Puerta del Alcázar gate and across the Plaza de Santa María, is **Saint Peter's Church**, with its impressive rose window. To the left is the Calle del Duque de Alba which leads (400 meters) to the **Convento de San José**, the first convent founded by Santa Teresa—now home to a museum of mementos about her life.

*Ávila*

To reach **Segovia**, return to the A6 freeway and cross over it to continue on the N110. Segovia was an important city even before the Romans came in 80 B.C. It was occupied by the Moors between the 8th and 11th centuries, and was reconquered by the Christians in 1085. Segovia claims one of the finest **Roman aqueducts** in existence today, and it still functions to bring water from the Riofrío River to the city. Thought to have been built in the 1st or 2nd century A.D., it is constructed, without mortar, of granite from the nearby mountains. It is almost a kilometer long and over 27 meters above the ground at its highest point as it crosses the Plaza de Azoguejo. Park by the aqueduct and head into the town.

In the old city are narrow, picturesque streets that deserve a half-day walking tour and intermingled with the sightseeing, you find lots of interesting shops. The **Church of Saint Stephen** is a lovely Romanesque building from the 13th century. Farther down is the **cathedral**, said to be the last Gothic cathedral built in Spain. East another block is Saint Martin's (12th century), and a couple of blocks farther on is one of the most unique mansions in Segovia, the **Casa de los Picos**, a 15th-century home adorned with diamond-shaped stones. Northwest of there is the Plaza del Conde de Cheste with its numerous palaces. If you head south from here, you find yourself back where the aqueduct crosses the Plaza del Azoguejo.

*Alcázar, Segovia*

The highlight of Segovia is the 14th-century **Alcázar** castle. Dramatically situated like a ship on the high sea, it is a sight not soon forgotten. This is the castle used in the film *Camelot*, from whose ramparts Lancelot launches into the song *C'est moi* before crossing the English Channel to join King Arthur's knights of the round table. Probably the most-photographed edifice in Spain, it is surprisingly barren inside—the tour is most memorable for its views. In 1474, Castilian King Henry IV's sister, Isabella, was here proclaimed Queen of Castile (which at that time included most of the western half of Spain and Andalusia). Isabella's marriage to Ferdinand, heir of Aragón, laid the groundwork for the creation of the modern nation.

A tour around the outside of the city walls to the north affords some excellent perspectives on the setting. Bear left from the aqueduct and you pass the old Moneda (Mint) and the Monasterio del Parral, on the left bank of the Eresma River. After crossing the bridge, bear left, then right to the **Church of the Vera Cruz**, from where you can enjoy a spectacular view of the city. To wind up your sightseeing with more city views, return to town via the Cuesta de los Hoyos.

Drive northeast on N110 for about 25 kilometers and turn left, following the signs for **Pedraza de la Sierra**, which is about 10 kilometers farther. Whereas El Escorial, Ávila, and Segovia are well-known tourist destinations, many have never heard of Pedraza, a fact that makes it even more fun to visit. This walled, medieval, hilltop village is a jewel. From the moment you enter through the lower gate, time stands still as you meander through the maze of little streets. There are no well-known sights to visit, although there is a brooding castle where the sons of King François I of France were once held captive. The main attraction here is the town itself. The heart of Pedraza is its picturesque **Plaza Mayor**, faced by houses that date back to the 16th century. The small side streets have restaurants and a couple of boutiques.

# Seville Highlights

*The Cathedral and Giralda, Seville*

We should preface this section highlighting Seville with a frank admission of prejudice. It is one of our favorite cities, chock-full of fond memories of good times and good friends. Every time we return we fall under Seville's spell—and it won't surprise us a bit if you're enchanted, too. It is not that Seville is totally different from other Spanish cities, it is just that the town and its inhabitants are the quintessence of Spain. We strongly suggest several days in Seville. You need time to see its many sights, as well as time to wander along the orange-tree-lined streets and soak up the special feeling that the city imparts to its guests.

PACING: Just to get a flavor of Seville you need to stay for two nights—allow more if you include visits to museums.

After settling in your hotel, you must first visit the **cathedral**, one of the largest Gothic churches in the world, ranking in size with Saint Peter's in Rome and Saint Paul's in London. It was constructed between 1402 and 1506 on the site of a mosque. In the elaborate Royal Chapel at the east end is buried Alfonso X, "The Wise," one of Spain's most brilliant medieval monarchs, who supervised the codification of existing Roman law in the 13th century. When his son Sancho rebelled, Seville remained loyal to Alfonso. Alfonso's gratified statement *"No me ha dejado"* (It has not deserted me) is the basis for the rebus symbol you are bound to notice painted and carved all over the city: a double knot (called a *madeja*) between the syllables "no" and "do," thus producing *No madeja do,* which is pronounced approximately the same as *No me ha dejado.* Ferdinand III, later Saint Ferdinand, who freed Seville from Moorish domination, is buried in a silver shrine in front of the altar. On one side, in an ornate mausoleum, is one of the tombs of Christopher Columbus (the other is in Santo Domingo in the Caribbean—both cities claim to have his real remains).

Just outside the east entrance to the cathedral is the best known of Seville's architectural sights, the **Giralda**. Originally it was the mosque's minaret and was retained when the church was built. Be sure to enter and ascend the ramp up the 70-meter spire (stairs were not used in order to allow horses access). The view of the city is outstanding, especially in the late afternoon. The name *Giralda* means weather vane and refers to the weather vane on the top, which was added in the 16th century.

On the opposite side of the cathedral from the Giralda is an impressive Renaissance building—originally built to be a customs house but later converted into the **Archives of the Indies**—which contains most of the documents (comprised of some 86,000,000 pages spanning 400 years) pertaining to the discovery and conquest of America. Students of Colonial Spanish American history still come across undocumented material when they make pilgrimages here for a rich feast of research.

*Alcázar, Seville*

On the north side of the cathedral (a pleasant spot to sit and watch Seville go by) there are cafés that are slightly more tranquil than those along Avenida de la Constitución. To the south of the cathedral is the **Alcázar**—not as impressive as the Alhambra in Granada, but a lovely and refreshingly cool spot to spend a hot afternoon. Most of it was restored by King Pedro "The Cruel" (14th century), but he used Moorish architects and thus retained much of its authenticity.

If you leave the Alcázar by way of the southeast corner of the *Patio de las Banderas* (Flag Court), you are in the old Jewish Quarter, the **Barrio de Santa Cruz**. Looking something like a set for an opera, this is a mixture of old whitewashed houses and shops—all, it seems, with flowers tumbling from wrought-iron windows and balconies. The painter Murillo is buried in the Plaza de Santa Cruz and the house where he died is in the nearby Plaza de Alfaro. Southeast of these two plazas, hugging the Alcázar walls, are the lovely **Murillo Gardens** (*Jardines de Murillo*), where painters are often engrossed in capturing the setting on canvas.

North from the cathedral you can stroll a few long blocks down the Avenida de la Constitución to the **Plaza de San Francisco** behind the city hall (*Ayuntamiento*), a center of outdoor events during Holy Week. Running parallel to Sierpes and out of the Plaza Nueva is Calle Tetuán, another major shopping street.

At the north end of Sierpes, turn left on Calle Alfonso XII, after which a few blocks' walk brings you to the **Museo de Bellas Artes** (Fine Arts Museum), housing one of the most important collections in Spain with well-presented paintings of El Greco, Zurbarán, Velázquez, and Murillo, among others.

On Calle San Fernando is a golden 18th-century building, once a tobacco factory, where Bizet's beautiful and fiery Carmen worked. This is now the **University of Seville**. Feel free, if it is open, to go in and stroll its wide hallways through the collection of interior patios. Upstairs (to the right of the main entrance) you can find the university bar, where students and faculty convene for a between-class cognac, beer, coffee, or sandwich. A visit here gives you an insight into Spanish academic life.

Behind the university is the entrance to the **Parque de María Luisa** (laid out by a former princess of Spain), a popular local retreat from the summer heat. Here you'll discover the **Plaza de España**, a large, semicircle complete with boat rides and tiled niches representing each of the provinces of Spain—where Spanish families like to have their pictures taken in front of their "hometown" plaque. This plaza was constructed for the International Exposition in Seville in 1929, as were several other buildings in the park, as well as the Hotel Alfonso XIII. In the Plaza de América, farther down, is the **Museo Arqueológico** with a very regional collection of Roman antiquities and an arts-and-crafts museum. If you fancy being covered with doves, there is a spot where a lady sells you some seeds which, when held out in your hand, attract dozens of the white birds to perch greedily on your arms, shoulders, and head—this makes a fun picture to take home. There are also, of course, numerous spots to sit and people watch.

You must not miss the **Casa Pilatos**, a stunning palace built in 1540 for the Marqués of Tarifa. The name derives from Pontius Pilate's home in Jerusalem (which supposedly the

Marqués visited and admired). The palace is a delight—filled with brilliantly colored tiles, sunny courtyards filled with flowers, lacy balustrades, and Roman statues. A bit far off the beaten path (but within walking distance), the Casa Pilatos is usually not brimming with tourists.

The major festivals in Seville are Holy Week and the Feria (Fair) de Sevilla (about the second week after Easter). Although both are absolutely spectacular events, do not dream of getting a hotel reservation then, unless you plan a year in advance. And be aware that things can get pretty wild during the ten days of the Feria.

If time allows, you can take several good side trips from Seville:

CARMONA: Head northeast out of town on NIV through fertile hills to the ancient city of Carmona (35 kilometers), which still retains some of its ramparts and much of its old-world ambiance. The Puerta de Sevilla, a curious architectural blend of Roman and Moorish, opens onto the old town, where whitewashed alleyways and stone gateways lead to private patios of what were once noble mansions. The plaza is lined with 17th- and 18th-century houses. In the patio of the town hall (Calle San Salvador) there is a large Roman mosaic. Stroll down the nearby Calle Santa María de Gracia to the Puerta de Córdoba (built into the Roman wall in the 17th century diametrically opposite the Puerta de Sevilla) for a lovely view over a golden plain of wheat fields. The **Parador de Carmona** (see listing).

ITALICA: Just 10 kilometers north of Seville on N630, a little past the town of Santiponce, is the Roman town of Italica, founded in 205 B.C. by Scipio Africanus and birthplace of emperors Trajan and Hadrian. Still being excavated and restored, its baths, mosaics, and amphitheater are interesting and well worth the short drive (especially if you will not get the chance to visit the incredibly impressive Roman ruins at Mérida). Open-air dramatic performances are occasionally given in the amphitheater here (check with the tourist office on Avenida de la Constitución in Seville for a schedule if you are interested).

JEREZ DE LA FRONTERA: If you have an interest in going sherry tasting in Jerez, the sherry capital of the world, it is easily visited from Seville, being just a quick 67 kilometers south on the freeway (see the description in the *Andalusian Adventures* itinerary).

*Jerez de la Frontera*

138

# *Places to Stay*

The Hotel Aigua Blava (located on Spain's most dramatic stretch of coast, the beautiful Costa Brava) has a prime position on a promontory overlooking an incredibly blue inlet dotted with boats and rocky beaches. The Capella family converted their home into a small hotel in 1940 after it was returned to them following the disastrous Civil War. The original owner, the much-loved Xiquet Sabater who warmly welcomed all the guests, died in 1995, but his family has taken over the management and continues to run the hotel in the same friendly manner. Now a fairly large hotel, the Aigua Blava retains the atmosphere of several homes jumbled together around flowered terraces and rinconcitos (little corners). Decorated by family members, each room is unique—from simple to elaborate—and many have sea views and terraces (for a surcharge). Set under a slanted ceiling, the Chez Xiquet room (containing family memorabilia) looks out to a large terrace and a fantastic view. For any room, however, reservations should be made well in advance during high season, as many guests return here year after year for their week or two in the sun. For a relaxing sojourn in an enchanting seaside spot with a family atmosphere, you can't go wrong at the Aigua Blava. *Directions:* Follow signs for Begur, then for Aigua Blava. Once in Aigua Blava, follow signs for Fornells until you reach the hotel.

❄ ☕ 💳 ☎ @ ♈ P ⑪ ≈ 🏃 🖼 ⚓ ⚓ 🎿 🐎 ⚓

*HOTEL AIGUA BLAVA*
*Manager: Josep Ma de Vehi*
*Playa de Fornells*
*Aiguablava 17255 Begur, Spain*
*Tel: 772-624-562, Fax: 972-622-112*
*85 Rooms, Double: €164–€234*
*Open: late Feb to early Nov, Credit cards: all major*
*Region: Catalonia, Michelin Map: 574*
*www.karenbrown.com/aiguablava.html*

On the high, isolated, tree-covered point of Esmuts, overlooking the open sea on one side and a turquoise bay on the other, sits the Parador de Aigua Blava—a secluded hideaway for the visitor seeking every comfort on the Costa Brava. Unlike most paradors, this one does not strive for an antique ambiance. The attractive public rooms are airy and open, accented in bright, spring colors; and the bedrooms are spacious and bright with red-tiled floors, most with terraces and lovely views of either the ocean or the bay. There are six extra-large, special rooms (habitaciones especiales), with large round bathtubs, separate, sunken showers, and exercise areas featuring exercycles and weights. There is, in addition, a public exercise/game room downstairs with saunas. Guests here are two minutes by a footpath from the beach on the bay, or can save the effort and choose to lounge around the lovely fresh-water pool overlooking the ocean. For a short or long stay, this contemporary parador above the idyllic, white town of Aiguablava is an excellent choice. *Directions:* Follow signs for Begur then Aiguablava until you see the Posada signposts.

*PARADOR DE AIGUABLAVA*
*Playa de Aiguablava*
*Aiguablava 17255 Begur, Spain*
*Tel: 972-622-162, Fax: 972-622-166*
*78 Rooms, Double: €135–€155\**
*\*Breakfast not included: €14*
*Open: all year, Credit cards: all major*
*Region: Catalonia, Michelin Map: 574*
*www.karenbrown.com/paradordeaiguablava.html*

This spectacular parador crowns the tiny fortified town of Alarcón on the rocky central meseta. Perched on a promontory, this dramatic 8th-century Arab fortress resembles an island, surrounded by the deep, natural gorges created by the looping Júcar River below. The fairytale castle is beautifully restored and retains a considerable portion of its original construction, including crenellated towers, ramparts, and the vigilant castle keep, featuring a guestroom on each floor. You can all but hear the rattling of swords borne by the Knights of the Order of Saint James, who readied themselves here to combat the Moors during the Reconquest. The main lounge off the entry patio is awe-inspiring: its towering stone- and wood-beamed ceiling arches over the room. The three bedrooms in the keep are "special" rooms with canopied beds. Whether you stay in them or one of the ten more traditional parador rooms you will be thrilled by this little hideaway. Be sure to take a turn around the ramparts—it will make you realize why the Moors chose it as a stronghold and wonder how the Christians ever wrested it from them. The adjoining village with its cobbled streets, whitewashed houses, a few shops and restaurants is particularly delightful. *Directions:* Exit the A3 (Madrid—Valencia freeway) at km 186 for the 15 km drive to the NIII which you take in the direction of Motilla. Take the first right for Alarcón.

*PARADOR DE ALARCÓN*
*Manager: Juan Antonio Choza Fernandez*
*Avenida Amigos de Los Castillos s/n*
*16213 Alarcón, Spain*
*Tel: 969-330-315, Fax: 969-330-303*
*14 Rooms, Double: €200*
*Open: all year, Credit cards: all major*
*Region: Castilla-La Mancha, Michelin Map: 575*
*www.karenbrown.com/alarcon.html*

The Parador de Albacete is located in the flat countryside just outside Albacete, a city well known for its archaeological museum. The hotel is not an historic monument, but it has the appealing ambiance of a Spanish hacienda. The whitewashed building, accented by wrought-iron lamps and a terra cotta roof, is constructed around a large central courtyard with a fountain, wrapped on four sides by a window-enclosed, wide hallway with a polished red-tiled floor. Shuttered windows, beamed ceilings and rustic furniture add to the old-world feel. The guestrooms and bathrooms are especially spacious with those on the upper floor having balconies. The cafeteria/bar is a popular gathering spot. The airy dining room, with its country style chairs, serves La Mancha specialties. Behind the hotel, set in a grassy lawn, is a large swimming pool, which offers a cool respite on a hot summer day. There are also two tennis courts and a pitch and putt course on the grassy lawn. *Directions:* The parador is to the south of the city. Exit the A30 (Alabacete to Murcia freeway) at the first exit, km 254 signpost Albacete. The parador is close to, and clearly signed from, the exit.

*PARADOR DE ALBACETE*
*02000 Albacete, Spain*
*Tel: 967-245-321, Fax: 967-243-271*
*70 Rooms, Double: €95–€115\**
*\*Breakfast not included: €13*
*Open: all year, Credit cards: all major*
*Region: Castilla-La Mancha, Michelin Map: 575*
*www.karenbrown.com/albacete.html*

On the top of a hill, dominating the town of Alcañiz and the beautifully fertile Maestrazgo valley, the Parador de Alcañiz is installed in a majestic, 18th-century, Aragonese palace, once a 12th-century castle. Its double rooms have extensive views framed by thick castle walls and wooden windows (some windows set so high that steps have been built into the walls to reach them), lovely rustic wood furnishings, pale-blue bedspreads and burnished red-tile floors highlighted by colorfully patterned rugs. All of the rooms have air conditioning, television, and mini-bar. Due to the spaciousness of the beamed hallways, sitting areas, beautiful, high-ceilinged dining room, and handsome lounge, the palace has deceptively few rooms to accommodate guests. Room 1 (a large corner bedroom with sweeping views in two directions) is especially outstanding. A 12th-century tower, which was constructed when the Knights of the Order of Calatrava were based here, is found on the grounds. A small cloister and the remains of walls dating from the 12th through the 15th centuries also share the hotel's dramatic hilltop setting. A 5-minute walk finds you at the central square with inviting cafes with tables and chairs set out facing the cathedral. *Directions:* You can see the parador (in the castle) from many miles away. Cross the river heading for the old part of town and watch for parador signs directing you to the hotel high above the town.

*PARADOR DE ALCAÑIZ*
*Castillo de Calatravos s/n*
*44600 Alcañiz, Spain*
*Tel: 978-830-400, Fax: 978-830-366*
*37 Rooms, Double: €130–€140\**
*\*Breakfast not included: €13*
*Open: all year, Credit cards: all major*
*Region: Aragon, Michelin Map: 574*
*www.karenbrown.com/alcaniz.html*

Gregorio Sánchez and his family moved from Madrid to Asturias where they totally renovated his family home and turned it into a small hotel—an awesome task that took two years to accomplish. The result is an absolute gem. From Panes, you wind up a narrow road, past cows grazing in the fields, to the very top of a hill where suddenly you come upon a tiny, remote village—no more than a cluster of houses, surrounded by the magnificent, natural landscapes of the Picos de Europa. The prettiest of these homes is La Casona de Alevia, an appealing, 17th-century stone farmhouse. Inside, loving care is shown in every detail and a cozy warmth exudes from every room. The renovation was accomplished with great skill, installing all the modern amenities to make a stay here one of absolute comfort, yet meticulously retaining the original rustic appeal and authentic architectural details. Downstairs are two lounges, one a comfortable parlor with a fireplace and the other a library/games room. Antiques abound, including a display on the walls of antique, handmade chestnut-farming implements. A central open staircase with a skylight above leads up to the nine guestrooms, each individually decorated with an abundance of family antiques and exquisite antique lace at the windows. *Directions:* In Panes, turn beside the bridge for Alevia, then immediately left (the village is above you) for the 3 km drive to Alevia. The hotel is on the left beside the square.

*LA CASONA DE ALEVIA*
*Owners: Lupe & Gregorio Sánchez*
*Alevia 33579 Panes, Spain*
*Tel: 985-414-176, Fax: 985-414-224*
*9 Rooms, Double: €70–€85\**
*\*Breakfast not included: €7*
*Closed: mid-Jan to mid-Feb, Credit cards: MC, VS*
*Region: Asturias, Michelin Map: 572*
*www.karenbrown.com/alevia.html*

For a rustic hideaway tucked away from the beaten path in a sheltered valley in the beautiful mountains of Asturias, La Tahona is an exceptional find. Besnes (where La Tahona is located) is a tiny hamlet that only appears on the most detailed maps—the closest town is Alles. The isolated location is what makes this inn so remarkable. La Tahona is not a fancy hotel in any way, nor does it pretend to be, but it shines in its simplicity. It's an appealing, two-story stone building with a red-tiled roof, deep in the woods beside a small stream. The rustic charm continues when you step inside the reception area, which opens up to the rustic restaurant—painted in blue with yellow curtains and little tables draped with blue cloths topped with crisp white linens—all overlooking the forest and a babbling brook. The staircase, lined with antique farm implements, leads down to a guest lounge. There are thirteen simple, little rooms in this building, which in days-of-yore was a bakery. The rest of the rooms are divided between an old mill down the road and two additional houses. *Directions:* From the AS114 (which runs between Cangas and Panes), take the small road north toward Alles. In less than a kilometer, turn left on the cobbled lane that leads to Besnes and La Tahona.

*LA TAHONA DE BESNES*
*Manager: Alberto Diaz*
*Alles 33578 Besnes, Spain*
*Tel & Fax: 985-415-749*
*25 Rooms, Double: €70–€115\**
*\*Breakfast not included: €5.70*
*Closed: Jan 10 to 31, Credit cards: all major*
*Region: Asturias, Michelin Map: 572*
*www.karenbrown.com/tahona.html*

Surprisingly, this parador is not a bona fide restoration of the 16th-century original, but was in fact built in 1979. Principally the entry and attached church are all that remain of the former 1596 convent. However, the newness is impossible to detect and you will marvel at the attention to detail. Everything—from the bricks and the windows to the rough stones used for the floor—were custom made. Elegant antiques abound in the public rooms. Cozy, quiet sitting areas, often with fireplaces, are located on each floor and lovely patios are spaced invitingly around the premises. The bedrooms are impressive, with ancient-looking windows and quaint wooden beds surrounded by pretty ceramic-tiled walls instead of headboards. The other furnishings are harmonious in style and color, contrasting delightfully with the whitewashed walls. The bar is holds giant clay vats that extend from the lower sitting area through the floor above. Surrounding the vats are rough wooden tables, which complete the ancient bodega atmosphere. In warm weather dinner is served on the patio. After a day sightseeing the pool is a welcome respite. It is just a couple of minutes walk to the heart of this historic town. *Directions:* On entering the town on the CM412 from Valdepeñas the parador is signpost to the left (before you get to the center of town). Turn right at the park and the parador is at the northern end of the park encircled by a high brick wall.

*PARADOR DE ALMAGRO*
*Ronda de San Francisco*
*13270 Almagro, Spain*
*Tel: 926-860-100, Fax: 926-860-150*
*54 Rooms, Double: €130–€140\**
*\*Breakfast not included: €13*
*Open: all year, Credit cards: all major*
*Region: Castilla-La Mancha, Michelin Map: 575*
*www.karenbrown.com/almagro.html*

This 1980s addition to the parador chain is of modern, whitewashed construction, built on a high point in town and overlooking the green sea of the Antequera plain. Just half an hour from Málaga and one hour from Granada, it offers a restful, rural alternative to city sounds and pace, in a town with no less than thirty-eight churches and three remarkable prehistoric dolmens. The dining room and vast lounge are on split levels, complemented by a blond-wood cathedral ceiling, Oriental carpets, and contemporary furniture. Wall-to-wall windows afford expansive countryside views from both. An immaculate blue-and-white hallway leads past a tiny, sunlit interior patio to the guestrooms, all identical—with good-size, white-tile baths, brick-red, terra-cotta floors with beige-weave rugs, pastel-print bedspreads, and wood and leather furnishings. All the rooms have lovely views, though if you request "una habitación en la segunda planta con vista de la vega" you'll get the best visual orientation. A large swimming pool is set on the grassy lawn. If you make a rest stop here, don't fail to visit nearby El Torcal, an incredible natural display of rock formations. *Directions:* The parador sits above the town and is well-signposted.

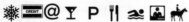

*PARADOR DE ANTEQUERA*
*Paseo García de Olmo*
*29200 Antequera, Spain*
*Tel: 952-840-261, Fax: 952-841-312*
*55 Rooms, Double: €95–€115\**
*\*Breakfast not included: €13*
*Open: all year, Credit cards: all major*
*Region: Andalusia, Michelin Map: 578*
*www.karenbrown.com/antequera.html*

Situated on cliffs high above a bend in the River Guadalete, Arcos de la Frontera commands a spectacular location. It's one of the most famous of the Pueblos Blancos (white towns) with its cobbled streets leading up to the old town square and its 15th-century church. Just a two minute walk from the plaza, down a narrow street from the market, you find the Hotel El Convento. As you might guess from the name, this small hotel was originally a convent, dating back to the 17th century. From the street you enter into the reception area, which also serves as the breakfast room, with a beamed ceiling, half-tiled walls and terra cotta floors. We loved to take our morning repast on the large outdoor patio with its birds' eye view across the valley. The same skywide panorama is enjoyed by most of the bedrooms, each very nicely kitted out in a non-fussy country style. Be sure to request one with a terrace. All the bedrooms have telephone, TV, air conditioning, and a modern bathroom. We had an excellent dinner at the hotel's restaurant located just down the street in the 17th century Palacio Valdespino. The restaurant, which specializes in authentic local cooking, oozes charm and hospitality. *Directions:* Arriving in Arcos follow signs for "centro" onto the narrow one-way system going steeply uphill. Pass through a narrow stone arch and turn right into the square. Walk down the alley beside the parador and first right will bring you to the hotel.

*HOTEL EL CONVENTO*
*Manager: José Antonio Roldán*
*Owner: María Moreno*
*Maldonado, 2*
*11630 Arcos de la Frontera, Spain*
*Tel: 956-702-333, Fax: 956-704-128*
*11 Rooms, Double: €55–€85\**
*\*Breakfast not included: €6*
*Closed: 15 days in Jan, Credit cards: all major*
*Region: Andalusia, Michelin Map: 578*
*www.karenbrown.com/convento.html*

This wonderfully situated hotel was built on the site of an old mansion in the center of the hilltop white town of Arcos. You would never suspect that it is a "modern" building for it was built to blend in perfectly with the other buildings on the historic Plaza del Cabildo: the Santa Maria church, the castle, and the town hall. You enter to a center courtyard with elegant arches, grille-windows, fountain, ochre colored walls and an old tiled stone well. Beyond lies the dining room whose wall of windows faces the dramatic view across the plains far below. The same view is enjoyed from the terrace and the lounge with its enormous picture window. Bedrooms are found off elegant hallways with either open-beamed or lovely vaulted ceilings. The rooms I saw were particularly spacious. Some overlook the town's picturesque main square, but it is well worth the extra tarrif to secure one with a terrace overlooking the valley far below. From your hilltop perch you can walk to everything in Arcos. *Directions:* Arcos is 30 km from Jerez on the A382. Follow signs for "centro" onto the narrow one-way system going steeply uphill. Pass through a narrow stone arch and turn right into the square beside the parador. Park in front to unload and purchase a parking ticket. There is usually an attendant on the square to assist you in finding a parking space.

*PARADOR DE ARCOS DE LA FRONTERA*
*Plaza del Cabildo s/n*
*11630 Arcos de la Frontera, Spain*
*Tel: 956-700-500, Fax: 956-701-116*
*24 Rooms, Double: €130–€140\**
*\*Breakfast not included: €13*
*Open: all year, Credit cards: all major*
*Region: Andalusia, Michelin Map: 578*
*www.karenbrown.com/frontera.html*

The Áran Valley, located in the high Pyrenees, is such a favorite target for skiers and sports enthusiasts that many of its once-picturesque villages are now buried behind giant condominium complexes. Happily, the tiny hamlet of Artíes, with stone houses lining its narrow winding streets, still retains much of its old-world charm. Driving into town, you cannot miss the parador—it faces directly onto the main road. The hotel has a cheerful, friendly look with honey-colored stone walls and a steeply pitched gray-tile roof, accented by two rows of whimsical gables. The original parador, which had only a few rooms, was built into the Casa de Portolá, the house of Don Gaspar de Portolá (a famous Spanish captain of the Dragoons, who in the 18th century explored California, founded the Mission of San Diego, and went on to become the first Governor of Baja California). In recent years, the parador has been greatly expanded. However a small chapel and the medieval core of the original mansion are still incorporated into one wing of the hotel. The decor is predominantly modern with dark-gray slate floors, contemporary chairs and sofas, and some abstract paintings. Relieving the newness of the decor are concessions to the inn's heritage, such as an antique grandfather clock, heavy, wrought-iron chandeliers, and a beamed ceiling in the spacious dining room.

*PARADOR DE ARTÍES*
*25599 Artíes, Spain*
*Tel: 973-640-801, Fax: 973-641-001*
*57 Rooms, Double: €115–€135\**
*\*Breakfast not included: €13*
*Open: all year, Credit cards: all major*
*Region: Catalonia, Michelin Map: 574*
*www.karenbrown.com/arties.html*

The Hostería de Bracamonte was the home of Don Juan Teherán y Monjaraz, mayor of Ávila during the glory days of the 16th century. Typical of the surrounding properties, this golden-stone mansion presents a severe façade to the street while inside all is most attractive—you find lots of rustic appeal, with stone walls, wooden beams, little tables set with flowers, and soft lighting. Up the broad staircase, you find a parade of absolutely delightful bedrooms. The loveliest of these rooms are 125, 123, 122, 112, and 111—we simply just could not choose between them. All are spacious, very nicely decorated and several have balconies. If you are traveling with children, request room 125, a two-story suite with a bedroom downstairs and a master bedroom upstairs. The restaurant specializes in typical Castillian dishes served in a most congenial atmosphere.Since the hotel has been bought by a corporation we have received a complaint about warmth of welcome and the standard of the food served in the restarant. We hope that these are just teething pains as new management takes over. *Directions:* Enter the city at the gate adjacent to the cathedral. Continue straight. When the road forks, go left, take the first right (very sharp), and the hotel is on your right.

CREDIT  P  ⊪  🏇

*HOSTERÍA DE BRACAMONTE*
*Bracamonte 6*
*05001 Ávila, Spain*
*Tel: 920-251-280, Fax: 920-253-838*
*22 Rooms, Double: €61–€73\**
*\*Breakfast not included: €6*
*Open: all year, Credit cards: MC, VS*
*Region: Castilla y León, Michelin Map: 575*
*www.karenbrown.com/bracamonte.html*

The Parador de Ávila is tucked within the walls of Ávila, the first fortified Romanesque city in Europe. Partially installed within the 15th-century noble home of Piedras Albas, both the renovated palace and its new addition are in keeping with the original architectural style. The massive granite, limestone, and wrought-iron staircase off the lobby, and granite and adobe floors testify to the success of this intention. Bedrooms in the wing of rooms that have been tastefully added to the palace are very spacious, airy and pleasingly decorated. A quiet lounge with comfortable sofas is found just off the bustling bar, which also sets out tables and chairs on the shaded patio. The garden extends to the ramparts and, while you are staying here, be sure to allow time to stroll along them. The dining room offers wonderful views of the garden, walls, and tower where storks nest. It specializes in local cuisine: roast suckling pig, El Barco beans, and Yemas de Santa Theresa (a dessert made with egg yolks). *Directions:* Follow the road that circles Ávila's walls until you see the signpost directing you through the western-facing gate to the parador.

*PARADOR DE ÁVILA*
*Calle Marqués Canales de Chozas, 2*
*05001 Ávila, Spain*
*Tel: 920-211-340, Fax: 920-226-166*
*61 Rooms, Double: €115–€125\**
*\*Breakfast not included: €13*
*Open: all year, Credit cards: all major*
*Region: Castilla y León, Michelin Map: 575*
*www.karenbrown.com/avila.html*

This fortress parador on the sea is undoubtedly one of the most remarkable in Spain. Isolated on a tiny, craggy peninsula just southwest of Baiona, it is encircled by the ramparts of the former fortress of Monte Real, which protected it on three sides from the wild, crashing sea. Because it is one of the larger paradors, it is one of the busier ones, and there is always lots of action in the lively bar and the spacious dining room. With its massive, stone stairway and original, stone-domed ceiling, the lobby is stunning; and the interior patio with its fountain is delightful. The bedrooms with wooden floors and ceilings are large and charmingly furnished, and most of them have spectacular views to the sea. Easily, several days could be enjoyed in this romantic, luxurious hotel with its dramatic backdrop of the clear Atlantic Ocean. A walk around the ramparts gives you fabulous vistas of the ocean and the port city of Baiona. *Directions:* From Vigo, take the freeway AG 51 to Baiona Sud, which brings you to a large, oceanside roundabout where you turn north. The parador is clearly visible on the peninsula ahead of you.

*PARADOR DE BAIONA*
*36300 Baiona, Spain*
*Tel: 986-355-000, Fax: 986-355-076*
*122 Rooms, Double: €180\**
*\*Breakfast not included: €16*
*Open: all year, Credit cards: all major*
*Region: Galicia, Michelin Map: 571*
*www.karenbrown.com/baiona.html*

Hotel Mar i Vent is without doubt one of the best values in Mallorca. For less than you pay for a room in most hotels, you also have breakfast and dinner included in the rate. This superbly run, small hotel has been in the Vives family for three generations. Originally it was owned by the grandfather of Francesc Vives, who is now manager. As was customary, his grandfather had to own a house before he could marry his sweetheart, so he went to America and saved enough money for a simple, stone house in the small village of Banyalbufar, high in the hills above the sea. There were no cars or roads in those days, but travelers sometimes happened by who needed a place to spend the night. With a kind heart, grandfather Vives took them in and his wife fed them. The village priest suggested that they open their home as a wayside inn, and today the same genuine hospitality exists. Francesc's pretty wife, Juana María, helps at the reception; his father, Tony, makes all guests feel special; his mother, Francisca, prepares the home-cooked meals; and aunt Juanita helps, too! Although this hotel is inexpensive, a high quality of service and accommodation exists. Each room is nicely decorated and has a terrace or balcony with a view over the terraced fields to the sea. The hotel is built into the hillside and on the lowest level is a large pool cantilevered over the cliffs with a panoramic view.

*HOTEL MAR I VENT*
*Owners: Vives family*
*Calle Major, 49*
*Banyalbufar 07191 Mallorca, Spain*
*Tel: 971-618-000, Fax: 971-618-201*
*29 Rooms, Double: €98–€150*
*Open: Feb to Dec, Credit cards: MC, VS*
*Region: Balearic Islands, Michelin Map: 579*
*www.karenbrown.com/marivent.html*

As implied by the name, this magnificent old edifice was once the palatial home of the Fuster family. Constructed in the early 20th century and now listed as Landmark Building by the city, it has been completely renovated and restored as an impeccable, modern hotel, carefully retaining most of the carved stone, marble, and wrought iron architectural features of a bygone era. Overlooking a verdant, tree-lined plaza at the end of Passeig de Gracia, it is located a short walk from the bustling shops and restaurants of Las Ramblas. The ground-floor salon bar with its Gaudí-inspired chairs and stunning combination of dark woods, gold-vaulted ceiling, original stone columns, and sumptuously comfortable, dark-crimson plush seating, sets the tone for the rest of the hotel. Rooms and suites come in a variety of sizes, none of them small. All are beautifully appointed with the creature comforts required by today's discerning traveler, and decorated in earth tones highlighted by splashes of rich color, wood paneling, plush designer fabrics, and fresh flowers. Large, modern bathrooms are finished in white and gray marble, many with deep whirlpool tubs. The rooftop pool, gymnasium, and restaurant all provide panoramic views across the city. Alternatively, the elegantly decorated first floor restaurant provides a view across the plaza. *Directions:* On the plaza at the end of Passeig de Gràcia.

*HOTEL CASA FUSTER*
*Manager: Ferran Rojo*
*Passeig de Gràcia, 132*
*08008 Barcelona, Spain*
*Tel: 932-553-000, Fax: 932-553-002*
*96 Rooms, Double: €588–€3,010\**
*\*Breakfast not included: €25*
*Open: all year, Credit cards: all major*
*Region: Catalonia, Michelin Map: 574*
*www.karenbrown.com/fuster.html*

It's hard to do justice to the many attributes of Hotel Claris in the space available. The expansive, marble-floored lobby, its copper-fronted reception desk of white poplar burl, and the interior waterfall and reflecting pool are merely harbingers of what is to come. Constructed around a glass-topped central atrium, natural light pervades throughout. Guest rooms are individually decorated, sumptuously appointed, and accented with the owner's personal collection of original art and Egyptian antiques. Fresh flowers, monogrammed linens and towels, complimentary wine on arrival, and, for the suites, a daily selection of bath salts and body oils—for either relaxation or invigoration—is part of the turn down service. The rooftop gymnasium and pool offer spectacular views of the city, as does the glass-roofed terrace restaurant. On days when the weather is not conducive to dining al fresco, retreat to the stylish, ground-floor Bar and Restaurant East 47 featuring original artwork by Andy Warhol. A special, exclusive treat for hotel guests is free access to the owner's private museum, containing an astonishing collection of Egyptian artifacts. Need wheels but don't want the hassle of a rental car? . . . Borrow the courtesy car available gratis to guests (there is a small charge for fuel) on a half-day basis and take a self-guided tour of the city. *Directions:* On the corner of Pau Claris and Valencia in the heart of Barcelona.

*HOTEL CLARIS*
*Manager: José Luis Fernández*
*Pau Claris, 150*
*08009 Barcelona, Spain*
*Tel: 934-876-262, Fax: 932-157-970*
*120 Rooms, Double: €430–€1,096\**
*\*Breakfast not included: €20*
*Open: all year, Credit cards: all major*
*Region: Catalonia, Michelin Map: 574*
*www.karenbrown.com/claris.html*

The Colón is a stately hotel with elegant touches, built in 1951, right in the middle of the enchanting Gothic Quarter (Barrio Gótico) of Barcelona, facing onto a promenade. The lobby is entered by a broad, brown marble stairway. The public rooms are decorated in neutral tones and furnished with comfortable chairs, antiques, collectibles, and interesting artwork. Linger awhile, and watch the passersby in front of the massive cathedral across the street. On certain days, local folklore buffs gather here for a session of the regional dance, the sardana (ask at the hotel desk for the current schedule). Some 34 of its rooms, a few with terraces, overlook the city's famous cathedral. When making reservations, request a room with a terrace, which will afford you a memorable view of the cathedral and a preferable, quieter location on one of the upper floors; and, if the budget allows, a suite or double room with a sitting area—for more money, but also more space. All of the rooms have wonderful high ceilings and are accented with old-world touches that lend an intimate feeling to this fairly big hotel. The Colón is a good, not-too-expensive hotel that enjoys an incomparable location. When you unload your luggage inquire about nearby parking. *Directions:* Follow directions to the cathedral. The hotel is directly across the square.

*HOTEL COLÓN*
*Avenida de la Catedral, 7*
*08002 Barcelona, Spain*
*Tel: 933-011-404, Fax: 933-172-915*
*145 Rooms, Double: €100–€350\**
*\*Breakfast not included: €15*
*Open: all year, Credit cards: all major*
*Region: Catalonia, Michelin Map: 574*
*www.karenbrown.com/colon.html*

Situated in the heart of the Quadrat d'Or, an area famed for Catalonia's exuberant brand of Art Nouveau, and a few minutes walk from the shops and restaurants of La Rambla, the Hotel Condes consists of two buildings on a corner facing Gaudi's La Pedrera. Formerly two palaces built in the late 1800s, they have been renovated and enlarged to provide a first class base from which to explore the city. Overall, our favorite is the "Monument" building, slightly older of the two, which has been sensitively renovated to include the original spiral staircase (take a rest on the "banquita" or use the elevator) and the splendid, old, wooden front door, complete with the original brass knocker from its days as an apartment building. The solarium, gym, and small splash pool on the roof provide a pleasant oasis away from the bustling streets below. All rooms have balconies except those on the first floor. The newer "Centre" building was constructed within the original façade and, while it lacks the rooftop facilities offered in Monument, it probably offers the nicest accommodation. The deluxe terrace rooms on the seventh floor with large, private, outdoor terraces provide magnificent views across the city. As might be expected of a modern hotel, all the guestrooms are stylishly appointed with every convenience, luxurious linens, bathrobes, and superb bathrooms. *Directions:* On the corner of Passeig de Gracia and Mallorca in the heart of downtown.

*HOTEL CONDES DE BARCELONA*
*Manager: Lorenzo Luvio*
*Passeig de Gràcia 73-75*
*08008 Barcelona, Spain*
*Tel: 934-450-000, Fax: 934-453-223*
*235 Rooms, Double: €165–€325\**
*\*Breakfast not included: €19*
*Open: all year, Credit cards: all major*
*Region: Catalonia, Michelin Map: 574*
*www.karenbrown.com/condesdeb.html*

The Hotel Inglaterra is perfectly located only a few steps from Las Ramblas and Plaza Universitat in the Triángulo de Oro (the Golden Triangle). The marble columns, large bay window, and wrought-iron balconies are appealing features that make the hotel's exterior stand out from the other modern hotels and surrounding buildings. You enter through wide, glass doors into a light, airy reception area and lobby with opulent marble floors, stainless-steel elevator, and state-of-the-art lighting fixtures. This entrance combined with the art-deco style, the plush velvet sofa, leather-fronted reception desk, and original marble staircase, lends an inviting feel. The well-appointed bedrooms, all paneled with light-wood walls and adorned with Chinese character paintings above the beds, offer balconies and ample built-in closet space. Original paintings by Catalan artists, Lluis Lleó and Armengol, can also be found throughout the hotel's guestrooms and public areas. Bathrooms are gleaming with marble floors and walls, and granite countertops. Room 601 is a real bargain—it is the largest of the 55 guestrooms and has a spacious, private balcony adjoining the hotel's rooftop terrace. On the second floor (Spanish first), you find the sunny bar-café where breakfast is served. For a moderately priced hotel with a superb location and friendly staff, you can't go wrong with the Hotel Inglaterra. *Directions:* Located just off Plaza Universitat.

*HOTEL INGLATERRA*
*Manager: Gemma Ravasi*
*Pelayo, 14*
*08001 Barcelona, Spain*
*Tel: 935-051-100, Fax: 935-051-109*
*60 Rooms, Double: €250–€370\**
*\*Breakfast not included: €12*
*Open: all year, Credit cards: all major*
*Region: Catalonia, Michelin Map: 574*
*www.karenbrown.com/inglaterra.html*

"Palace" denotes luxury, and this lovely old lady lives up to her name. The 1919 hotel, with a prime location in the heart of Barcelona near the popular Las Ramblas, has undergone extensive remodeling and the old rooms have only gained in ambiance. The walls are painted in soft colors and climb to ceilings that are at least 4 meters high. The bedrooms are immense by modern hotel standards and furnished handsomely in old-world style. Salvador Dali's favorite room, and ours, is number 110 with a sunken Roman bath and its bed tucked into an alcove. The renovation of the Palace Hotel's public rooms is masterful; the resulting lobby, central hall, lounges, and excellent restaurants are elegant without being intimidating. Gleaming marble floors, shiny, solid brass fixtures, stunning crystal chandeliers, gilded mirrors, bathtubs you sink into, subdued piano music, finest quality linens, turn-down service at night—this all adds up to nostalgic, old-fashioned luxury and refined grace. The service is nothing short of perfection, and the English-speaking concierges go out of their way to anticipate your needs—a real asset in this city with so much to offer. You will feel pampered at the Palace and that is a feeling hard to come by in large city hotels these days. *Directions:* Facing the Gran Via and Roger de Lluvia in the heart of Barcelona.

*PALACE HOTEL*
*Manager: Javier Gener*
*Gran Vía de les Corts Catalanes, 668*
*08010 Barcelona, Spain*
*Tel: 935-101-130, Fax: 933-180-148*
*120 Rooms, Double: €421–€2,690\**
*\*Breakfast not included: €27*
*Open: all year, Credit cards: all major*
*Region: Catalonia, Michelin Map: 574*
*www.karenbrown.com/palace.html*

Deep in the countryside of almond and olive groves, yet only a 15-minute drive from Ronda, Molino del Santo makes the perfect hub from which to venture out each day to explore Andalusia and beyond (guests often make a daytrip to Gibraltar). Quite truthfully, you might forget all thoughts of sightseeing because the Molino del Santo is such a gem you won't want to leave—rates that include dinner and afternoon tea are available. Originally an old grain and olive mill, the property was converted into an outstanding, friendly little resort by Pauline Elkin and Andy Chapell (formerly schoolteachers in England). The charming old water mill now houses the reception area, lounge, bar, and dining room. Guests enjoy eating on the flower-bedecked terrace listening to the millstream as it rushes by. Sparkling white-walled guestrooms in cozy cottages, most with their own terrace, have been added over the years—three are large enough to accommodate families All is simply but very tastefully decorated. The solar-heated pool and the immaculately kept gardens display the same touch of perfection. If you enjoy casual informality, for both price and ambiance, Molino del Santo is absolute perfection. *Directions:* From Ronda take the A376 towards Seville and after leaving the town take the first left for the 11 km drive to Benaoján. The mill is signpost in lower Benaoján by the river—not in the village on the hill.

*MOLINO DEL SANTO*
*Owners: Pauline Elkin & Andy Chapell*
*Bda. Estacion s/n*
*29370 Benaoján, Spain*
*Tel: 952-167-151, Fax: 952-167-327*
*18 Rooms, Double: €80–€180*
*Open: mid-Feb to mid-Nov, Credit cards: MC, VS*
*Region: Andalusia, Michelin Map: 578*
*www.karenbrown.com/molinodelsanto.html*

This 12th-century palace on the edge of a bustling metropolis was practically destroyed by the French in 1808, but was rescued and restored by the government as a historical monument. Ferdinand and Isabella stayed here on their pilgrimage to Santiago. Of the original castle, there remains only the Torreón. In the tower cellar, you find the bar reconstructed from the original foundation, reached down a stone stairway with thick stone walls. The bars-vaulted, painted, 11-meter-high wooden ceiling has massive beams which support a huge, antique iron chandelier. A door from the bar leads onto the grassy terrace where you find the swimming pool. The spacious bedrooms flank long, broad hallways and have a rustic, almost "western" ambiance with tile floors and leather furnishings. They have lovely views of the town and countryside. The bedrooms on the upper two floors have terraces, while those on the ground floor are poolside. The vaulted dining room has a wall of windows looking out across the escarpment to the countryside. Be sure to visit the Salón Artesonado whose Mudéjar ceiling was brought here from the town of San Román del Valle in León and lovingly reassembled. *Directions:* Benevente is a small town at the junction of the N52 and A6. The parador is well signed as you approach town.

▦ P ⫪ ≈ 🚶

*PARADOR DE BENAVENTE*
*49600 Benavente, Spain*
*Tel: 980-630-304, Fax: 980-630-303*
*30 Rooms, Double: €115–€145\**
*\*Breakfast not included: €13*
*Open: all year, Credit cards: all major*
*Region: Castilla y León, Michelin Map: 575*
*www.karenbrown.com/benavente.html*

Tucked at the top of a narrow, steep, graveled road in the beautiful hills of the Basque countryside and surrounded by nature, this is a simple inn that reminded me of something we might recommend in the Swiss Alps. The decor is simple, fresh, and pretty, and so as not to compete with the surrounding natural beauty, light pine is used for the furnishings and the beds are topped by crisp, white duvets. With no other buildings in sight, the cozy guestrooms open up to bucolic views and a few even enjoy their own small balcony. Although bedrooms are small, guests can relax in a sitting room with tables and chairs and a cozy niche in front of a wonderful corner fireplace off the first-floor entry. The hotel's restaurant has two dining rooms, one an enclosed terrace whose tables enjoy wonderful views, the other a cozy interior room with tables set up against stone walls. Even though the inn, located just outside Jauntsarats, is in a quiet spot (though actually just five minutes from the autoroute and 35 kilometers from Pamplona), I suggest you make a reservation in advance since you might find that the person at the reception desk speaks only Basque. If time allows, pay a visit to nearby Beruete, a charming village of geranium-bedecked houses clustering around a village church against a gorgeous mountain backdrop.

*HOTEL PERUSKENEA*
*Owner: José Maria Astiz Nuin*
*31806 Beruete, Spain*
*Tel: 948-503-370, Fax: 948-503-284*
*9 Rooms, Double: €80–€100\**
*\*Breakfast not included: €10*
*Open: all year, Credit cards: all major*
*Region: Navarra, Michelin Map: 573*
*www.karenbrown.com/peruskenea.html*

The setting of the Parador de Bielsa is nothing less than sensational. From Bielsa, the road weaves down a beautiful, narrow valley, following the River Cinca for 14 kilometers, until the way is blocked by granite walls of some of the highest mountains in the Pyrenees. The hotel is perched on the side of the hill, looking across the rushing stream and idyllic meadow to a glacial backdrop of mountains laced with waterfalls. The gray stone building (of relatively new construction) blends well with the rugged landscape. The interior also blends in perfectly—the ambiance is that of a rustic mountain lodge. Throughout the hotel good taste prevails in every detail. Handwoven carpets sit on polished pine floors, the light fixtures are of heavy, black wrought-iron, the ceilings are supported by thick beams, the antique wood-paneled walls are accented by handsome oil paintings and framed prints. Green plants flourish in their window settings and comfortable brown leather sofas and chairs form cozy areas for friends to gather before the massive fireplace. The guestrooms have wood-paneled headboards, wrought-iron reading lamps, and sturdy wooden desks and chairs. Ask for the third floor for an unforgettable view.

*PARADOR DE BIELSA*
*22350 Bielsa–Valle de Pineta, Spain*
*Tel: 974-501-011, Fax: 974-501-188*
*24 Rooms, Double: €115–€145\**
*\*Breakfast not included: €13*
*Closed: mid-Jan to mid-Mar, Credit cards: all major*
*Region: Aragon, Michelin Map: 574*
*www.karenbrown.com/bielsa.html*

The Guggenheim Museum in Bilbao has turned this busy city into a sightseeing destination and there is no better place to stay—handily a five minute walk from the museum—than the Hotel López de Haro. This 5-star hotel exudes refined elegance. The décor is extremely tasteful with traditional furniture and fabrics used throughout. Bedrooms are priced by size from small doubles to luxurious suites. The color scheme varies on each floor and—a wonderful advantage for women—there is one floor dedicated to lady travelers. The clubby bar is adjacent to the breakfast room, where on weekends buffet style lunches are served. There's a real sense of occasion to dining in the Club Nautico restaurant, a popular dining venue for both locals and guests. While the focus of your sightseeing is the Guggenheim, be sure to visit Bilbao's other museums of fine art and folk art. *Directions:* Leave the A6 at Bilbao Oeste, follow signs for "centro" until you see hotel signs. Park in front of the hotel to unload luggage and your car will be taken to the car park. The traffic can be overwhelming, so be prepared to get lost.

*HOTEL LÓPEZ DE HARO*
*Manager: Marian Anasagasti*
*Obispo Orueta, 2*
*48009 Bilbao, Spain*
*Tel: 944-235-500, Fax: 944-234-500*
*53 Rooms, Double: €140–€390\**
*\*Breakfast not included: €16*
*Open: all year, Credit cards: all major*
*Region: País Vasco, Michelin Map: 573*
*www.karenbrown.com/lopezdeharo.html*

Cáceres is best appreciated by staying overnight and there is no better place to stay than the Parador de Cáceres, which occupies an entire city block of the quaint, walled old quarter of the town (a national monument). Once within its medieval gates, you are suddenly immersed in a well-preserved city that, in its heyday, was home to many wealthy Spaniards who made their fortunes in the New World. The 14th-century Parador de Cáceres, just off the Plaza de San Mateo, was built by Don Diego García de Ulloa. Like most of the mansions in town, it has a façade of cut stone with ornamental wrought-iron balconies stretching over the narrow street. Once through the massive doors and up a few steps, you enter an open courtyard and then the lobby. One of the nicest features of the hotel is its dining room, which spills out onto a shaded terrace overlooking the garden—a perfect spot for romantic dinners and summer breakfasts. Bedrooms are large and attractive with tiled floors, white walls, and wooden furniture. *Directions:* Be patient following parador signs through this sprawling, traffic-filled city. Eventually you enter the cobbled streets of the old quarter only to find the road barred by bollards. Press the button beside them and announce "parador"—the bollards magically sink into the ground and you find the parador just up the street on your left. You will be directed to parking.

*PARADOR DE CÁCERES*
*Calle Ancha, 6*
*10003 Cáceres, Spain*
*Tel: 927-211-759, Fax: 927-211-729*
*31 Rooms, Double: €130–€140\**
*\*Breakfast not included: €13*
*Open: all year, Credit cards: all major*
*Region: Extremadura, Michelin Map: 576*
*www.karenbrown.com/caceres.html*

One of the most dramatic paradors in the country, the Parador de Cardona has dominated the fortified town of Cardona for centuries from its 460-meter-high hilltop setting. This site was chosen as a home by the Duke in the 10th century and, although much of the construction is recent, the period flavor and authentic nature of the original 9th-century fortified building have been maintained. Behind the hotel you find a unique 2nd-century tower and 11th-century church along with a beautiful Roman patio from which you can get a bird's-eye view of the unusual salt hills, the pueblo, and the Pyrenees. The bedrooms, many with four-poster beds, red-wine tile floors, and dark wooden furniture, are ample in size and were totally renovated in 1996. The restaurant is spectacularly situated in a forever-long, dramatic, vaulted-ceilinged room. The ochre-toned walls create a warm glow in the evening, making dinner a special occasion. Although out of the way, this parador offers a memorable night's stay in a carefully renovated historic setting with all the modern comforts of home.

*PARADOR DE CARDONA*
*Castillo s/n*
*08261 Cardona, Spain*
*Tel: 938-691-275, Fax: 938-691-636*
*54 Rooms, Double: €135–€145\**
*\*Breakfast not included: €14*
*Open: all year, Credit cards: all major*
*Region: Catalonia, Michelin Map: 574*
*www.karenbrown.com/cardona.html*

The Parador de Carmona is ideally located in a small, ancient town imbued with medieval ambiance, but still only 30 minutes from downtown Seville. This is one of three castles built in the walled town of Carmona and its conversion into a parador is a real beauty. Long ago decorated by the same Moorish architects responsible for the famous Alcázar in Seville, the restoration has preserved the original Moslem flavor while adding more modern appointments. You will be charmed from the beginning by the entry through the castle gate into the courtyard surrounded by the restored castle walls. Entry into the building itself transports you into the Moorish past, the fantastic patio with its tiled floor, impressive fountain, and slender, graceful arches and columns. You will be delighted by the intricately patterned, colorful ceramic-tile decor throughout the hotel. The large guestrooms, decorated in traditional Spanish style, maintain the reliably high standards of the paradors. Request one of the rooms with a terrace—and feast your eyes on the wonderful view from the hilltop vantage point over the vast plains below. The same panorama can be enjoyed from the terrace outside the bar. A swimming pool is cleverly tucked into the ramparts. *Directions:* From Seville take the NIV highway in the direction of Cordoba/Madrid. After 25 km exit for Carmona and follow signs for "Centro Historico" and the parador is well signposted.

❄️ 💳 🛗 P 🍴 ≈ 🎿 🥾 🏇 🏄

*PARADOR DE CARMONA*
*41410 Carmona, Spain*
*Tel: 954-141-010, Fax: 954-141-712*
*63 Rooms, Double: €145–€155\**
*\*Breakfast not included: €14*
*Open: all year, Credit cards: all major*
*Region: Andalusia, Michelin Map: 578*
*www.karenbrown.com/carmona.html*

The Parador de Cazorla is definitely off the beaten path—do not plan to stay here just as a convenient overnight stop, but rather as a sightseeing experience in itself, and a place to go walking in the mountains. The setting on a small plateau with a sweeping vista of pine-covered mountains is absolutely fabulous. On the grassy terrace in front of the hotel there is a large swimming pool that captures the same lovely view. The hotel is built to resemble a very large Andalusian farmhouse with a white stucco façade and red-tiled roof. Inside, the ambiance is appropriately simple. The lounge has comfortable armchairs and historic hunting prints on the walls. The dining room has high-backed upholstered chairs, wrought-iron chandeliers, and French doors leading to a spectacular terrace with marvelous views of the mountains. The bedrooms are spacious and nicely decorated with country style furniture. Ask for a room with a view—most of them have this. Beyond the terrace is a children's playground and a swimming pool. *Directions:* The address reads Cazorla, but it is actually 25 kilometers away in the heart of the Cazorla Sierra nature reserve. Upon reaching Cazorla, follow the signs to the park—the road climbs up from the valley and into the mountains—keep your eyes peeled for a right hand turn onto the parador's 5 km driveway. The road is well signposted, but be sure to arrive in daylight.

*PARADOR DE CAZORLA*
*23470 Cazorla, Spain*
*Tel: 953-727-075, Fax: 953-727-077*
*33 Rooms, Double: €95–€125\**
*\*Breakfast not included: €13*
*Closed: mid-Dec to mid-Feb, Credit cards: all major*
*Region: Andalusia, Michelin Map: 578*
*www.karenbrown.com/cazorla.html*

Imaginatively and extensively renovated, this parador is a real beauty. It is located just off the main plaza in the charming, historic town of Chinchón (justifiably famous for its anise liqueur). The circular plaza, with its many overhanging wood balconies, is very picturesque and magically transforms into a bullring for festivals. The parador is installed in a 17th-century Augustinian monastery, and fountains, hanging and terraced gardens, reflecting pools, and worn stone patios soothe the secular guest here with the same tranquility once treasured by its previous religious residents. The pale-brick-paved central cloister features a glass-enclosed colonnade lined with antiques and hung with tapestries. The guestrooms are simple and lovely, floored in red tile, with whitewashed walls and colorful wooden beds topped with spreads. The rooms in the old section overlooking the garden are particularly attractive, and room 8, with a private sitting room and balcony, is superior. The cheerful dining room is accented with colorful azulejos (tiles) and offers an interesting variety of dishes. A lovely swimming pool is found on one of the lower terraces in the garden. Try to fit in a visit to the historic restaurant Mesón Cuevas de Vino at the top of town, well-known locally for its traditional grills and sangría. *Directions:* Follow signs for "centro" and the parador is on your right just before you enter the circular central plaza.

❅ ♨ CREDIT ☎ Υ P ⑪ ≈ ⌂ ⅋ ⅋

*PARADOR DE CHINCHÓN*
*Avenida Generalísimo, 1*
*28370 Chinchón, Spain*
*Tel: 918-940-836, Fax: 918-940-908*
*38 Rooms, Double: €135–€145\**
*\*Breakfast not included: €14*
*Open: all year, Credit cards: all major*
*Region: Madrid, Michelin Map: 576*
*www.karenbrown.com/chinchon.html*

On rare occasions we discover a small hotel that is so perfect it seems too good to be true. This is definitely the case with the Posada del Valle. This charming, 19th-century stone farmhouse is tucked onto the south side of a hill with a breathtaking, stunning view. In one direction, the jagged peaks of the Picos de Europa soar into the sky; in the other direction, rows of limestone mountains melt endlessly into the horizon. In all hotels, warmth of welcome is the most important ingredient, and here you will truly be welcomed with an open heart. Your hosts, Joanne and Nigel Burch, originally from Britain, have lived for many years in Spain and have a sincere love of their adopted land, particularly Asturias. Joanne cooks dinner—be sure to book in advance—which often includes their organic "Xaldo" lamb. All the bedrooms are delightful; our favorites are the Sueve rooms with their king-size beds. If you enjoy simple inns with romantic charm, a stupendous setting, rustic appeal, delicious food, and great heart; you will love it. Guided walks are often available. Nigel and Joanne produce a brochure offering enough activities to keep you busy for a month. *Directions:* Leave N634 at Arriondas and enter the town center. Take AS260 out of Arriondas, following signs to Colunga and Mirador del Fito. After 1 km, turn right at the sign for Collia and Torre. Go straight through Collia. The hotel is 300 meters on the left, down a steep cement driveway.

*HOTEL POSADA DEL VALLE*
*Owners: Joanne & Nigel Burch*
*33549 Collia, Spain*
*Tel: 985-841-157, Fax: 985-841-559*
*12 Rooms, Double: €61–€84\**
*\*Breakfast not included: €8*
*Open: Apr to Nov 1, Credit cards: MC, VS*
*Region: Asturias, Michelin Map: 572*
*www.karenbrown.com/posadadelvalle.html*

The Hotel Albucasis is just a short walk to the colorful mosque and all the other sightseeing in the heart of this historic city. Although centrally located in the bustling Barrio de la Judería with its maze of narrow, twisting streets, whitewashed houses, and wrought-iron balconies, the hotel is remarkably quiet. Reflecting the Arabic and Roman style, the Albucasis faces onto its own small courtyard with potted plants and fresh white walls laced with greenery. From the courtyard you enter into the reception area, which also serves as the bar and breakfast lounge where coffee, juice and croissants are served in the morning. The decor is very simple and uncluttered with white walls, terra cotta floors, round tables and their wooden chairs. The hotel is a mixture of double and twin bedded rooms, the latter being the largest—all similar in decor with wooden headboards and matching desk and chair. Although not large, the rooms are of ample size, and the tiled bathrooms are not too cramped. Best of all, this small hotel is spotless and the staff is very helpful. We ate an excellent dinner just up the street at El Churrasco. *Directions:* Even if you have the most detailed of maps the hotel is absolutely impossible to drive to. Your best is to park your car as close as possible to the mosque (mexquita), and first find the hotel on foot. They will give you a detailed driving map so that you can bring your car to the hotel's garage.

*HOTEL ALBUCASIS*
*Owner: Alfonso Salas Camacho*
*Buen Pastor, 11*
*14003 Córdoba, Spain*
*Tel & Fax: 957-478-625*
*15 Rooms, Double: €75–€80\**
*\*Breakfast not included: €6*
*Closed: Jan, Credit cards: MC, VS*
*Region: Andalusia, Michelin Map: 578*
*www.karenbrown.com/albucasis.html*

The grounds of this parador include acres of grassy hillside, a huge swimming pool overlooking the city, and tree-shaded areas ideal for relaxing in the heat of the day—the perfect place for those who want to soak up a little sun. It's a modern parador with lots of amenities. The public rooms seem to cover almost as many acres as the lawn and command spectacular views of the valley and the city. Appointments are delightfully traditional, with occasional tapestries and old-style chandeliers to remind you of the past. The spacious bedrooms are furnished in contemporary Spanish style, and it is well worth paying a little more money to enjoy the same gorgeous view you see from the lobby and dining room—over the lawn and trees to the city below—from your balcony. The vista is especially attractive at night. All this natural (and man-made) air-conditioned luxury is still only a ten minute taxi ride from the Mezquita and the fascinating and colorful old Jewish Quarter. The old city is the most wonderful place to visit but a driver's nightmare so leave your car at the parador. *Directions:* We thought the parador difficult to find when coming from the city and would suggest requesting detailed instructions to fit the direction of your arrival. Parador staff told us that the parador is signpost on an exit from the N432 which heads north from Córdoba towards Badajoz. There's ample parking around the hotel.

❄ 🏊 🚗 💳 ⬆⬇ P ⑂ ≈ 🏃 🏃‍♂️

*PARADOR DE CÓRDOBA*
*Avenida de la Arruzafa s/n, Carretera de El Brillante*
*14012 Córdoba, Spain*
*Tel: 957-275-900, Fax: 957-280-409*
*94 Rooms, Double: €130–€140\**
*\*Breakfast not included: €13*
*Open: all year, Credit cards: all major*
*Region: Andalusia, Michelin Map: 578*
*www.karenbrown.com/cordoba.html*

Have you ever wished you had friends in Spain who owned a romantic hideaway where you could spend your holiday? Wish no more. Staying at Finca Listonero, you will feel like a pampered guest in a private home—and indeed you are. Finca Listonero is the home of Graeme Gibson (originally from Australia) and David Rice (originally from Ireland), who for many years owned an extremely popular restaurant on the Costa del Sol, followed by an equally successful restaurant in Sydney. Now, in Spain, they have found their dream—a 300-year-old farmhouse tucked up in the hills, not far from the quaint Moorish coastal town of Mojacar. Graeme is an interior designer, and David a talented chef—a perfect combination for their latest venture. The farmhouse, painted a deep rosy-pink, enhanced by bright-green shutters and accented by a profusion of potted plants, is a happy sight. Inside, the cheerful use of color continues: deep rose and green remain predominant, but other colors are used boldly throughout. Art Nouveau, European, and Oriental antiques; English fabrics; Spanish tiles; and hand-loomed carpets are cleverly combined to create a welcoming ambiance. Each bedroom has its own color scheme—the Blue Room, featuring pretty English floral fabric, is especially inviting. Finca Listonero makes a good place to relax after a few days in Granada (a two-hour drive away). Note: Plan to dine here—David's meals are truly memorable.

*FINCA LISTONERO*
*Owners: Graeme Gibson & David Rice*
*Cortijo Grande 04639 Turre, Spain*
*Tel & Fax: 950-479-094*
*7 Rooms, Double: €75–€95*
*Open: all year, Credit cards: MC, VS*
*Region: Andalusia, Michelin Map: 578*
*www.karenbrown.com/listonero.html*

You cannot help falling in love with the Hotel del Oso, superbly located in the glorious mountain range called Picos de Europa. Although it is officially rated two stars, many deluxe hotels could take lessons from this gem. Rarely do you find such a combination of warmth of welcome, faultless housekeeping, superb cuisine, and beautiful displays of flowers. Undoubtedly this degree of excellence is the work of the Rivas family. Sr. Rivas designed the hotel, which, although of new construction, maintains a traditional air, blending in with the other beige stone buildings in the region. His charming, friendly wife is the talented chef, and people come from afar to sample her fabulous food (specialties are regional dishes). However, the greatest asset is what few other hotels can offer—four wonderful, talented daughters (Ana, Irene, Teresa, and Cari) who assist in every aspect of the running of the hotel. Their sparkle and genuine hospitality would be difficult to duplicate. On the ground floor there is a wood-paneled reception room, a large dining room, and a cozy bar which opens up to a terrace where tables overlook a crystal-clear stream. The guestrooms are located on two upper floors (each level has its own sitting room). Each of the bedrooms has the same furniture—only the matching fabrics used on the spreads, curtains, and cushions vary. Ask for one of the rooms numbered 209 to 213—these have some of the best mountain views.

*HOTEL DEL OSO*
*Manager: Ana Rivas Gonzalez*
*Cosgaya 39539 Potes, Spain*
*Tel: 942-733-018, Fax: 942-733-036*
*36 Rooms, Double: €65–€75\**
*\*Breakfast not included: €10*
*Closed: Jan to mid-Feb, Credit cards: MC, VS*
*Region: Cantabria, Michelin Map: 572*
*www.karenbrown.com/oso.html*

One of the latest stars to be added to the Spanish parador group is set in the spectacular 16th-century Convento de San Pablo. The hotel, crowning a rocky promontory, faces across the gorge to Cuenca, a breathtaking town hewn out of the rocks. When staying at the Parador de Cuenca, you can leave your car parked at the parador and take the long footbridge that spans the gorge between two giant outcrops of rock. The interior has been restored with skill to preserve the authentic soul of the old convent. The cloister still remains as the garden in the core of the hotel. The colonnaded walkway (which wraps around the cloister on four sides) now serves as a lounge area for guests. The bar, entered through an ornately decorated portal, has dark-green wicker chairs with cushions in green and terra cotta, repeating the color in the potted palms and tiled floor. The vaulted ceiling is elaborately frescoed. In one of the wings there is a beautifully restored, tiny chapel. The dining room is dramatic, with a row of tiered chandeliers highlighting the intricately paneled ceiling. The guestrooms are decorated with reproduction painted headboards and floral-patterned draperies which are color-coordinated with bedspreads and chair coverings. *Directions:* Arriving in Cuenca follow pink signs for Casas Colgadas (hanging houses) until you see parador signs. The parador is not in the historic city but across the gorge. There is lots of parking.

*PARADOR DE CUENCA*
*Paseo Hoz del Huécar s/n*
*16001 Cuenca, Spain*
*Tel: 969-232-320, Fax: 969-232-534*
*63 Rooms, Double: €135–€145\**
*\*Breakfast not included: €14*
*Open: all year, Credit cards: all major*
*Region: Castilla-La Mancha, Michelin Map: 575*
*www.karenbrown.com/cuenca.html*

The Posada de San José, located in the heart of the walled city of Cuenca, is a gem tucked onto a tiny cobbled lane just off the Plaza Mayor. The entrance is easy to miss—just an antique doorway with a niche above it featuring a charming statue of San José holding the infant Christ. Once inside you find the hotel terraces down the hillside with staircases leading up and down, twisting and turning, with lots of interesting nooks and crannies. The bedrooms are comfortably furnished and many have thick stucco walls, beamed ceilings and old tiled floors. Best of all most of them have stunning views across the Huecar gorge to the Convento de San Pablo. Several of them have balconies. Rooms 11, 12, 31 and 33 are more luxurious suites with separate bath and shower and a most spacious bedroom/sitting room decorated in contemporary décor. We loved our rooms: 15 a twin with a spacious terrace and 22 a double four-poster with French windows opening to the view. Tapas, light suppers and breakfast are served in its welcoming little restaurant whose wall of windows frames the breathtaking views. Owner Jennifer Morter (raised in Canada) speaks perfect English. *Directions:* Arriving in Cuenca it is vital that you follow pink signs for "Casco Antiguo" into the old town. Go through the Plaza Major (cathedral) and straight—the third alley on your right has the hotel at the end—park on the street to unload and you will be directed to parking.

*POSADA DE SAN JOSÉ*
*Owner: Jennifer Morter*
*Julian Romero 4*
*16001 Cuenca, Spain*
*Tel: 969-211-300, Fax: 969-230-365*
*31 Rooms, Double: €75–€148\**
*\*Breakfast not included: €9*
*Open: all year, Credit cards: all major*
*Region: Castilla-La Mancha, Michelin Map: 575*
*www.karenbrown.com/sanjose.html*

La Residencia, perched high in the hills with views to the sea yet just steps from the quaint village of Deia, is a faultless hideaway. This gem of a hotel, nestled in 35 acres, is imaginatively created from three 16th, 17th, and 18th century farmhouses built of the golden-tan stone of the region. In keeping with its past, the decor is elegantly simple with white walls accented by beautiful antiques and bouquets of fresh flowers. Check-in is handled quietly and without fuss at an antique desk. Nearby are intimate lounges and bars where guests can sit quietly with friends as if in a private home. However, most guests "live" outdoors—the hotel has its own private club by the sea, serviced by a shuttle bus. There is a leisure center with indoor pool, two tennis courts with cushioned surface and a resident coach, Jacuzzi, gym, beauty center, bar, and terraces for those who don't want to leave the property. The manicured gardens offer an exquisite retreat with secluded shady nooks. The hotel is built on a hillside with two swimming pools tucked onto terraces. Next to the lower pool is a bar where guests can order lunch and sample fresh fish of the day. For those who want to dine elegantly there is a gourmet restaurant, El Olivo, while the more informal restaurant, Son Fony, offers local cuisine. The bedrooms are all fabulously furnished. The suites, three with their own private pool, are stunning; but even the standard doubles overlooking the garden are outstanding.

*LA RESIDENCIA*
*Manager: John Rogers*
*Deia 07179 Mallorca, Spain*
*Tel: 971-639-011, Fax: 971-639-370*
*59 Rooms, Double: €475–€2,550*
*Open: all year, Credit cards: all major*
*Region: Balearic Islands, Michelin Map: 579*
*www.karenbrown.com/residencia.html*

Converted to a luxury hotel just a few years ago from the private home of the Terry family who owned the neighboring bodega, The Hotel Duques de Medinaceli affords travelers very elegant and exquisite accommodation. The hotel boasts 28 suites that are all identified by plaques and named for the famous guests that have resided there. The Hotel Duques de Medinaceli is refined, lovely and very historical—almost a museum in terms of the artwork that graces its walls—but it also has the ambiance and warmth of a private home with a rich and inviting décor. The entry of the hotel is an impressive tiled courtyard with columns and a fountain. At the far end is the reception with a pretty sitting area that wraps around a historical botanical garden. Heavy drapes curtain the floor to ceiling windows that frame the beauty of the outdoors. Beyond the reception is a gorgeous dining room, whose décor and table settings compliment the culinary excellence of the kitchen. Guestrooms are sequestered behind handsome carved doors and are all individual in layout and amenities, and very regal in appointment. Don't complete your stay without a visit to the chapel and the private patio terrace, Los Olivos, named for the ancient olive trees that shade its tables. *Directions:* Take the A4 from Seville to Jerez and the second Jerez exit, Jerez sud, for the 25 km drive to El Puerto de Santa María.

❄ ⚲ 🖃 ♨ @ ♈ P ♜ ≈ 🖼 ☗ ⚓ 🧍 ⚗ ❦

*HOTEL DUQUES DE MEDINACELI*
*Owner: José Antonio Lopez Esteras*
*Plaza de los Jazmines, No. 2*
*11500 El Puerto de Santa María, Spain*
*Tel: 956-860-777, Fax: 956-542-687*
*28 Rooms, Double: €176–€280\**
*\*Breakfast not included: €19.80*
*Open: all year, Credit cards: all major*
*Region: Cádiz, Michelin Map: 578*
*www.karenbrown.com/duques.html*

El Puerto de Santa María is a lovely port town located on the Bay of Cádiz. Columbus returned here from the new world on the Santa Maria. Home to commercial fishermen, restaurants and outdoor cafes feature a wonderful bounty of seafood. At the heart of town, situated on a lovely cobbled street lined with orange trees, the Hotel Monasterio San Miguel, commissioned in 1727 by the Duque of Medinaceli, was converted to a hotel just over a decade ago. In this wonderful old cloister built round a central courtyard and fountain with handsome tile floors, arched doorways, high-vaulted beamed ceilings, wrought-iron fixtures, heavy old wooden doors, a bounty of windows, and handsome furnishings, guests will enjoy both historical ambiance and modern-day comforts with personal and attentive service from its professional staff. We enjoyed a lovely two-room suite in the main house that overlooked the central courtyard. Also popular are the rooms in the adjacent, three-story addition with their own balconies and views over the pool and rooftops to the river. Under stone-arched ceilings, the restaurant, Las Bóvedas, offers exceptional cuisine. The more informal Les Capuchinas offers a very reasonable menu at tables located just off the cozy bar. *Directions:* Take the A4 freeway from Seville to the second exit for Jerez, Jerez sud. From the exit it is a 25 km drive to El Puerto de Santa Maria where you find the hotel on the right.

*HOTEL MONASTERIO SAN MIGUEL*
*Owner: José Antonio Lopez Esteras*
*Calle Larga Virgen de los Milagros 27*
*11500 El Puerto de Santa María, Spain*
*Tel: 956-540-440, Fax: 956-542-604*
*165 Rooms, Double: €152–€320\**
*\*Breakfast not included: €13*
*Open: all year, Credit cards: all major*
*Region: Cádiz, Michelin Map: 578*
*www.karenbrown.com/sanmiguel.html*

The San Román de Escalante is a member of Relais & Châteaux and prides itself on giving guests complete privacy—the gates are only opened for guests and there are no signs indicating where the hotel is located. Once inside the gates, you will be impressed with the complex of one- and two-story buildings, in a mélange of stone, brick, and stucco topped with gorgeous weathered tiles, set in a large garden filled with sculptures. The 17th-century mansion contains several inviting public areas including a library (behind stained-glass doors) and five lovely bedrooms. Our preference is the bedrooms in the courtyard with spacious high-beamed rooms, traditionally furnished and hung with modern art, their picture window and terrace overlooking pastoral views. A secluded pool is located in a walled garden. Everywhere there is an abundance of art: sculpture, paintings, and statuary. The hotel is located in the rural hamlet of Castillo, adjacent to the gorgeous Cantabrian coast with its magnificent prehistoric caves and charming villages. Bilbao and the Guggenheim Museum are an hour's drive away. *Directions:* Leave the A6 at exit 188 and follow signs for Gama, where you turn for Escalante. In the center of the village, turn left for Castillo. The hotel is on your right after 2 km.

*SAN ROMÁN DE ESCALANTE*
*Owner: Juan Melis*
*Manager: Rubén Fernández*
*Castello, km 2*
*Escalante 39795 Cantabria, Spain*
*Tel: 942-677-728, Fax: 942-677-643*
*16 Rooms, Double: €122–€200\**
*\*Breakfast not included: €12*
*Open: all year, Credit cards: all major*
*Region: Cantabria, Michelin Map: 572*
*www.karenbrown.com/escalante.html*

If idyllic peace and solitude is your goal, look no further. Situated a scant five kilometers off a national highway, winding up an easily negotiable single-track road, Cal Teixdó is a remarkable find. Owned and operated by the Tapies family—with the same attention to detail that they apply to its "big brother", (the Castell de Ciutat in nearby Seu d'Urgell) amid the peace of an unspoiled village in the heart of the Pyrenees. The hotel has been cleverly integrated with the old slate-roofed and rough stone-walled farm buildings. The restaurant in the old hayloft, the guests' sitting room with comfy leather sofas, the reception area, and a cozy bar (open to residents and locals alike) are all found in the converted barn below. The guestrooms, all named after herbs, are individually decorated in a casual, country style. We particularly liked the rooms in the adjacent farmhouse with their top-of-the-line bathrooms, spacious bedroom, sitting area with sofa that converts to an extra bed, and terrace with spectacular views over the countryside to the mountains. The staff will happily assist you in your choice of outdoor activities including golf, ballooning, walking, cycling, archery—even transporting you up the mountain to their well-equipped activity center. The well-stocked cellars feature over 200 bins of regional wines. *Directions:* From Seu d'Urgell, take the N260 towards Puigcerda for 5 km and turn left up a small mountain road for the 5 km drive to Estamariu.

❄ ☕ 🛷 💳 P ❖ 🏌 🚶 🎿 ♿

*CAL TEIXDÓ*
*Owners: Tapies family*
*Sol de Villa*
*Estamariu, Seu d'Urgell, Spain*
*Tel: 973-360-121, Fax: 973-362-267*
*14 Rooms, Double: €90–€200*
*Restaurant closed Mon & Tue, Mar to Jun & Oct to Dec*
*Closed: Jan 15 to Mar 01, Credit cards: all major*
*Region: Catalonia, Michelin Map: 574*
*www.karenbrown.com/teixido.html*

This parador has a distinctly different flavor from most of the other paradors in Spain. Instead of presenting an old-world look, there is an unpretentious, rather masculine, nautical ambiance—a most appropriate theme for its waterfront position. The square, three-story building (painted white with stone trim around the windows) is not very old, but definitely has a traditional feel. The setting (particularly if you are interested in ships) is very interesting: the hotel sits on a high embankment overlooking Ferrol's long row of naval yards, and beyond to the commercial docks. A wide terrace in front of the hotel has benches, rose gardens, a gigantic anchor, and several antique canons—poised guarding the harbor. To the right of the lobby (which has a handsome floor with a harlequin pattern of alternating large dark-gray and beige marble tiles) is a large lounge, which looks a bit like a men's club, with dark-red leather chairs and sofas, potted palms, fresh flowers, nautical prints on the walls, and a marvelous antique oil painting of two ships in the midst of battle. A sunny dining room with bentwood chairs set around small tables and two entire walls of windows overlooks the harbor. The guestrooms are spacious and traditional in decor. Number 25, a corner room, is especially large and has a great view of the harbor.

*PARADOR DE FERROL*
*Plaza Eduardo Pondal*
*15401 Ferrol, Spain*
*Tel: 981-356-720, Fax: 981-356-721*
*38 Rooms, Double: €115–€145\**
*\*Breakfast not included: €13*
*Open: all year, Credit cards: all major*
*Region: Galicia, Michelin Map: 571*
*www.karenbrown.com/ferrol.html*

The Parador de Fuente Dé (which means "thunder of the gods") sits high on a mountain plateau surrounded by the soaring granite peaks of the Picos de Europa. Although the setting is dramatic, the exterior of the hotel looks a little dreary. Although one stone part is attractive, there is a modern, three-story wing stretching to the side that lacks much character. However, don't be put off by first impressions. Inside, the hotel is remarkably pleasant. This is a parador that attracts guests who love the outdoors and enjoy being close to nature, and the cozy bar and various lounges are appropriately decorated with a welcoming, informal flair. Nothing is elegant, nor should it be—instead, there is a mountain-lodge ambiance and a feeling that no one needs to get dressed up. If the weather is not conducive to being outdoors, there is a large games room where you can wile away the hours waiting for the sun to come out. The beamed-ceiling dining room is attractive and serves good, hearty meals featuring specialties of the region. The spacious guestrooms are remarkably nice. Many have enclosed balconies with windows that can open up if the day is warm and excellent large bathrooms, some with double sinks. There is a cable car that leaves from near the hotel offering magnificent views of the peaks of the Picos de Europa. *Directions:* From Panes, go south on N621 to Potes and then follow signs to Fuente Dé. The large hotel is on the right-hand side of the road.

*PARADOR DE FUENTE DÉ*
*39588 Fuente Dé, Spain*
*Tel: 942-736-651, Fax: 942-736-654*
*30 Rooms, Double: €115\**
*\*Breakfast not included: €13*
*Closed: mid-Nov to mid-Mar, Credit cards: all major*
*Region: Cantabria, Michelin Map: 572*
*www.karenbrown.com/fuente.html*

The Hotel Rebeco shares the same high mountain plateau as the Parador de Fuente Dé (they are opposite each other). Each has its own particular attributes: whereas the guestrooms at the parador are larger and the bathrooms more commodious, the Hotel Rebeco has a cozier ambiance and a more attractive façade. The hotel is built of sturdy blocks of gray granite, blended well into the rugged landscape and sets the mood of a mountain lodge. Inside, the furnishings are appropriately simple—anything ornate or fancy would seem completely out of character in this hotel that attracts those who love the outdoors and want to come back to a warm fire and a hearty dinner. There is a cozy bar to the right of the reception area and, to the left, is an attractive dining room set with wooden tables and chairs. This is a spacious room, but not so large as to lose a friendly ambiance. The guestrooms, located upstairs, are not large but they are all pleasantly decorated, again with a rustic decor appropriate to the style of the building. The fact that this is a hotel where the family is definitely involved is demonstrated by all the needlework "paintings" of flowers, birds, people, animals, and scenery on the walls—the owner's wife, Conception Cuesta, is an incredibly talented and prolific artist with the needle. *Directions:* From Panes, go south on N621 to Potes and then follow signs to Fuente Dé. The hotel is on the left, just before the cable car.

☰ P ⑪ ⚐

*HOTEL REBECO*
*Owner: Ottomar Casado Polantinos*
*Ctra. Fuente Dé s/n*
*39588 Fuente Dé, Spain*
*Tel: 942-736-601, Fax: 942-736-600*
*30 Rooms, Double: €65\**
*\*Breakfast not included: €12*
*Open: all year, Credit cards: all major*
*Region: Cantabria, Michelin Map: 572*
*www.karenbrown.com/rebeco.html*

The Parador de Granada is the most popular parador in Spain—obtaining a room is well nigh impossible in the high season unless reservations are made months in advance. An excellent alternative is the Hotel Alhambra Palace, a deluxe, well-located hotel with splendid views. From here you can gaze out from your room over the historic city of Granada through Moorish arched windows. Opened in 1910, the Alhambra Palace has long been a mainstay of the Alhambra hotels. Andrés Segovia, the famous Spanish guitarist, played his first concert here, and it remains a favorite hotel choice in Granada for most visiting dignitaries. The sumptuous decor of the public rooms is enchantingly, almost overwhelmingly, Moorish—from the intricately carved ceilings and unusual decorative touches, to the symmetrically placed arched doorways and colorful tiled walls. The bedrooms are large and comfortable: several of the junior suites are big enough to accommodate a family of four. The hotel is air-conditioned—a blessing in Granada's hot summer months. Savor one of the best views in Spain from the expansive bar area or the outdoor terrace. The hotel has a prime location: just down the road from the entrance to the Alhambra. *Directions:* Do not follow signs for Granada Centro. Take exit (km) 132 of Route A44, signposted Alhambra, which (follow signposts) takes you 6 km to the Alhambra complex. Stay to the left when you come to the paid parking.

❄ CREDIT ❙❙ 🚶 🐎

*HOTEL ALHAMBRA PALACE*
*Manager: Fernando Maldonnado*
*Peña Partida, 2*
*18009 Granada, Spain*
*Tel: 958-221-468, Fax: 958-226-404*
*129 Rooms, Double: €185–€275\**
*\*Breakfast not included: €15*
*Open: all year, Credit cards: all major*
*Region: Andalusia, Michelin Map: 578*
*www.karenbrown.com/alhambra.html*

Although officially holding just a one-star rating, the Hotel America is, in our estimation, far superior in many ways to some so-called "superior" class hotels. Its most outstanding feature is its location. You cannot be any closer to the portion of the Alhambra reserved for paying sightseers—the Hotel America is on the citadel grounds, just steps away from the entrance. But the America has more than location. The pretty, cream-colored stucco, three-story building with red-tiled roof is enhanced by lacy vines and black wrought-iron light fixtures. To the left of reception is a sitting area with a cozy clutter of old-fashioned furniture. On balmy days, guests' favorite place to congregate is the inner courtyard—an inviting small oasis enhanced by blue-and-white-tile tables and an overhead leafy trellis. The only meals served are breakfast and lunch. Bedrooms are very nice and have air conditioning, which makes them very attractive for an afternoon rest on a hot summer day. Remember that this is a simple hotel, so if you are fussy and like everything just perfect, this is not the place for you. However, the Hotel America makes an excellent choice for a cozy, family-run hotel with an unbeatable location. *Directions:* Do not follow signs for Granada Centro. Take exit (km) 133 off the N323 signposted Alhambra. Follow signposts for 6 km to the Alhambra complex. Stay to the left when you come to the paid parking. Hotel America is next to the parador.

*HOTEL AMERICA*
*Owner: Rafael Garzón*
*Real de la Alhambra, 53*
*18009 Granada, Spain*
*Tel: 958-227-471, Fax: 958-227-470*
*17 Rooms, Double: €115–€189\**
*\*Breakfast not included: €8*
*Open: Mar to Nov, Credit cards: MC, VS*
*Region: Andalusia, Michelin Map: 578*
*www.karenbrown.com/america.html*

This is Spain's most famous and popular parador, and reservations must be secured at least six to eight months in advance. Installed in a 15th-century convent, restoration has been carried out so as to retain much of the original structure, including the chapel where Queen Isabella was first buried before being moved to the cathedral downtown. Outside, lovely Alhambra-style gardens and walks blend well with the neighboring marvel. Inside, the decor is a mixture of Moorish and Christian. The former shows up in wonderful ceilings, carved doors, ceramic tile, and the graceful arches in the beautiful interior patio. The public rooms are rich in antique religious art objects—paintings, sculpture, and colorful tapestries. The guestrooms are comfortably unostentatious, with period accents and views varying from excellent to ordinary. The dining room is in a style apart—its walls lined with handsome, contemporary, abstract art. An outstanding feature of the parador is its secluded location within the Alhambra: an oasis of calm in the usually bustling tourist area. *Directions:* Do not follow signs for Granada Centro. Take exit (km) 133 off the N323 signposted Alhambra. Follow signposts for 6 km to the Alhambra complex. Stay to the left when you come to the paid parking.

*PARADOR DE GRANADA*
*Real de la Alhambra s/n*
*18009 Granada, Spain*
*Tel: 958-221-440, Fax: 958-222-264*
*38 Rooms, Double: €260\**
*\*Breakfast not included: €16*
*Open: all year, Credit cards: all major*
*Region: Andalusia, Michelin Map: 578*
*www.karenbrown.com/granada.html*

The Parador de Gredos, built in 1926 as a hunting lodge for King Alfonso XIII, was the very first parador and today it still remains a real winner. Surrounded by pine forests, mountains, large rock formations, green meadows, and rushing streams, the hotel is a favorite weekend getaway for residents of Madrid. The parador's charm is not immediately apparent: at first glance, it appears as a large, rather sterile, gray stone building with a French gray-tile mansard roof. Once you are inside, the charm of the hotel emerges. A portrait of Alfonso XIII hangs in the lobby surrounded by just the kind of sturdy country-style furniture that you expect to find in a hunting lodge. The floors are wood-planked, the ceilings timbered, and large paintings of hunting scenes and trophies hang on the walls. Several of the bedrooms have four-posters and several of those on the upper floor have balconies overlooking the forest and distant mountains—the same view that is enjoyed from the broad stone terrace, attractively set with wicker chairs. Children enjoy a large play yard with gym sets and slides. Walking is a popular pastime hereabouts.

※ ☕ ⚕ 💳 ☎ 🛗 @ ⅄ P ⑪ 🚶 🖼 ⚓ 🏌 🚶‍♂️ 🐎 ⛵

*PARADOR DE GREDOS*
*05635 Gredos, Spain*
*Tel: 920-348-048, Fax: 920-348-205*
*74 Rooms, Double: €95–€115\**
*\*Breakfast not included: €13*
*Open: all year, Credit cards: all major*
*Region: Castilla y León, Michelin Map: 575*
*www.karenbrown.com/gredos.html*

Shadowed by the famous monastery's towers, this inn was a Hieronymite hospital and pharmacy in the 16th century, but since the days of Ferdinand and Isabella has sheltered those who came to worship. Until 1960 visitors exchanged a daily donation of a mere 50 pesetas for accommodation. Still today, there is nothing comparable in Guadalupe—or anywhere else—for value received and atmosphere, so follow the footsteps of the faithful to this hostelry. Sharing and managing the edifice is an active Franciscan religious order, whose guides regularly conduct an insiders' tour of their monastery, museum, and cathedral, a crazy and wonderful mixture of Mudéjar and Gothic architecture. The hotel bedrooms overlook the original stone-arched and paved hospital patio. Most rooms have incredibly high wooden ceilings, often with intricate patterns. Several can accommodate three or four people. Some have an extra room, a loft with two extra beds, or are large enough for four single beds. If you want to be treated like visiting royalty, request room 120, which is always assigned to high-ranking clergy, or room 108, a grand baroque suite with sitting room and bedroom. The shaded courtyard or paneled dining room are excellent places to eat. *Directions:* Guadalupe is located in the mountains directly to the east of Trujillo and south of Oropesa. The Hospedería is to the left of the monastery—the largest building in town.

*HOSPEDERÍA EL REAL MONASTERIO*
*Manager: Javier Córdoba de Julian*
*Plaza Juan Carlos I*
*10140 Guadalupe, Spain*
*Tel: 927-367-000, Fax: 927-367-177*
*47 Rooms, Double: €60–€145\**
*\*Breakfast not included: €6.50*
*Open: all year, Credit cards: MC, VS*
*Region: Extremadura, Michelin Map: 576*
*www.karenbrown.com/monasterio.html*

Built in the 14th century as a hospital to shelter and minister to pilgrims who came to venerate the famous Black Virgin of Guadalupe, this parador now provides admirably for the needs of the modern-day visitor. It is located directly across the street from the Franciscan monastery in a village from which the Catholic monarchs granted permission for Columbus' ships to depart for the New World. Whitewashed, with red roof tiles, the parador invites you to enjoy its cool, Moorish gardens sheltering a sparkling turquoise fountain, and to dine on its outdoor terrace overlooking a tiled Mudéjar fountain. Thanks to the local craftsmen, colorful tile is found throughout the hotel: the interior patio is especially lovely. When it was remodeled several years ago 20 rooms were added, all with garden-view terraces, which faithfully maintain the period ambiance. However, the old rooms with low, stone doorways are still the favorites—some have canopied beds, fireplaces, and balconies (ask for "una habitación antigua con terraza"). But, no matter what the room, this is a special inn set in a tranquil and picturesque locale. *Directions:* Guadalupe is located in the mountains directly to the east of Trujillo and south of Oropesa. Facing the monastery the parador is on your right, on a side street just off the square.

*PARADOR DE GUADALUPE*
*Marqués de la Romana, 12*
*10140 Guadalupe, Spain*
*Tel: 927-367-075, Fax: 927-367-076*
*41 Rooms, Double: €115–€125\**
*\*Breakfast not included: €13*
*Open: all year, Credit cards: all major*
*Region: Extremadura, Michelin Map: 576*
*www.karenbrown.com/guadalupe.html*

Just a twenty minute drive from Seville in distance, yet a world away in atmosphere, lies the Hotel Cortijo Aguila Real, crowning the rise of a small hill. When the owner bought the property it had fallen into serious disrepair but he saw the great potential of this handsome, white farmhouse that had been the showplace of the whole region. In fact, the wealthy landowner who built the Cortijo owned all the surrounding countryside—even including the town of Guillena. In typical Andalusian style, you enter the property through a gate in the whitewashed walls into a large courtyard. Facing onto the courtyard is the family chapel, which is now used for special events such as weddings, as are a great many of the buildings that surround the courtyard. Guests have their private wing accessed from the courtyard where a door leads into a library with chairs facing the fireplace (early-morning coffee is available here), a spacious living room, and a dining room, El Águila, whose wall of windows gives distant views of the Seville skyline. The bedrooms open to a patio next to the gardens. Each of the bedrooms is named after a flower and all are most attractively decorated. In the gardens you find a swimming pool. *Directions:* From Seville take SE-30 towards Mérida —A66. Exit 798 for Guillena A460, go through the town, and take the right-hand fork towards Burguillos A461. You find the hotel on your right at km 4.

※ ⚡ 💳 ☎ @ P ⊩ ≈ ⬧ ♿ ⊥ ⅄ 🖈

*HOTEL CORTIJO AGUILA REAL*
*Owner: Aguila Real S.L.*
*41210 Guillena, Spain*
*Tel: 955-785-006, Fax: 955-784-330*
*15 Rooms, Double: €88–€209.35\**
*\*Breakfast not included: €12.82*
*Open: all year, Credit cards: all major*
*Region: Andalusia, Michelin Map: 578*
*www.karenbrown.com/aguilareal.html*

With the 14th-century ramparts secluding its garden and terrace, the Hotel Obispo has a perfect location for exploring this interesting, medieval town. A wide, stone staircase leads up from the courtyard to the reception lounge, where you may well be greeted by the owner, Victor Alza, who takes a very personal interest in the running of his delightful little hotel. Down a few stairs finds you in the vaulted, stone sitting room leading to the airy breakfast room, which opens up to the sheltered garden terrace. If you do not want an elaborate evening meal, you can also enjoy dinner here. Each of the guestrooms has its own personality with a color scheme set by the color of the walls (in pink, blue, green, or yellow). I particularly liked room 201, a standard room with a courtyard view, and rooms 204 and 205, superior rooms with long balconies that overlook the harbor. The same view is enjoyed from the terrace—the perfect place to relax with a drink after a long day of sightseeing. *Directions:* Arriving in Hondarrabia, skirt the towns walls (follow signs to "centro") to the third roundabout (has fountains—often not working) where you double-back and make a right-hand turn (press the button and the hotel will lower the bollard). Parking is in the courtyard or the hotel's private garage.

❄ ☕ 💳 @ ▽ P 🍴 🖼 ⚓ 🚶 🚶‍♂️ 🏄

*HOTEL OBISPO*
*Owner: Victor Alza Lekuona*
*Obispo Square, 1*
*20280 Hondarribia, Spain*
*Tel: 943-645-400, Fax: 943-642-386*
*16 Rooms, Double: €125–€156*
*Open: all year, Credit cards: all major*
*Region: País Vasco, Michelin Map: 573*
*www.karenbrown.com/obispo.html*

Just before the Plaza de Armas, in the shadow of the beautiful parish church of Santa Maria de Asunción, you find the Hotel Pampinot. From the outside, the austere stone façade looks similar to the other 16th- and 17th-century gray stone mansions that line the narrow street—just a small hotel sign indicates you have found the proper house. Inside, a surprise awaits: the stern exterior does not hint at the opulence within. The reception is a spacious area with a massive stone floor and exposed stone walls, which set off to perfection two large altar pieces, intricately and colorfully painted, dominating the facing walls. Beyond the entrance lobby, a delightful little bar is tucked into a large stone niche under the stairs. A wide staircase, with iron railings topped by a polished brass banister, leads up to the guestrooms. There are only eight—four on each level—with each room having an elaborately painted ceiling depicting clouds and a variety of birds and cherubs—one even has colorful, frolicking parrots. Rumor has it that María Theresa stayed here on her way to marry Louis XIV of France. *Directions:* On arriving in Hondarribia, follow signs for "parador" into the walled city. The hotel is on your right, before reaching the parador. Parking is on the street.

P ⊥ ⊼ ⋀⋀ ⅃

*HOTEL PAMPINOT*     **Cover painting**
*Manager: Javier Irigoien*
*Calle Mayor, 5*
*20280 Hondarribia, Spain*
*Tel: 943-640-600, Fax: 943-645-128*
*8 Rooms, Double: €105–€155\**
*\*Breakfast not included: €14*
*Open: all year, Credit cards: all major*
*Region: País Vasco, Michelin Map: 573*
*www.karenbrown.com/pampinot.html*

The Parador de Hondarribia is located at the heart of the picturesque, medieval walled-town of Hondarribia (also called Fuenterrabía). Installed in a 12th-century castle, overlooking a square lined by brightly colored houses, the imposing stone castle was at one time occupied by Ferdinand and Isabella and also their grandson, Charles V. The building's incredible 3-meter thick walls have withstood countless assaults over the centuries. An outstanding feature of the parador is its stone-paved lobby featuring lances, cannon, suits of armor, tapestries, and a remarkable, soaring 15-meter ceiling, overlooked through stone arches by a cozy lounge with a beamed ceiling. The interior glass-enclosed, flower-filled courtyard has comfortable wicker chairs, where you relax and enjoy a drink before going in to dinner. One side of the courtyard is the crumbling remains of the original stone wall. Beyond the inner courtyard, a broad outdoor terrace overlooks the boat-filled harbor. Not only are the setting and structure of this parador outstanding, but the public rooms rival those of the finest hotels in Spain. This is a very popular parador, be sure to book well in advance. *Directions:* Arriving in Hondarribia, follow signposts to the parador through the first city gate that you come to. The parador has parking to the rear.

*PARADOR DE HONDARRIBIA*
*Plaza de Armas, 14*
*20280 Hondarribia, Spain*
*Tel: 943-645-500, Fax: 943-642-153*
*36 Rooms, Double: €200\**
*\*Breakfast not included: €13*
*Open: all year, Credit cards: all major*
*Region: País Vasco, Michelin Map: 573*
*www.karenbrown.com/hondarribia.html*

The engaging Parador de Jaén crowns the ridge of Cerro (hill) de Santa Catalina, the patron saint of Jaén, and flanks the 13th-century Arabic fortress after which it is named and whose architecture it imitates. It is immediately apparent that much imaginative effort went into the construction of this "copycat" castle-hotel. The public rooms feature cavernous fireplaces, recessed windows, and tapestry-hung, stone-brick walls soaring to carved-wood or granite ceilings. The drawing room is especially dramatic with 20-meter-tall crossed arches. The high-ceilinged guestrooms are spacious and bright, with rough-hewn brick floors trimmed in green tile, leather and wood furniture, cheery spreads and throw rugs, and shiny green-and-white-tiled baths. Each has a roomy terrace commanding panoramic vistas over the city, the fertile Guadalquivir river valley, and an endless expanse of undulating hills studded with the olive groves. There is a large swimming pool on the ramparts. Tranquil will define your stay here, which should be combined with a visit to the Arab baths and the barrio de Magdalena in Jaén, which spreads out in the valley below the hotel. *Directions:* Do not go into the city of Jaén. The parador sits high atop the Cerro de Santa Catalina, next to the castle of Santa Catalina, 5 km from the center of the city. We took the N323 (direction Motril) and exited for the A316 (Baeza) then took this road away from Baeza and we picked up parador signs.

❄ 💳 🏨 P ¶ ≈

*PARADOR DE JAÉN*
*23001 Jaén, Spain*
*Tel: 953-230-000, Fax: 953-230-930*
*45 Rooms, Double: €135–€145\**
*\*Breakfast not included: €14*
*Open: all year, Credit cards: all major*
*Region: Andalusia, Michelin Map: 578*
*www.karenbrown.com/jaen.html*

In the 15th century, the Counts of Oropesa built a fortress surrounded by gardens on the hillside above the fertile, tobacco-growing Tiétar Valley. Their noble home is now the Parador de Jarandilla de la Vera, beautifully preserved, with odd-shaped towers, ramparts, and a drawbridge completing the late-medieval picture. Charles V once briefly resided here, and the dramatic large fireplace in the lounge was added at his request, since he found the castle chilly in winter. Cross the former drawbridge and you find a garden shaded with olive trees, a swimming pool, and a children's play yard. The cool, stone-paved inner courtyard has ivy-covered walls and a placid central pool, overlooked by a terraced second-floor lounge with fireplace and lovely antiques. Guestrooms are found in the castle and an added wing of traditional rooms. The high ceilings, rich wood floors, and antique furnishings of the spacious castle chambers lend an atmosphere impossible to duplicate. This is an absolutely charming hilltop hideaway. *Directions:* Jarandilla de la Vera is situated between Plasencia and Arenas on the EX203. The parador is well-signposted in the center of town.

*PARADOR DE JARANDILLA DE LA VERA*
*Carretera de Plasencia*
*10450 Jarandilla de la Vera, Spain*
*Tel: 927-560-117, Fax: 927-560-088*
*53 Rooms, Double: €115–€140\**
*\*Breakfast not included: €13*
*Open: all year, Credit cards: all major*
*Region: Extremadura, Michelin Map: 576*
*www.karenbrown.com/jarandilla.html*

Whereas many of the beach towns on Spain's popular Costa Blanca are dominated by towering hotels and condominium projects, somehow Jávea has managed to keep a low profile. There is a small, pretty curve of sandy beach, the Platja de l'Arenal, rimmed by shops and restaurants. Embracing one end of the crescent of sand is a tiny rocky promontory that is home to the Parador de Jávea. The front of the hotel—a curved white-stucco, five-story building—looks like a typical beach hotel but on the inside, the true merits of the hotel emerge. The spacious reception area opens onto the lounge with a wall of windows looking out to the terrace and garden. The decor is simple but pleasing, with Spanish hand-loomed rugs accenting cream-colored marble floors, locally made cane furniture, large paintings on the walls, and a profusion of green plants. Beyond lies a terrace and an expanse of meticulously tended lawn (dotted with palm trees), which stretches out to the sea. Of course there's a swimming pool with loungers dotted beneath umbrellas in the shade of the palms. The bedrooms are spacious, furnished with contemporary, furniture, and all have a balcony with a spectacular view of the curve of sand to the distant rocky headland. *Directions:* Take exit 62 off the E15 and drive the 15 km into Javea (Xàbia). Arriving in the city follow signs for Cap de la Nau (pink) and the parador which is located on Platja de l'Arenal.

❄ ⚷ 💳 ♿ 🍴 @ ⅄ P ⅋ ≋ ⛵ ⚒ ⚓ 🏃 🚶 🐎 ⚓ 🍇

*PARADOR DE JÁVEA*
*Av. Mediterraneo, 7*
*03730 Jávea (Xàbia), Spain*
*Tel: 965-790-200, Fax: 965-790-308*
*70 Rooms, Double: €145–€155\**
*\*Breakfast not included: €14*
*Open: all year, Credit cards: all major*
*Region: Valencia, Michelin Map: 577*
*www.karenbrown.com/javea.html*

The Parador Hostal de San Marcos is elegantly installed in what was originally an elaborate, stone monastery commissioned by Ferdinand at the beginning of the 16th century. Before its conversion to a hotel in 1965, it was used as a military prison and stable, seeing lots of activity during the Civil War. Behind its immense façade are over 200 rooms. The rest of the space is occupied by an exquisite stone patio peopled with statues of saints, an archaeological museum, a chapel, spacious lounges, hallways lavishly furnished with antiques, and a modern restaurant offering a delectable dinner menu (we enjoyed superb scallops "vieiras"). A few suites discovered off a maze of creaky, worn hallways are large and comfortable with high ceilings, old-world ambiance, and antique furnishings—a real treat. To the rear is a 1965 extension where rooms and several suites are found down long, broad corridors. With balconies overlooking a quiet garden, these spacious rooms and suites maintain a traditional Spanish flavor. You get a real feel for historic León staying here. *Directions:* Arriving in town, follow pink signposts to San Marcos, located on the river, to the parador. Park in front to unload and you will be directed to the car park at the rear of the building.

*PARADOR HOSTAL DE SAN MARCOS*
*Plaza San Marcos, 7*
*24001 León, Spain*
*Tel: 987-237-300, Fax: 987-233-458*
*227 Rooms, Double: €180\**
*\*Breakfast not included: €17*
*Open: all year, Credit cards: all major*
*Region: Castilla y León, Michelin Map: 575*
*www.karenbrown.com/sanmarcos.html*

Occupying an impressive position at one end of Plaza Mayor, as befits the former palace of the Duke of Lerma whom history has defined as a somewhat reprobate favorite of Philip III, the parador has been completely renovated complete with indoor pool, gym, and spa facilities. The result is a magnificent hotel that combines modern luxury and haute cuisine with an architectural heritage dating back to the 17th century. Guestrooms surround the central courtyard, replete with original Tuscan and Ionic columns, now enclosed to provide a comfortable sitting area in which to enjoy a pre-dinner drink or relaxing break from the summer heat. Spaciousness pervades: high ceilings, large rooms, tall windows. Terra-cotta tiled floors contrast with beige walls and dark wood paneling. Marble-and-tile bathrooms are provided with a plentiful supply of toiletries, sumptuous white towels, and matching robes. A beautifully carpeted wooden staircase leads down to the twin restaurants, both with magnificent stone vaulted ceilings. Breakfast is served on the third floor—we recommend a table on the balcony watching early-morning activities in the village. If your taste runs to a little local cuisine, we strongly recommend Asador Casa Brigante, specializing in oven-roasted baby lamb, local produce, and regional wines, situated close by on the main square. *Directions:* On the Plaza Mayor. Lerma is 36 km from Burgos via the N1.

*PARADOR DE LERMA*
*Plaza Mayor, 1*
*09340 Lerma, Spain*
*Tel: 947-177-110, Fax: 947-170-685*
*Double: €145–€155\**
*\*Breakfast not included: €14*
*Open: all year, Credit cards: all major*
*Region: Castilla y León, Michelin Map: 575*
*www.karenbrown.com/lerma.html*

When Alfonso XIII held his cabinet meetings here in the gray stone Eguilior Palace, who would have dreamed that it would be transformed into the luxurious, modern parador that it is today. The austere palace has been extended to the rear by two modern wings housing the majority of the bedrooms, the dining and breakfast rooms, a gymnasium, and a parking garage. While the exteriors present a great contrast between the historic and the modern, inside the décor is unabashedly contemporary with a decidedly art deco flavor. Enjoy drinks and a casual lunch in the bar, on the garden terrace, or in the grand entry hall. Spend the afternoon by the pool, playing tennis and paddleboard, or go sightseeing along the coast. Dinner napkins are the size of small tablecloths and the dinner staff, wearing large bistro-style aprons, happily discuss the dinner menu which (thankfully for those not conversant with regional Spanish) is translated into English. Bedrooms and bathrooms are top-of-the-line modern with high ceilings. Several rooms in the palace have sun terraces, though I preferred the spacious rooms at the end of the corridor with their octagonal sitting areas and sofas that convert into a bed for a child. *Directions:* Leave the A8 at exit 173 for Limpias and take the road towards Burgos. The parador is well-signed 1 km south of the village on your right.

❄ ⚓ 💳 P ⅋ 🍴 ≈ 🏃 🖼 ⚓ 🚶

*PARADOR DE LIMPIAS*
*Owner: Jose Carlos Campos Regaldo*
*39820 Limpias, Spain*
*Tel: 942-628-900, Fax: 942-634-333*
*65 Rooms, Double: €135–€145\**
*\*Breakfast not included: €14*
*Open: all year, Credit cards: all major*
*Region: Cantabria, Michelin Map: 572*
*www.karenbrown.com/limpias.html*

The Hotel Llafranch has been welcoming visitors to the quaint, former fishing village of Llafranc since 1956. The three-star hotel, its exterior freshly painted white, fronts onto the main tree-lined promenade, offering enchanting views of the beach and nearby harbor. The terraced bar and restaurant, stretched across the front of the building, and the outdoor dining area, situated in the hotel's adjacent plaza, offer shady areas of respite from the sun and are ideal for people watching. Within the bar and lounge area are photos and paintings of celebrities who have stayed here—we spotted Rock Hudson and Kirk Douglas. The main, more formal, dining room specializes in seafood, while the terrace offers more casual dining with the specials of the day being posted on a blackboard and a short tourist menu. The bedrooms are simply, but tastefully, furnished, decorated with wood accents and tiled floors. While some rooms are painted all in white attractively contrasted by rich wood tones, others are painted in bright colors complemented with delightful hand-painted furniture. Several rooms have balconies; rooms to the side are larger and still have ocean views. *Directions:* Llafranc is located between Begur and Palafrugell. Follow signs for either of these towns until you see signs for Llafranc. The hotel is on the waterfront next to the square. Park outside to unload, hotel parking is a two minute drive away.

*HOTEL LLAFRANCH*
*Manager: Juan Carlos Bisbe*
*Passeig Cypsela, 16*
*17211 Llafranc, Spain*
*Tel: 972-300-208, Fax: 972-305-259*
*28 Rooms, Double: €121–€153*
*Open: all year, Credit cards: all major*
*Region: Catalonia, Michelin Map: 574*
*www.karenbrown.com/llafranch.html*

This deluxe resort is an experience unto itself, spectacularly situated on over 1,000 acres of scenic countryside. No detail has been overlooked to offer every convenience in a distinctive atmosphere combining characteristic Andalusian style with contemporary elegance. Graceful Moorish arches, carved-wood ceilings, tiled patios, grilled terraces, marble fountains, and blossoming gardens surround the pampered guest in this intimate hideaway. Amenities that come with the exquisite accommodation here include spa equipment and programs, indoor and outdoor swimming pools, saunas, Jacuzzi, tennis, horseback riding, and quads. There are concerts and a staff that outnumbers the clientele. Each spacious guestroom is unique, richly and imaginatively decorated in soft colors, with a large bathroom (featuring both bath and shower), and either a balcony or garden patio from which you can enjoy the tranquil landscape. There are decadent suites and sumptuous Imperial suites. In addition, you have your choice of two dining spots, one of which, La Finca, has gained justifiable regional renown. The hotel will make reservations for tickets for the Alhambra in Granada. *Directions:* Not in Loja—Loja is the postal address. Exit the A92 (Granada and Antequera road) at km 175 and follow the road north for 1 km to the Barcelo La Bobadilla's entry on your right. Follow the driveway for 3 km to the hotel.

*BARCELO LA BOBADILLA*
*Manager: Enrique Castellanos*
*18300 Loja, Spain*
*Tel: 958-321-861, Fax: 958-321-810*
*70 Rooms, Double: €296–€1,405*
*Open: all year, Credit cards: all major*
*Region: Andalusia, Michelin Map: 578*
*www.karenbrown.com/bobadilla.html*

The Hotel Arosa, situated in a large building in the heart of Madrid, provides excellent accommodation at a price that is very good value for money. The only part of the hotel at street level is the small lobby (serviced by a doorman)—the actual hotel is on the upper levels, with two elevators taking you up to the different floors. The quaint elevator on the right—a tiny, five-sided affair—is unique, obviously constructed to fit the precise space available. Found on the third floor (Spanish second) is the reception, which opens up to a most attractive sitting area and snack bar/breakfast room, an oasis of cool and quiet in the heart of this noisy, bustling city. Individually decorated bedrooms are found off broad corridors, with the majority having a most attractive modern minimalist decor and sparkling modern glass-and-marble bathrooms. While all the rooms we saw were spacious for a city hotel, we were particularly impressed by room 708, which, in addition to being a larger room, has French doors opening onto a balcony with a table and chairs perfectly located for watching the action on the street below. Although there are some dodgy-looking side streets a few blocks away, the location is very good: a few minutes by foot to the chic Puerta del Sol (a shopper's paradise) and the Plaza Mayor with its charming cafés. The Best Western Arosa remains one of Madrid's best buys. *Directions:* Just off Grand Via within easy walking distance to several metro stations.

*BEST WESTERN HOTEL AROSA*
*Owner: Fernando de León*
*Calle Salud, 21*
*28013 Madrid, Spain*
*Tel: 915-321-600, Fax: 915-313-127*
*125 Rooms, Double: €124–€180\**
*\*Breakfast not included: €14*
*Open: all year, Credit cards: all major*
*Region: Madrid, Michelin Map: 576*
*www.karenbrown.com/arosa.html*

Located in the very heart of Madrid, conveniently close to its famous theaters and a few minutes' walk from the attractions of both the Puerta del Sol and the Plaza Mayor, the Catalonia Moratin successfully combines modern décor and the old building's architectural features. With its impressive old five-story wooden staircase and soaring, glass-topped entrance hall, the original structure dates back to the 18th century but was completely renovated in 2002. Bedrooms come in a variety of configurations and sizes dictated by shape of the old building but, by European standards, even the smallest is more than ample. Plainly, but tastefully, decorated in pale earth tones accented with light wooden paneling, the rooms are fully equipped with all modern creature comforts. Tile-and-marble bathrooms are provided with a plentiful array of basic toiletries, fluffy white towels, and matching robes. A bar just off the main reception area offers a welcome respite from the clamor of the city streets. Downstairs the restaurant provides a wide-ranging breakfast buffet and is also open and reasonably priced for dinner. *Directions:* Five minutes' walk east of the Plaza Mayor, central Madrid.

*HOTEL CATALONIA MORATIN*
*Manager: Paula Camblor*
*Atocha, 23*
*28012 Madrid, Spain*
*Tel: 913-697-171, Fax: 913-601-231*
*63 Rooms, Double: €165–€198\**
*\*Breakfast not included: €13*
*Open: all year, Credit cards: all major*
*Region: Madrid, Michelin Map: 576*
*www.karenbrown.com/catalonia.html*

Frequently referred to as one of the world's top ten hotels, The Ritz, across the street from the Prado Museum, is all one could ask for in a world-class hotel. The opulent old-world decor has been restored and creates a belle epoque ambiance. The restoration is based on extensive research to ensure that the decor re-creates exactly its 1910 glory. A statue of Diana that had graced the upper hall bar was retrieved, restored, and replaced where it had stood for the first 40 years of the hotel's existence. The expanse of lobby and grand hall behind it are magnificent. The restaurant, which features regional specialties, is hung with dramatic tapestries, which were refurbished by the original makers, the Royal Tapestry Factory. There is a delightful outdoor garden, an oasis of greenery, where guests relax on old-fashioned, white-wicker chairs. The bedrooms are spectacular in their decor and the same glorious hand-woven carpet that adorns the rest of the hotel has been custom-woven to fit each one. Everything, from the striking gold bathroom fixtures to the tasteful and handsome furnishings, will make you feel pampered. There is also a fitness center with sauna and massage. The Ritz successfully combines the luxury of the contemporary world with turn-of-the-last-century elegance. It provides all the comfort and facilities any guest could desire.

☰ ☎ ♿ 🏋 ♉ 🍴

*THE RITZ*
*Manager: Anton Küng*
*Plaza de la Lealtad, 5*
*28014 Madrid, Spain*
*Tel: 917-016-767, Fax: 917-016-776*
*165 Rooms, Double: €510–€4,650\**
*\*Breakfast not included: €30*
*Open: all year, Credit cards: all major*
*Region: Madrid, Michelin Map: 576*
*www.karenbrown.com/theritz.html*

Situated just off the plaza that shares its name, Hotel Santo Domingo, a typical European city hotel, blends modern convenience and efficiency with a museum-like array of original art, antiques, and collectibles. The heat and bustle of the street are left behind when you enter the air-conditioned tranquility of the brightly decorated lobby, furnished with smart but comfortable sofas and armchairs. A small bar is tucked away in the back next to the somewhat formidably named Restaurante Inquisicion, its neat wrought-iron chairs and tables presided over by an impressive old door displayed in the corner. As might be expected of accommodations retrofitted into an old building, no two guestrooms are the same. The common theme, however, is very pleasant. All are comfortably furnished, tastefully decorated in pastel shades with wallpapered highlights, and equipped with nicely appointed marble-and-tile bathrooms. Two small elevators service the lobby, transporting guests to corridors filled with an impressive collection of oil paintings, collages of old lace, and collectibles. Situated just a few minutes' easy walk away from the Palacio Real and Plaza Mayor, the Santo Domingo is conveniently close to all the attractions of historic Madrid. *Directions:* On the northwest corner of Plaza Santo Domingo, central Madrid.

*HOTEL SANTO DOMINGO*
*Manager: Antonio Nunez*
*Plaza Santo Domingo, 13*
*28013 Madrid, Spain*
*Tel: 915-479-800, Fax: 915-475-995*
*120 Rooms, Double: €155–€325\**
*\*Breakfast not included: €11.75*
*Open: all year, Credit cards: all major*
*Region: Madrid, Michelin Map: 576*
*www.karenbrown.com/santodomingo.html*

The Hotel Villa Real, facing a tiny plaza just off the beautiful tree-lined Paseo de la Castellana, is a rare jewel—a tranquil oasis in the heart of Madrid's famous triangle (formed by the Thyssen Bornemisza Museum, the Prado Museum, and the Reina Sofia Museum). Appropriately, the hotel has museum pieces of its own: Andy Warhol's Marilyns in the bar, an ancient Roman sculpture by the front door, several large Roman mosaics, and ancient urns in the breakfast room. Yet there is nothing museumlike about this hotel, which is furnished throughout with sleek modern furniture enhanced by some whimsical sculptures. This is one of those rare hotels where we prefer the standard rooms, which are actually mini-suites, with the beds on one level and three steps leading down to a cozy sitting area with comfortable sofa, upholstered chairs, writing desk, and television. Most of the rooms even have a small balcony where you can step outside to enjoy the magic of Madrid. Our favorite rooms overlook the tiny Plaza de las Cortes. The Hotel Villa Real's goal "to ensure that whoever visits us will find a family atmosphere in which they can feel truly at home" is without a doubt fulfilled.

*HOTEL VILLA REAL*
*Manager: Félix García Hernán*
*Plaza de Las Cortes, 10*
*28014 Madrid, Spain*
*Tel: 914-203-767, Fax: 914-202-547*
*115 Rooms, Double: €165–€389\**
*\*Breakfast not included: €21*
*Open: all year, Credit cards: all major*
*Region: Madrid, Michelin Map: 576*
*www.karenbrown.com/villareal.html*

Situated on Mount Gibralfaro, high above the sprawling port of Málaga, this premier parador commands a stunning view. Installed in an old stone mansion with wrought-iron grilles and arcaded wrap-around galleries, the hotel is surrounded by hillside greenery and located within easy walking distance of a ruined Moorish fortress that once guarded this proud town. If you want to stay along the Costa del Sol, this marvelous parador is truly choice for excellence of accommodation, ambiance, and, above all, the incredible setting with views the broad bay. Bedrooms are contemporary in style, with those on the third floor commanding spectacular views across the adjacent bullring to the harbor. Ground-floor rooms look into trees and are larger, with enough room for a sofa bed for a child. After a day's sightseeing take a dip in the small rooftop swimming pool. The terrace restaurant, which houses three original Picasso paintings, is an extremely appealing dining spot during warm weather (as evidenced by the number of locals who make the trip up the steep hill to dine). This parador is very popular, so be sure to book well in advance during the high season. *Directions:* Follow signposts for Málaga Este and Almaria until you see the Castillo Gibralfaro sign.

❋ ▭ⓒ ⌸ P ▯ ≋ ♿ ⚓ ⛳

*PARADOR DE MÁLAGA GIBRALFARO*
*Camino del Castillo de Gibralfaro*
*29016 Málaga, Spain*
*Tel: 952-221-902, Fax: 952-221-904*
*38 Rooms, Double: €145–€155\**
*\*Breakfast not included: €14*
*Open: all year, Credit cards: all major*
*Region: Andalusia, Michelin Map: 578*
*www.karenbrown.com/malaga.html*

The Parador de Málaga Golf is not actually in Málaga, but well-located just a short drive west of town. A tree lined driveway winds through the golf course to the Andalusian style white stucco parador with its typical red roof. You would never guess that you were adjacent to a busy freeway and outlet mall. You enter into a one-story-wing where the reception area, dining room, and lounges are located. The guestrooms are found in two wings stretching out from these public areas, forming a U. In the center is a large lawn accented palm trees, and a swimming pool. The open end of the U faces the sea across the golf course where there's a long, sandy beach. Bedrooms are on the larger size with each having color-coordinated fabrics on the chairs, bedspreads, and drapes. As an added bonus, all the bedrooms have either a balcony or patio facing the gardens and pool. As the name might suggest, the emphasis of this parador is on golf and many guests come to play the course that surrounds the hotel. As a hotel guest you get a 50% discount on the green fees. It is not a destination hotel but it certainly makes an excellent place to stay either your first or last night in Spain if you are flying into or out of Malaga airport. *Directions:* Parador de Málaga Golf is easy to find. It is signposted just after leaving the airport and also from the Coin/Aeropurto exit from the A7 E15 Malaga to Cadiz freeway.

❄ 💳 P ¶ ≈ 🏃 ⛷ ⚓ 🕺

*PARADOR DE MÁLAGA GOLF*
*Autovía-Málaga-Algeciras*
*29080 Málaga, Spain*
*Tel: 952-381-255, Fax: 952-388-963*
*60 Rooms, Double: €135–€155\**
*\*Breakfast not included: €14*
*Open: all year, Credit cards: all major*
*Region: Andalusia, Michelin Map: 578*
*www.karenbrown.com/malagagolf.html*

Tucked high in a mountain valley, Meranges is one of the few remaining unspoiled Catalan villages in the Pyrenees. Clinging to the hillside is just a cluster of charming old gray stone buildings weighted down with heavy slate roofs. Laura's mother spent her childhood summers here in this remote valley with her grandparents—in the same farmhouse where her grandfather was born. She and her husband later moved to this idyllic hamlet, purchased the 200-year-old farmhouse and opened it as a small hotel and appealing small restaurant. The bedrooms are all simple, but extremely charming and in absolute keeping with the nature of the building. Happily, nothing is contrived or too cute. The walls are painted a fresh white, the floors are of pine, the ceilings have natural beams. The only decoration on the walls is a display of beautiful black-and-white photographs of the region, all taken by a local priest (now well up in his years) whose hobby was capturing on film the animals, people, and landscape he knows so well. The former sheep stable has been transformed into a cozy restaurant where stone walls and a low, beamed ceiling set a romantic stage. Along with the lovely mountain setting, it is this restaurant (featuring Catalan country-style cooking) that draws guests.

☕ ✂ 💳 @ P � 🏃 🏃‍♂️ 🐎 ⛷

*HOTEL CAN BORRELL*
*Owners: Laura Forn & Oliver Verdaguer*
*C/ Retorn, 3*
*17539 Meranges, Spain*
*Tel: 972-880-033, Fax: 972-880-144*
*9 Rooms, Double: €79–€150*
*Closed: mid-week Jan to May, Credit cards: MC, VS*
*Region: Catalonia, Michelin Map: 574*
*www.karenbrown.com/canborrell.html*

The Parador de Mérida is installed in a historic church-convent-hospital-jail dating back to the 17th century. There is, in addition, strong archaeological evidence pointing to the conclusion that this was originally the site of the Concordia Temple of Augustus during the Roman occupation of Mérida. There are ancient artifacts scattered throughout the large, whitewashed hotel—all discovered nearby. The architecture is a crazy mix: for example, in the gorgeous, Andalusian interior patio you will discover elegant Mudéjar-style pillars with Roman and Visigothic stones, and the stunning front sitting room was the convent chapel. The whitewashed rooms with dark Spanish furniture are very attractive, and many have domed ceilings and colorful rugs brightening the red-tile floors. Bedrooms at the back have balconies and overlook the delightful Moorish gardens and its adjacent swimming pool. Facilities also include a gym and a sauna. This unusual parador has an excellent location: from here you can walk to everything at the heart of the city. *Directions:* Patience is needed to follow the parador signs, which bring you through the traffic-clogged streets to the heart of the town. Behind the parador is a large underground parking garage.

❄ 💳 🏨 🏋 P 🍽 ≈ 🕴

*PARADOR DE MÉRIDA*
*Plaza de la Constitución, 3*
*06800 Mérida, Spain*
*Tel: 924-313-800, Fax: 924-319-208*
*82 Rooms, Double: €130–€140\**
*\*Breakfast not included: €13*
*Open: all year, Credit cards: all major*
*Region: Extremadura, Michelin Map: 576*
*www.karenbrown.com/merida.html*

The quaint town of Molló is situated in the beautiful Camprodon Valley in the high Pyrenees. Driving into town, you are drawn to the charming Tyrolean-style Hotel Calitxó, with colorful potted plants hanging from every window and terrace and surrounded by lush lawns, hedges, and trees. Once you enter the wood-paneled lounge area, an inviting room with a large fireplace and comfortable sofas and reading chairs, you are greeted by the warm and welcoming staff, who truly go out of their way to ensure a comfortable and enjoyable stay for each guest. The restaurant, popular with local patrons, is known for its hearty, sumptuous Catalan dishes and friendly service. The adjacent bar area is an ideal spot for an after-dinner drink or warm cup of coffee after a day of skiing. The inexpensively priced en suite bedrooms, rustic in decor, are very simple and not glamorous in any sense, but each room offers a comfortable night's stay and a terrace from which to enjoy the unforgettable views. When making reservations request one of the 12 suites—these are larger, offering spacious bathrooms and terraces, and the same spectacular vistas. The natural splendor of the grounds and surrounding area offers ample opportunity for outdoor activities at all times of the year—nearby skiing in winter, horseback riding, fishing, and hiking trails in summer. Your visit to this extraordinary mountain retreat is sure to be memorable.

*HOTEL CALITXÓ*
*Owner: Josep Solé*
*El Serrat s/n*
*17868 Molló, Spain*
*Tel: 972-740-386, Fax: 972-740-746*
*26 Rooms, Double: €82–€145*
*Open: all year, Credit cards: MC, VS*
*Region: Catalonia, Michelin Map: 574*
*www.karenbrown.com/calitxo.html*

Words cannot prepare you for the magical setting of the Hotel Hacienda Na Xamena. As you approach, the road gradually climbs through a gentle forest of pines to a sparkling white building. When you check in, the Hacienda seems lovely, but not so different from other luxury hotels: it is only when you open the door into your bedroom that the absolute splendor of the Hacienda unfolds. The hotel is built into the hillside and what appears at first to be a one-story structure actually cascades down the hill with six floors of guestrooms—each with a view to die for. Views just don't get any better. Spread before you are giant cliffs of granite that plunge into the sea, forming idyllic, small coves where the blue sea dances in the sunlight. All of the bedrooms have either a terrace or a balcony. The superior rooms and suites have large Jacuzzi tubs in front of picture windows. If your heart is not set on relaxing in your bath while soaking in the view, the standard rooms offer the same amenities, but the Jacuzzi is in the bathroom. The public areas combine the feel of Ibiza with a touch of Andalusia, reflected in two inner courtyards, one with palm trees, the other with a covered pool. There is a tennis court and two more swimming pools, one is equipped for hydrotherapy, the other is romantically perched on the cliff overlooking the sea.

❄ ⛷ 💳 📷 🐕 🏨 🏋 @ 🍸 P 🍴 ♘ ≈ 🚶 🖼 ⛳ ⛱ 🏌 🚶‍♂ ⛴

*HOTEL HACIENDA NA XAMENA*
*Manager: Sabine Lipszyc*
*Na Xamena 07815 San Miguel, Ibiza, Spain*
*Tel: 971-334-500, Fax: 971-334-514*
*65 Rooms, Double: €225–€1,736\**
*\*Breakfast not included: €20*
*Open: Apr to Nov, Credit cards: all major*
*Region: Balearic Islands, Michelin Map: 579*
*www.karenbrown.com/hacienda.html*

The Parador de Nerja is a modern hotel perched at the edge of a 30-meter cliff overlooking the blue Mediterranean. As you first see it from the road, the hotel seems unexceptional, but as soon as the glass doors part to admit you to the lobby you will be thrilled. Before you lies a formal garden with flowerbeds and a fountain at its center, bounded by shady walkways and beyond a grand sweep of lawn dotted with interesting trees, bulbous roots stretching to the clifftop. Loungers are placed under the trees and umbrellas. The dining room has a wall of glass that captures the magnificent ocean view—a vista that is also enjoyed from the large shaded patio. All but six of the bedrooms have spectacular ocean views from their patios and balconies. There are two splendid suites and eleven junior suites with Jacuzzi tubs. Many of the rooms are large enough to accommodate an extra bed. It's a perfect place to enjoy a beach holiday. Handily an elevator takes you down the cliff to a beautiful expanse of beach with ample bars, restaurants and boat rental facilities. Being less than an hours drive from Malaga airport it's a handy first or last stop. You'll be glad you stayed several days and if you simply must go sightseeing Granada is a mere hour and a half's drive away. *Directions:* Exit the E15 N340 (Malaga to Almeria) at Nerja and going towards town you will find the parador signposted.

*PARADOR DE NERJA*
*Manager: Alfonso Rubio*
*Avenida Rodríguez Acosta s/n*
*29780 Nerja, Spain*
*Tel: 952-520-050, Fax: 952-521-997*
*96 Rooms, Double: €135–€155\**
*\*Breakfast not included: €14*
*Open: all year, Credit cards: all major*
*Region: Andalusia, Michelin Map: 578*
*www.karenbrown.com/nerja.html*

Sitting at the head of a vast lake the village of Nuévalos is hidden among the steep mountains of the Sistema Ibérico. Beyond the village lies the Monasterio de Piedra, a large monastery, surrounded by a vast expanse of parkland with gorges, waterfalls, a grotto and lakes. Pathways meander through the park which is a very popular summer sightseeing destination. Guided tours are given of the oldest part of the monastery which dates back to 1194 when it was established by Cistertian monks. Handily for visitors a large portion of this large monastic establishment is now a hotel and a stay here gives you complimentary access to the parklands and the historic abbey. The hotels long antique-lined, arched-ceilinged marble hallways must be 6 meters wide and 10 meters high, through which it seems the slightest sound echoes endlessly. The incredible round windows that appear to be covered with parchment are actually made of alabaster. Off the corridors you find the simply furnished, wood-floored bedrooms in, not surprisingly, the original monks' cells. Bedrooms overlook the parkland, an interior patio or the cloister. Meals are taken in the former refectory a grand high ceilinged room. Your stay here is guaranteed to be unforgettable. *Directions:* Exit the E90, Madrid to Zaragoza freeway at km 231 for the 23 km drive to Nuévalos and continue up the road to the monastery.

*MONASTERIO DE PIEDRA*
*Manager: Aurora Segovia Villa*
*50210 Nuévalos, Spain*
*Tel: 902-196-052, Fax: 976-849-054*
*61 Rooms, Double: €126*
*Open: all year, Credit cards: all major*
*Region: Aragon, Michelin Map: 574*
*www.karenbrown.com/piedra.html*

Olite was the medieval capital of the Kingdom of Navarre, and Charles III made this castle fortress his summer residence in the early 15th century. Part of the extensive original dwelling has been incorporated into a luxurious parador offering the modern-day traveler unique lodging in this ancient walled town. Situated next to a tiny, elaborate church on a tranquil, grassy plaza, the parador has an austere stone façade. Once inside, you will be delighted with the opulent décor: warm red-tile floors topped with plush handwoven rugs, elegant sofas and chairs, suits of armor, and grand antiques. There's a real sense of occasion to dining in the restaurant with its massive stone arches. Simpler dinner fare, lunch, and snacks are served in the cozy coffee shop/bar. Several of the bedrooms are in the historic building. They are wonderful with canopied beds and wood floors, some with exposed, stone walls dating back hundreds of years, and two (rooms 106 and 107) have massive stone fireplaces. The "new" rooms are particularly nice (and larger), decorated in subtle earth colors with traditional Spanish wood furniture and floors. If you prefer to stay in the old section, be sure you request "la parte vieja" when making your reservation. *Directions:* Arriving in Olite, circle the town until you see the parador signs directing you through the stone arch to the old part of town.

❄ 💳 🛗 🍴 🏃

*PARADOR DE OLITE*
*Plaza de los Teobaldos, 2*
*31390 Olite, Spain*
*Tel: 948-740-000, Fax: 948-740-201*
*43 Rooms, Double: €130–€140\**
*\*Breakfast not included: €13*
*Open: all year, Credit cards: all major*
*Region: Navarra, Michelin Map: 573*
*www.karenbrown.com/olite.html*

The Hotel de la Reconquista is a real classic. From the first glance, you will know this is not an ordinary hotel. The exterior is stunning—a superb 18th-century masterpiece, justifiably designated a national monument. The front of the two-story building is made of pretty ochre-colored stone. Wrought iron balconies adorn the formal line of windows and a magnificent crest is mounted above the entrance. Inside the splendor continues: the entrance hall opens to an enormous, arcaded courtyard (with a patterned red carpet and blue velvet chairs and sofas) roofed in glass, creating a lounge that is protected from the sun and rain. This is where guests gather for a cup of tea or an aperitif before dinner, surrounded by an old-fashioned, understated elegance of a bygone era. Beyond the first courtyard, there is a second garden courtyard; and beyond that, even a third. Throughout, the decor reflects a formal grandeur with gorgeous large mirrors, beautiful antique chests, fine oil paintings, grandfather clocks, fresh flowers, and green plants. The walls and hallways to the guestrooms are covered in a rich, red fabric. The bedrooms are tastefully decorated in a traditional style, many with antique accents. *Directions:* Follow directions to the center of town, which brings you to the one-way system around the large, central square, San Francisco park. Locate Uria, the main shopping street on the square, turn left (around the park) and second right. The hotel is in front of you.

*HOTEL DE LA RECONQUISTA*
*Manager: Ramón Felip*
*Gil de Jaz, 16*
*33004 Oviedo, Spain*
*Tel: 985-241-100 or 985-239-529*
*Fax: 985-241-166 or 985-246-011*
*142 Rooms, Double: €146–€241\**
*\*Breakfast not included: €19*
*Open: all year, Credit cards: all major*
*Region: Asturias, Michelin Map: 572*
*www.karenbrown.com/reconquista.html*

This hideaway midway between Seville and Córdoba was a Franciscan monastery from the 16th to the 19th centuries, sheltering and educating monks on their way to missions in the New World, including Fray Junípero Serra, famous evangelizer of California. In 1828, when church property was being confiscated by the state, the monastery passed into private hands—and subsequent ruin. It was eventually inherited by the Moreno family who, restored it over a three-year period, opening the hotel to the public in 1987. (The family also raises fighting bulls, and the manager will happily arrange a visit to their ranch, if you're interested.) Tucked behind whitewashed walls in the heart of the non-touristy Andalusian town of Palma del Río, you'll discover an excellent restaurant, a high ceilinged sitting room/bar with decorative wooden ceiling and decoratively painted walls as well as the cloistered patio supporting a gallery around which the guestrooms are situated. The twin-bedded, air-conditioned rooms are simple and comfortable, decorated in earth tones with dark-wood furniture and trim. They have colorfully tiled baths and small sitting areas. Beyond the kitchen gardens is a large swimming pool surrounded by lawn with loungers strategically placed under shady trees. The Monasterio offers unique, economical accommodation not far off the beaten track. *Directions:* The Hospedería is next to the main church in the center of the town.

*MONASTERIO DE SAN FRANCISCO*
*Manager: Francisco Jose Mulero Molino*
*Avenida Pío XII, no. 35*
*Palma del Río 14700 Córdoba, Spain*
*Tel: 957-710-183, Fax: 957-710-236*
*35 Rooms, Double: €116*
*Open: all year, Credit cards: all major*
*Region: Andalusia, Michelin Map: 578*
*www.karenbrown.com/sanfrancisco.html*

In the 14th century King Henry granted the medieval town of Oropesa, with its ancient castle, to Don García Alvarez de Toledo, who gradually restored the castle and added to it, as did his descendants. It really is a mighty-looking fortress—hard to believe that at one time it served as the town's bullring. There's plenty of room to spread out in this parador which has lots of spacious public rooms. This spaciousness extends to the traditionally decorated bedrooms, many of which overlook the fertile Sierra de Gredos Valley: the others look over the interior patio. The quality of the food is particularly important here as the parador is home to an international cooking school. The dining room is laid out on two levels, with skylights, painted-wood ceiling, and large picture windows. In the lounge areas, cozy leather furniture and antiques cluster around big stone fireplaces. In the basement is a tiny cell where Saint Peter of Alcántara chose to stay when he visited here—it is intriguing, but he might have chosen differently could he have seen the accommodations available now. *Directions:* You will have no problem finding the parador since it is the largest building in town.

*PARADOR DE OROPESA*
*Plaza del Palacio, 1*
*45560 Oropesa, Spain*
*Tel: 925-430-000, Fax: 925-430-777*
*48 Rooms, Double: €115–€130\**
*\*Breakfast not included: €13*
*Open: all year, Credit cards: all major*
*Region: Castilla-La Mancha, Michelin Map: 575*
*www.karenbrown.com/oropesa.html*

The little town of Osuna is conveniently located between Seville, Cordoba, Granada, and Malaga, making it an ideal base for exploring much of Andalusia. The outer limits of the town are plain indeed compared to the architectural gems concealed within the older section. San Pedro has been declared one of the most beautiful streets in Europe by UNESCO, and it is here that you will find the nicely restored Palacio Marqués de la Gomera. Just beyond the massive front door, its archway adorned with ornately carved stonework and pillars, lies the central courtyard, watched over by the original marble-and-gilt chapel in the corner. Reception, dining rooms, and a bar occupy the remainder of the ground floor. The latter features photographs of director Franco Zeffirelli and the cast of his movie on the life of Maria Callas, filmed almost exclusively on location in the Palacio. Upstairs, around the glassed-in courtyard balcony, are the guestrooms. As you might expect, no two are the same in either size or character, but all are nicely appointed and comfortable with antique headboards, exposed beams, and tiled floors. All have modern bathrooms and the larger have whirlpool baths. A favorite was Number 5 with its circular windows providing views over the surrounding rooftops. *Directions:* Arriving on the A92 from Granada or Seville, take either the first or the last (but not the middle!) Osuna exit and follow signs to the hotel, up the hill in the old town.

*PALACIO MARQUÉS DE LA GOMERA*
*Manager: Francisco Alvarez*
*Calle San Pedro, 20*
*41640 Osuna, Spain*
*Tel: 954-812-223, Fax: 954-810-200*
*20 Rooms, Double: €96–€180\**
*\*Breakfast not included: €10*
*Open: all year, Credit cards: all major*
*Region: Andalusia, Michelin Map: 578*
*www.karenbrown.com/gomera.html*

La Posada de Don Mariano is a very nice family-run hotel that complements one of Spain's most beautiful villages. The two-story, sturdy stone home set on a quiet pedestrian street just off the Plaza Mayor is enriched by black wrought-iron lamps and balconies brimming with colorful pots of flowers. The reception area is small and simple. Probably one of the family members will be at the front desk to greet you since this is a family-owned and -operated hotel. Stairs lead to an upper level where there is a courtyard filled with flowers. About half of the bedrooms have balconies that overlook this pretty garden, while the others have views of the village and surrounding hills. Each of the bedrooms is individual in decor, but quite lovely—the drapes match the fabric on the bedspreads and chairs and even coordinate with the shower curtains. Every detail shows the attention of owners who truly care. Some of the guestrooms are small, but all are appealing—you cannot go wrong with any of them. One favorite is number 110, which has twin iron beds draped in a pretty peach-and-cream-colored fabric. Another winner is room 101, which has a four-poster bed and is decorated in tones of white—even including white flowers on the balcony. *Directions:* Follow the one-way system through the town and park near the castle. The Calle Mayor is the road that goes from the castle entrance into the town.

*LA POSADA DE DON MARIANO*
*Manager: Mariano Pascual*
*Calle Mayor, 14*
*40172 Pedraza de la Sierra, Spain*
*Tel: 921-509-886, Fax: 921-509-887*
*18 Rooms, Double: €85–€110\**
*\*Breakfast not included: €8*
*Open: all year, Credit cards: all major*
*Region: Castilla y León, Michelin Map: 575*
*www.karenbrown.com/donmariano.html*

The Aultre Naray is an appealing, small hotel nestled at the threshold of the gorgeous Picos de Europa in a region of spectacular, natural beauty. Peruyes is a cluster of houses and a delightful 18th-century church. Although the building has been totally reconstructed, the thick walls, beautiful arched entry, and robust masonry are typical of the country homes of the 19th century—and the age is verified by the date 1873 carved above the front door. On the ground floor you find a cozy bar, a dining room, a games room, and, best of all, an inviting sunroom with windows on three sides capturing the stunning view. The sunroom opens out to a charming garden enclosed by a stone wall. This is a favorite spot for guests to sit outside and savor the magnificent mountain views. In the core of the house, a handsome staircase leads to the guestrooms, which are on the two upper floors. We particularly admired rooms 8 and 9, larger, twin-bedded rooms; room 2, a small bedroom with a little sitting room; and room 6, a small bedroom with an enclosed balcony and fabulous view. Room 10 is a family room with two bedrooms. Hiking, canoeing, and fishing are available in the area; plus there are two golf courses nearby—the hotel will loan you a set of clubs. *Directions:* Peruyes is 1 km off the N636, signposted in Llano de Margolles, a small village between Llovio and Arriondas.

*AULTRE NARAY HOTEL*
*Manager: Susana Marks*
*Cangas de Onis*
*33547 Peruyes, Spain*
*Tel: 985-840-808, Fax: 985-840-848*
*11 Rooms, Double: €70–€115\**
*\*Breakfast not included: €5—€10*
*Open: all year, Credit cards: all major*
*Region: Asturias, Michelin Map: 572*
*www.karenbrown.com/aultre.html*

With a prime location along the River Muga amid lush pastures, El Moli was a working mill until fifty years ago. Pere Lladó and his wife purchased the abandoned mill and undertook an extensive restoration to create this delightful inn. The barrel-vaulted ceilings, exposed stone, and wooden beams create a rustic atmosphere throughout. You enter through a cozy bar, which opens up to the restaurant and its expansive vine-shaded patio. Weather permitting, it is a real treat to eat outside. Marc and Jordi Lladó, two of the talented chefs, both speak excellent English and can explain the traditional dishes offered on the menu. All of the bedrooms are most attractive, furnished in a rustic way that totally suits the old mill, and all have televisions with an English channel. Room 102 is a larger room with the largest bed and has a view of the river. The adjacent room 103, with both a double and twin bed, is the most spacious room and is ideal for those traveling with a child. Salvador Dali was born just down the road in Figueras, and the Dali museum here is one of Spain's most visited. Travel to the coast to visit Cadaqués near to where Dali lived, or inland to the medieval village of Besalú. *Directions:* Leave the A7 (Barcelona to France autopista) at exit 3 for Pont de Moulins. Go into the village and follow the river for 2 km to El Moli.

*EL MOLI*
*Owners: Pere Lladó family*
*Caretera Pont de Molins a las Escaulas*
*17706 Pont de Molins, Spain*
*Tel: 972-529-271, Fax: 972-529-101*
*8 Rooms, Double: €89–€99*
*Open: Feb 1 to Dec 23, Credit cards: all major*
*Region: Catalonia, Michelin Map: 574*
*www.karenbrown.com/moli.html*

Facing the same plaza as the Parador de Ronda, the Hotel Don Miguel has an equally outstanding setting overlooking the New Bridge and the dramatic gorge that slices the town of Ronda. This hotel is incorporated into what was once the home of the jailer who was in charge of the prison that was housed in the New Bridge. It has since grown to incorporate several adjacent houses. You enter the hotel from the Plaza de España. Several of the rooms are found in this house while others are located in adjacent houses on the Calle Rosario. For a good value for money place to stay I was particularly impressed with the quality of the bedrooms that come in two styles. Traditional rooms have rustic wooden headboards, tiled floors and white drapes and bedspreads while "new rooms" have wooden floors wrought iron headboards and rust and gold drapes and bedspreads. Several rooms are large enough to accommodate a third bed. A great many of the rooms overlook the gorge and several have balconies to enjoy the view. The same incredible view that is enjoyed from the patios of the restaurant. If the day is warm, dine outside on the terrace and watch the old stone bridge change colors in the glow of the sunset. *Directions:* Exit the A7 (Malaga to Algeciras freeway) at km 172 for the winding 47 km drive to Ronda. Arriving in town cross the bridge and hotel is on the right. Park in front to unload. The hotel has a garage.

*HOTEL DON MIGUEL*
*Owners: Miguel Coronel & Ursula Nohl*
*Plaza de España, 3*
*29400 Ronda, Spain*
*Tel: 952-877-722, Fax: 952-878-377*
*30 Rooms, Double: €85*
*Open: all year, Credit cards: all major*
*Region: Andalusia, Michelin Map: 578*
*www.karenbrown.com/donmiguel.html*

Even if the romantic town of Ronda were not worth a detour in its own right, this dramatic hotel would warrant one. The hotel is built onto the cliff above the "Tajo" (the gorge that splits the town) and from either inside or on the terrace by the swimming pool, you have views of the soaring arched bridge that miraculously crosses the impressive, 120-meter cleft formed by the Guadalevín river. You enter the honey-colored stone building into a sky-lit atrium where the reception desk is located. Beyond is a large seating area with comfortable sofas and chairs in tones of blue and yellow. The walls are a beige-colored brick and the floors white marble. The most attractive color scheme of blues, beiges, and yellows is continued throughout the hotel. There is no effort made to create an artificial antique ambiance. Rather, the furnishings are traditional in style with beautiful fabrics of excellent quality used on the sofas, chairs, and drapes in the public rooms and guestrooms. Each of the attractive bedrooms has a balcony. All the views are lovely, but for a truly memorable experience, ask for one of the corner rooms with two balconies that capture the sweeping view. *Directions:* Exit the A7 (Malaga to Algeciras freeway) at km 172 for the winding 47 km drive to Ronda. Arriving in town cross the bridge and parador is on the left. Pull onto the driveway which leads directly into the garage.

*PARADOR DE RONDA*
*Plaza España s/n*
*29400 Ronda, Spain*
*Tel: 952-877-500, Fax: 952-878-188*
*78 Rooms, Double: €145–€155\**
*\*Breakfast not included: €14*
*Open: all year, Credit cards: all major*
*Region: Andalusia, Michelin Map: 578*
*www.karenbrown.com/ronda.html*

The somewhat plain, golden-stone exterior of the Palacio de San Esteban belies the creature comforts to be found within. What was originally a convent has been meticulously transformed into a stylish, modern hotel, situated within comfortable walking distance of all the diverse attractions of the historical center of Salamanca. The entrance lobby overlooks a very comfortable residents' lounge. Books, magazines, and reference materials line one wall and a computer is provided for your Internet business. On the same level the El Monje restaurant, serving breakfast, lunch, and dinner, is a stunning mix of old and new, with stone walls, high-vaulted, wood-beamed ceilings, soft lighting, classic tile, and wood floors. Decoration of interconnecting hallways is sparse to the point of minimalism. Guestrooms are not overly large but extremely functional, with open beamed ceilings, dark wood accents, wood floors, and sisal carpeting. Windows open through the original thick stone walls, with several rooms overlooking the outdoor courtyard and patio. Nicely appointed, ultra-modern bathrooms are outfitted in marble and tile and feature avant-garde glass washbasins. Guest services include a free coffee shop and mini-bar as well as a fitness center. *Directions:* Not far from the river, adjacent to the heart of historic Salamanca.

*PALACIO DE SAN ESTEBAN*
*Manager: Elain Salanda*
*Arroyo de Santo Domingo, 3*
*37001 Salamanca, Spain*
*Tel: 923-262-296, Fax: 923-268-872*
*51 Rooms, Double: €100–€255\**
*\*Breakfast not included: €13*
*Open: all year, Credit cards: all major*
*Region: Castilla y León, Michelin Map: 575*
*www.karenbrown.com/esteban.html*

The Hotel Rector, located at the edge of the ancient walls of Salamanca, is one of Spain's finest small hotels with a special enhancement—gracious owners who oversee every detail. The handsome, three-story, beige-stone building (with beautiful, sculpted designs over the windows and doors, and black wrought-iron balconies) blends in perfectly with the typical old houses of the adjacent old town. It is steps away from the Roman bridge and just a seven-minute walk through the old town to the spectacular Plaza Mayor. The decor throughout is tasteful and traditional. The colors are mostly pastel, with accents of deep rose. A whimsical touch, just as you enter, is provided by two large arched windows with a colorful "Tiffany" glass effect. The reception area opens to a comfortable sitting area and leads to the hotel's parking garage. Nothing is on a grand scale—instead, there is a refined, understated elegance. The guestrooms are lovely, with the finest-quality, traditional-style furnishings and color-coordinating fabrics on the bedspreads and draperies. They all have large marble bathrooms. Breakfast is the only meal served and staff are happy to make recommendations on reasonably priced places to eat. *Directions:* Arriving from Madrid on the N501, cross the river, go first right, then left at the roundabout, and the Hotel Rector is on your left after 300 meters. Stop in front and you will be directed to parking.

*HOTEL RECTOR*
*Manager: Julian V. Almaraz*
*Rector Esperabé, 10*
*37008 Salamanca, Spain*
*Tel: 923-218-482, Fax: 923-214-008*
*14 Rooms, Double: €120–€175\**
*\*Breakfast not included: €12*
*Open: all year, Credit cards: all major*
*Region: Castilla y León, Michelin Map: 575*
*www.karenbrown.com/rector.html*

Pikes (pronounced Peekays) has its own special personality. Not your "run-of-the-mill" hotel at all, this intimate inn is a favorite hideaway of the world's rich and famous and it is not at all surprising that they flock here. Pikes offers 26 guestrooms, each decorated with a dramatic flair worthy of a stage setting. They are discreetly housed in a cluster of honey-beige-toned cottages that offer privacy. However, most of the guests I saw did not seem to be seeking seclusion, but were sunning by the swimming pool, playing tennis, taking advantage of the exercise room, or laughing with friends at the bar. An air of unpretentious informality prevails, conducive to guests becoming friends. Pathways crisscross through the beautifully tended gardens, which include walls of cascading bougainvillea, roses, hibiscus, geraniums, daisies, carnations, and fragrant lavender. The heart of the property is a 300-year-old finca (farmhouse) where the stunning dining room and bar offer authentic rustic charm. The thick stone walls, arched doorways, low, beamed ceilings, and old olive press create a romantic atmosphere for tables set with pretty linens, fresh flowers, and softly glowing candles. And, best of all, the food is outstanding. If you can tear yourself away from this oasis tucked into the low hills outside of San Antoni, there are beaches, golf, and sights to see nearby. *Directions:* The hotel is located 1.5 km E of San Antoni de Portmany.

❄ ✗ ☕ 🖼 ☎ 🐕 ✗ @ ⚓ P ⑈ ✿ ≈ 🏊 ⚓ 🚶 🐎 ⚓

*HOTEL PIKES*
*Owner: Anthony Pike*
*Calle Sa Vurera*
*San Antoni de Portmany 07820 Ibiza, Spain*
*Tel: 971-342-222, Fax: 971-342-312*
*27 Rooms, Double: €170–€775*
*Open: all year, Credit cards: all major*
*Region: Balearic Islands, Michelin Map: 579*
*www.karenbrown.com/pikes.html*

La Colina, a centuries-old finca (farmhouse)—one of only a few that still exist on the island—is a delightful small hotel. You enter into a large living room exuding a fresh and pretty rustic charm. In the corner is a fireplace with a cozy grouping of white slipcovered chairs, and a blue-and-white-striped sofa. The blue-and-white color scheme continues in the cheerful dining room, which has a flagstone floor and windows on three sides. The chef prepares excellent meals using fresh produce from the island. All of the individually decorated bedrooms are attractive. Number 14 (with a four-poster canopy bed and a view of the garden) is a special favorite. Ibiza has many moderately priced hotels, but most from the same cookie-cutter, modern white high-rises. In comparison, La Colina is truly a gem. Although not on the sea, it has a large swimming pool and makes a good base from which to venture out each day to explore Ibiza's many enchanting small beaches and coves. Guests come back year after year. *Directions:* The hotel is located 5 km SW of Santa Eulalia on PM810 to Ibiza.

*LA COLINA*
*Owners: Claudia & Ralph Gysi*
*Carretera Ibiza a Santa Eulalia*
*Santa Eulalia del Río 07840 Ibiza, Spain*
*Tel & Fax: 971-332-767*
*13 Rooms, Double: €95–€105*
*Open: Nov to Jan, Credit cards: MC, VS*
*Region: Balearic Islands, Michelin Map: 579*
*www.karenbrown.com/colina.html*

Looking for a spot for a morning coffee break, we happened upon this wonderful old ivy-covered complex and were so impressed that we wondered what took us so long to find it! The convent was converted to a hotel in the 90s and it still looks well appointed and well cared for. You enter into the courtyard and then pass through arched doors into a long, narrow hallway. Directly across from the entrance is the charming restaurant with tables set on old stone floors against beamed and exposed-stone walls—a very popular place with both tourists and locals. Along the hallway is an attractive bar, which also has tables set just outside on the lawn. Twenty-three bedrooms and two suites are accessed from the wing to the left of the entry, up a wide old staircase whose wall is painted with a dramatic historical mural. We saw two rooms, a standard room and a suite, and were impressed by their level of comfort (good lighting, televisions, telephones, modern bathrooms), appealing decor, and very reasonable price. The hotel is not air-conditioned but even on a hot summer day the combination of thick stone walls and natural ventilation through the open windows seemed adequate. *Directions:* Located 2 km east of the N611, about halfway between Palencia to the south and Torrelavega to the north, just south of the town of Aguilar de Campo in the village of Santa Maria de Mave.

CREDIT ☎ P ¶

*POSADA CONVENTO DE SANTA MARIA DE MAVE*
*Owners: Begoña & Ignacio Moral*
*Monasterio de Santa Maria de Mave*
*34402 Santa Maria de Mave, Spain*
*Tel: 979-123-611, Fax: 979-125-492*
*25 Rooms, Double: €75–€105\**
*\*Breakfast not included: €5*
*Open: all year, Credit cards: all major*
*Region: Castilla y León, Michelin Map: 575*
*www.karenbrown.com/mave.html*

What was once the Convent Las Oblatas has been refurbished and expanded to create a stylish, modern hotel—just a ten minutes walk from the Cathedral and all the attractions of the fascinating old town. The expansive, glass-fronted lobby in cool, earth tones sets the scene of casual elegance with comfortable seating and a display of modern art from local Galician artists. Size is all that differentiates the guestrooms: standard, superior, and suites, all furnished in a modern, minimalist style with light-wood floors, exposed beam ceilings, large beds, and crisp, white linens. We particularly liked Suite 302 in the old building with its private sitting room and views of the cathedral across the adjoining rooftops. Bathrooms are immaculate with terracotta tile, marble and glass; and include all the amenities. Juices, sodas, water, and beer stocked in the mini-bar are provided gratis. An airy, open, glass-sided gallery leads to the first and second floor rooms in the new building, which also houses the indoor swimming pool, steam room, sauna, and fitness center. Breakfast, lunch, and dinner are served in the expansive dining room which opens up to a terrace and large gardens. A residents' lounge provides free coffee, soft drinks, and snacks for late risers. *Directions:* Entering town from any direction, follow "centro ciudad" and parador signs until you see the signs to the hotel, which will lead you through the one-way system of streets surrounding the old town.

❄ 🚲 💳 🛗 👤 @ 🍸 P 🍴 🏊 🖼 🏃

*HOTEL AC PALACIO DEL CARMEN*
*Manager: Jose Sanchez*
*Oblatas s/n*
*15703 Santiago de Compostela, Spain*
*Tel: 981-552-444, Fax: 981-552-445*
*74 Rooms, Double: €130–€202\**
*\*Breakfast not included: €13*
*Open: all year, Credit cards: all major*
*Region: Galicia, Michelin Map: 571*
*www.karenbrown.com/palaciocarmen.html*

The Parador Hotel Dos Reis Católicos, one of the most magnificent inns in Spain, is without a doubt, one of the pearls of the parador chain. In the 15th century, the building housed a pilgrims' hospice, which nurtured the sick and sheltered the humble, who journeyed from all parts of Europe to visit the tomb of Saint James. The top-of-the-line parador has four interior patios—Matthew, Mark, Luke, and John—overlooked by enclosed third-floor gallery/lounge areas lined with antiques. The fabulous central court (where a music festival is held every August) has a 15-meter ceiling and beautiful stained-glass windows. Each room, hallway, ceiling, and floor is special. In addition to its rich history, the Dos Reis Católicos offers truly sumptuous accommodation for the modern pilgrim. No two rooms are exactly alike, and the attention to detail is unsurpassed, resulting in harmonious old-world ambiance. The green-marble bathrooms are immense, featuring separate bath and shower and heated towel racks. In a city that must be visited, this is a hotel that cannot be missed, even if you merely take a tour—it is the second most popular tourist attraction in Santiago after the cathedral. *Directions:* Follow signs for "centro." The Parador is well-signposted in the pedestrian zone, adjacent to the cathedral. Park in front and your car will be taken to the parking garage.

*PARADOR HOTEL DOS REIS CATÓLICOS*
*Plaza del Obradoiro, 1*
*15705 Santiago de Compostela, Spain*
*Tel: 981-582-200, Fax: 981-563-094*
*136 Rooms, Double: €205\**
*\*Breakfast not included: €17*
*Open: all year, Credit cards: all major*
*Region: Galicia, Michelin Map: 571*
*www.karenbrown.com/catolicos.html*

Ideally located at the heart of the enchanting, medieval village of Santillana del Mar is a five-star hotel whose accommodation surpasses any other property in town. The entry off the cobbled street is discreet. We first took notice of the building for its handsome arched wooden door and band of carved-stone coats of arms, before even realizing that it is a hotel. This is a very popular town, but as the hotel has only 15 guestrooms and no restaurant to draw additional patrons, the Casa del Marqués offers a luxurious escape from the crowds. We fell in love with it the minute we passed through the heavy wooden doors. The appointments are elegant with handsome antiques and beautiful paintings set against old, stone walls and exposed wooden beams. Just beyond the intimate reception area, you come to the breakfast room and then the attractive bar, Café Linaje. Settle with a book in one of the comfortable chairs in either the Salon del Noble with its handsome fireplace, or the Puerta del Maestra with its fireplace and door opening onto the pedestrian street. Guestrooms are spacious and comfortable with both sleeping and seating areas, and their decor plays handsomely on an old-world theme. *Directions:* Since you have a reservation at the hotel, you will be allowed to drive your car into the pedestrian zone. The hotel has parking in a gated courtyard to the rear.

❄ ☕ 🛎 CREDIT ☎ 🛗 @ Y P ⚓ 🚶 🐎 ⛵

*CASA DEL MARQUÉS*
*Manager: Angel Cuevas*
*C / Contón, 24*
*39330 Santillana del Mar, Spain*
*Tel & Fax: 942-818-888*
*15 Rooms, Double: €119–€386*
*Open: all year, Credit cards: all major*
*Region: Cantabria, Michelin Map: 572*
*www.karenbrown.com/marques.html*

Flanked by pretty gardens, the handsome stone façade of the Hotel Los Infantes blends beautifully with the medieval village of Santillana. The 18th-century façade of this typical mountain manor was moved stone-by-stone from the nearby town of Orena and faithfully reconstructed here. Over the doorway are two carved escutcheons—one bearing King Phillip V's coat of arms, the other that of Calderón, the original landlord. The walls of the reception area house a tremendous collection of wall clocks—thankfully none of them ticking. There's a spacious and very comfortable first-floor salon filled with antiques—the perfect place to relax. There are 28 bedrooms in the main house and 11 more in the annex. All the bedrooms we saw were very comfortable with modern bathrooms and, often, little terraces. We particularly admired rooms 303 and 204 larger and a bit more expensive room. Rooms 301 and 302 have a separate sitting area with a sofa that can be converted into an extra bed. Los Infantes offers reasonably priced accommodation in this delightful town. *Directions:* Hotel Los Infantes is on the main road adjacent to the pedestrian area.

*HOTEL LOS INFANTES*
*Manager: Marisa Mesones Gomez*
*Avenida Le Dorat, 1*
*39330 Santillana del Mar, Spain*
*Tel: 942-818-100, Fax: 942-840-103*
*48 Rooms, Double: €67–€113\**
*\*Breakfast not included: €5.15*
*Open: all year, Credit cards: all major*
*Region: Cantabria, Michelin Map: 572*
*www.karenbrown.com/infantes.html*

The Gil Blas, an imposing 17th-century stone manor with wrought iron balconies, is named after the infamous character in Le Sage's 18th-century novel. The parador sits on the cobblestoned main square in the heart of the enchanting, medieval village of Santillana del Mar. There are 26 rooms in the main house, plus 28 more in an annex across the road. The entrance into the original house opens onto a spacious, inner patio with massive stone walls and superb antiques. There is also a pretty interior garden where supper is served in warm weather. The hallways and charming sitting areas are planked with dark wood that gleams with the patina of age. The beautiful bedrooms are whitewashed and wood-beamed, and furnished with period pieces. Throughout, the decor is exceptional. The interior abounds with splendid antiques, which are tastefully combined with sofas and chairs covered with elegant fabrics. The Parador de Santillana del Mar Gil Blas is truly a jewel, further enhanced by being located in the quaint town of Santillana del Mar. *Directions:* Since you have a reservation at the parador, you will be allowed to drive your car into the pedestrian zone. The parador has side-street and garage parking.

*PARADOR DE SANTILLANA DEL MAR GIL BLAS*
*Plaza Ramón Pelayo, 8*
*39330 Santillana del Mar, Spain*
*Tel: 942-818-000, Fax: 942-818-391*
*54 Rooms, Double: €130–€140\**
*\*Breakfast not included: €13*
*Open: all year, Credit cards: all major*
*Region: Cantabria, Michelin Map: 572*
*www.karenbrown.com/santillana.html*

In the 12th century, Saint Dominico built a shelter and hospital on the site of an old palace belonging to the Kings of Navarre. His goal was humanitarian: a wayside hospice for pilgrims who passed through here on their arduous journey to Santiago. Today it houses a parador offering unique accommodation in the quaint old town in the heart of the Rioja wine country. The town of Haro, home to numerous fine bodegas, is only 16 kilometers away. The entrance of the hotel is through a small lobby into a vast lounge, buttressed by massive stone pillars and arches, with a wood-beamed ceiling and stained-glass skylight. The dining room is unusual, too, with dark, rough-hewn wood pillars throughout and the tables interspersed between them. The bedrooms are plain by parador standards, though they live up to them in size and comfort, with traditional Spanish wooden furniture and floors. Those in the old part are similar in decor to those in the new. Ask for one of the front-facing doubles, which have small terraces overlooking the quiet plaza, across to the cathedral and a church.

*PARADOR DE SANTO DOMINGO*
*Plaza del Santo, 3*
*26250 Santo Domingo, Spain*
*Tel: 941-340-300, Fax: 941-340-325*
*61 Rooms, Double: €135–€145\**
*\*Breakfast not included: €14*
*Open: all year, Credit cards: all major*
*Region: La Rioja, Michelin Map: 573*
*www.karenbrown.com/domingo.html*

238  *Places to Stay*

The walled city of Segovia, with its remarkable Roman aqueduct, outstanding castle, and narrow streets with interesting shops, is often visited as a day excursion from Madrid. If you have the luxury of time, you should enjoy Segovia more fully with an extended visit. For a wonderful place to stay, the 19th-century Infanta Isabel can't be beaten—this is a lovely hotel with an excellent location on the Plaza Mayor. From the moment you enter you will be enthralled by its charms: an airy lobby with sunny green-and-gold decor; a delightful bar that opens up to a casual bistro; a dimly-lit formal restaurant for romantic dinners; an attentive and very friendly staff. The bedrooms are smart and attractively decorated. Be sure to ask for a room with French doors that open onto a balcony overlooking the square and the majestic cathedral—these are truly special. *Directions:* Drive into the pedestrian heart of the city, following signs for "centro". The Hotel Infanta Isabel is to the left of the cathedral. Unload your bags and you will be directed to the hotel's car park.

*HOTEL INFANTA ISABEL*
*Owner: Enrique Cañada Cardo*
*Plaza Mayor*
*40001 Segovia, Spain*
*Tel: 921-461-300, Fax: 921-462-217*
*40 Rooms, Double: €83–€103\**
*\*Breakfast not included: €9*
*Open: all year, Credit cards: all major*
*Region: Castilla y León, Michelin Map: 575*
*www.karenbrown.com/isabel.html*

The Linajes is (not easily) found down one of the tiny stone streets that crisscross Segovia's quaint old quarter, the barrio of San Esteban, which sits on a hill above the modern city. The hotel, "The House of the Lineages" with its warm-stone and aged-wood façade, has at its heart an 11th-century palace of the noble Falconi family, whose escutcheon can still be seen over the arched entryway. Inside, there are several rooms that preserve the old-Castile flavor, with dark wood, beamed ceilings, and burnished-tile floors. An alcove off the lobby, decorated with antiques, looks into a glass-enclosed garden patio on one side and over the open terrace at the back, sharing its panoramic views over the city's monumental skyline. There are lovely views from many of the bedrooms, especially those at the rear of the hotel where it terraces down the hillside to the bar/cafeteria. There's a gymnasium, sauna and Jacuzzi for guests to use. *Directions:* Drive into the pedestrian heart of the city, following signs for "centro", pass in front of the cathedral, and continue to the Alcazar where you turn right. The hotel is above you on the right. Park on the street and walk up the steps. The hotel has a gated parking garage.

*HOTEL LOS LINAJES*
*Manager: Miguel Borreguero Rubio*
*Dr Velasco, 9*
*40003 Segovia, Spain*
*Tel: 921-460-475, Fax: 921-460-479*
*63 Rooms, Double: €89–€106\**
*\*Breakfast not included: €9.75*
*Open: all year, Credit cards: all major*
*Region: Castilla y León, Michelin Map: 575*
*www.karenbrown.com/linajes.html*

Segovia's parador is one of the few ultra-modern offerings within the government-run chain, but, in accordance with its consistently high standards, it is a cut above any other contemporary competitor in service and style. Situated on a hill outside Segovia, the parador commands spectacular panoramas of the golden, fortified city. The hotel's architecture is every bit as dramatic as its setting: huge brick and concrete slabs jut up and out at intriguing angles, topped by tiled roofs and surrounded by greenery. The angled brick-and-concrete motif is carried inside, where black-marble floors glisten beneath skylights in the enormous lobby. Picture windows frame Segovia beyond a garden terrace with a pretty pool (there's also an indoor one). The decor throughout is tasteful, Spanish-contemporary, the feeling open, airy, and bright. The bedrooms are spacious and decorated in earth tones, with pale wooden furniture. Each has a balcony that shares the incomparable city view. The combination of the modern and the historical has an unforgettable impact on the guest staying here. *Directions:* From Madrid take the N6 and exit at km 60 onto the N605 for Segovia. The parador is on your left just past the city sign and before you see the walled town across the valley.

*PARADOR DE SEGOVIA*
*Carretera de Valladolid s/n*
*40003 Segovia, Spain*
*Tel: 921-443-737, Fax: 921-437-362*
*113 Rooms, Double: €135–€145\**
*\*Breakfast not included: €14*
*Open: all year, Credit cards: all major*
*Region: Castilla y León, Michelin Map: 575*
*www.karenbrown.com/segovia.html*

Set high atop a hill dominating the Segre Valley on a fortified site dating back to the Bronze Age with spectacular views of the surrounding Pyrenees, the Castell was abandoned for years before being purchased by the Tapies family; who have restored and transformed it into not just a luxury hotel, but a complete destination. The rooms are all individually decorated and furnished in comfortable, country style. All the main floor rooms have balconies. Views from the dining room and terrace (a perfect place for afternoon tea or aperitifs) are spectacular. Enjoy exquisite, innovative food in the gastronomic restaurant Tapies or be traditional fare in the charming, more casual, restaurant Katia with spectacular views over the mountains. Explore the cavernous wine cellar with the sommelier to make your selection for dinner from over 700 wines. Relax in the large, dark wood-paneled library with its comfortable sofas, books and artwork. The accent is on relaxation and recreation: golf, ballooning, walking, cycling, and archery. For those less actively disposed, there are an outdoor pool and Jacuzzis for dipping between sunbathing and favorite books. Alternatively, simply indulge yourself in the luxurious spa with its indoor pool, saunas, Turkish and ice baths, and massage and treatment regimes. *Directions:* Located 1 km west of Seu d'Urgell high above the N260 in the direction of Lleida.

*EL CASTELL DE CIUTAT*
*Owners: Tapies family*
*Ctra N-260, km 229*
*25700 Seu d'Urgell, Spain*
*Tel: 973-350-000, Fax: 973-351-574*
*38 Rooms, Double: €195–€400*
*Open: all year, Credit cards: all major*
*Region: Catalonia, Michelin Map: 574*
*www.karenbrown.com/elcastell.html*

Constructed on the 14th-century site of the ancient church and convent of Santo Domingo, and next door to the Romanesque cathedral of La Seu d'Urgell (the oldest in Catalonia), this is nonetheless a parador whose byword is "modern." Graceful stone arches (reminiscent of the old cloisters that once stood here) form the foundation of a square central room, four stories high with a glass ceiling. With its chic modern décor, this room is especially stunning at night when the different colored walls of the corridors are softly lit casting a rainbow of colors around the room. The elegant dining room with its dark gray slate floor is complimented by soft shades of gray in its décor; and is especially appealing at night, when the tables are set with crisp white linen and the lighting is romantically dimmed. Bedrooms are delightfully modern and all are accompanied with a top-of-the-line bathroom. Several open onto a large terrace that faces the mountains. A spiral staircase leads down from the sun terrace to an indoor, heated swimming pool. There's also a fully equipped gymnasium for those who want to work out. The old town is at your doorstep and a short walk away from the river at the 1992 Olympic canoeing park, where you can go canoeing or whitewater rafting. *Directions:* The parador is adjacent to the cathedral. Below the parador is a parking garage.

❄ 💳 ▥ 🏋 P ⍟ ≈ 🚶 🎿 ⛷ ⚓

*PARADOR DE SEU D'URGELL*
*Santo Domingo, 6*
*25700 Seu d'Urgell, Spain*
*Tel: 973-352-000, Fax: 973-352-309*
*79 Rooms, Double: €115–€140\**
*\*Breakfast not included: €13*
*Open: all year, Credit cards: all major*
*Region: Catalonia, Michelin Map: 574*
*www.karenbrown.com/urgell.html*

The Casa Imperial was built in 1560 as the home of the steward of the adjacent Casa Pilatos, a stunning palace built for the Marqués of Tarifa—to which it is joined by an underground passage, and also served as a guesthouse for visiting dignitaries. Carmen Caballero and Jochen Knie purchased the mansion in the 1990s and undertook a two-year program of sensitive restoration, preserving all the lovely tilework and historic architectural features of this beautiful old home, which now offers five-star accommodation in a warm, friendly atmosphere. Some of the guestrooms have separate sitting room, bedroom, rooftop balcony or private patio. Because it was easier to obtain planning permission for self-catering, some sitting rooms have non-functioning kitchenettes, which serve as spacious in-room bars. Bathrooms have a Moorish flair, with rough-hewn hand-painted tubs and plaster walls decorated with delicate stenciling. Breakfast is served either in the old salon or in one of the Andalusian courtyards. The restaurant serves a selection of European and typical Andalusian dishes and provides 24-hour room service. The Hotel Casa Imperial sits directly behind the Casa Pilatos in the heart of the old city. The hotel will gladly send you a map outlining the route to its door. There are parking spaces outside the hotel or your car can be taken to a nearby private car park.

*HOTEL CASA IMPERIAL*
*Owners: Carmen Caballero & Jochen Knie*
*Imperial, 29*
*41003 Seville, Spain*
*Tel: 954-500-300, Fax: 954-500-330*
*26 Rooms, Double: €200–€420*
*Open: all year, Credit cards: all major*
*Region: Andalusia, Michelin Map: 578*
*www.karenbrown.com/imperial.html*

Found on one of Seville's narrowest streets, Las Casas de la Judería occupies the quietest of locations at the heart of Santa Cruz, the city's Jewish Quarter. The hotel comprises several mellow ochre-colored townhouses and a palace that in the 16th century was the home of the Duke of Béjar, Cervantes's patron and a member of one of the most famous Spanish aristocratic families. Now you can live like the dukes of old with all the modern conveniences of air conditioning, satellite TV, phone, and mini-bar, for the hotel has been completely renovated to ooze historic atmosphere while providing all the conveniences of the 21st century. There's even an underground car. Because the hotel's bedrooms are spread among several buildings (some of them are connected by underground passages) you have the feeling that you are staying in a small hotel. Bedrooms come in all shapes and the larger ones can accommodate a rollaway bed. *Directions:* For those who arrive by car, head for the Santa María la Blanca church (marked on tourist maps) off the Avenida Mendez Pelayo and just before the church (at the square) watch for a uniformed concierge at the entrance to a narrow street. He will take your car and check your baggage into your room. It is essential to have a detailed map of Seville in order to find this hotel.

*LAS CASAS DE LA JUDERÍA*
*Manager: Jesus Rojas Alcario*
*Plaza Santa María la Blanca*
*Callejón de Dos Hermanas, 7*
*41004 Seville, Spain*
*Tel: 954-415-150, Fax: 954-422-170*
*150 Rooms, Double: €140–€286\**
*\*Breakfast not included: €16*
*Open: all year, Credit cards: all major*
*Region: Andalusia, Michelin Map: 578*
*www.karenbrown.com/juderia.html*

Located between the squares of San Francisco and El Salvador at the heart of what has always been considered the mercantile center of Seville, the area where German bankers, Flemish and French merchants, and Genoese dealers traded, you find Las Casas de los Mercaderes. This hotel, owned by the Duke Ignacio Medina, offers quality accommodation in Seville at a mid-range price. Behind its modern façade the hotel opens up to an 18th-century courtyard with tall, elegant arches and wrought-iron balconies. While its heart is historic and its location even more so, the hotel is essentially modern, with contemporary bedrooms offering TVs, mini-bars, and sparkling bathrooms. You are enveloped by Las Casas de los Mercaderes' crisp, light, airy ambiance as soon as you step into the spacious marble lobby. As we set off to explore the surrounding pedestrian-only street area we were thrilled by the lack of "touristy" shops. A few minutes' walk finds you at the cathedral in the center of Seville. *Directions:* Be sure to have a detailed city map and ask the hotel for detailed directions via email, fax or mail before your arrival.

*LAS CASAS DE LOS MERCADERES*
*Manager: José Alfonso Morilla Espejo*
*Alvarez Quintero, 9–13*
*41004 Seville, Spain*
*Tel: 954-225-858, Fax: 954-229-884*
*47 Rooms, Double: €115–€151\**
*\*Breakfast not included: €15*
*Open: all year, Credit cards: all major*
*Region: Andalusia, Michelin Map: 578*
*www.karenbrown.com/mercaderes.html*

Las Casas del Rey de Baeza sits on a tiny square amidst the charming, narrow, cobbled streets at the heart of historic Seville. Behind its smart street-front façade the hotel opens to three inner courtyards where stark white walls contrast crisply with blue balconies hung with cascading plants. Nearly all of the bedrooms open up to these shaded cobbled courtyards decked with bygones and country antiques. Yet this is the most modern of hotels, with a new spa, an underground parking garage and a rooftop swimming pool with a solarium area. The spacious bedrooms are absolutely delightful, decorated in a tailored, contemporary style and containing every imaginable modern convenience. Each is accompanied by an absolutely top-of-the-line bathroom (most with shower). Relax on one of the shady patios or in the comfortable lounge with its leather sofas and chairs grouped round the fireplace. A sumptuous breakfast is served in the restaurant. *Directions:* Because of its location in the maze of narrow streets behind the Casa Pilatos, it is essential that you have a detailed map to reach the hotel by car. Follow posted signs to Plaza Ponce de Leon, across from the church take Santiago two blocks to the hotel's courtyard.

*LAS CASAS DEL REY DE BAEZA*
*Manager: Cristina Alvarez*
*c/Santiago*
*Plaza Jesús de la Redención, 2*
*41003 Seville, Spain*
*Tel: 954-561-496, Fax: 954-561-441*
*41 Rooms, Double: €195–€400\**
*\*Breakfast not included: €16*
*Open: all year, Credit cards: all major*
*Region: Andalusia, Michelin Map: 578*
*www.karenbrown.com/baeza.html*

Make a special effort to include the Parador de Sigüenza in your itinerary. The dramatic stone castle is perched romantically on a hillside overlooking an unspoiled cluster of old stone houses with red-tiled roofs. Happily, there are no modern buildings to interrupt the mood of the 12th century when the castle was a Moorish stronghold. The reconstruction was an overwhelming venture—take a look at the before and after photographs—you cannot help being impressed with what has been accomplished. Only the shell of the old castle remained, but the original walls have been repaired and the interior has been reconstructed with great care to preserve the original ambiance. Of course there are all the concessions to modern comforts for the traveler, but the decor (although perhaps too glamorous) is great fun. The lounge is an enormous baronial room with groupings of sofas and chairs that appear diminutive beneath the soaring ceiling with its beams, massive chandeliers, and a huge fireplace. The hotel, following the original plan, is built around a central patio where the old well still remains. The spacious guestrooms are uncluttered and not too over-decorated: the walls stark white, the floors red tile, the furniture tasteful rustic reproductions, and the matching draperies and spreads of fine quality. *Directions:* Exit the N11, Madrid to Zaragoza freeway, at km 104 for Sigüenza. Follow parador signs directing you to the castle overlooking the town.

*PARADOR DE SIGÜENZA*
*Plaza de Castillo s/n*
*19250 Sigüenza, Spain*
*Tel: 949-390-100, Fax: 949-391-364*
*81 Rooms, Double: €130–€140\**
*\*Breakfast not included: €13*
*Open: all year, Credit cards: all major*
*Region: Castilla-La Mancha, Michelin Map: 575*
*www.karenbrown.com/siguenza.html*

Next to the ramparts in the ancient fortified town of Sos del Rey Católico, birthplace of the catholic King Ferdinand, sits the parador that bears his name. This parador has a delightful, old-world ambiance that blends harmoniously with the centuries-old buildings around it. The setting is enchanting—overlooking a patchwork of fields stretching off to the distant mountains. It's a totally peaceful spot; perfect for exploring the narrow maze of streets lined with low, sunken doorways and stone escutcheons; and for venturing up to the nearby Sada Palace, where Ferdinand was born. In the lobby is a statue of the reyito (little king) alongside his mother, Juana Enriquez. Enjoy countryside views from the shaded terrace or while eating in the adjacent dining room with its wood-beamed ceiling, and elaborate iron chandeliers. Dining is a more casual affair than at many paradors with the staff dressed in local folk costumes. Our bedroom was very pleasing with its walls painted a muted salmon, its beige bedspreads and bed hanging, and its traditional, dark-wood furniture matching the large window shutters that swung open to a narrow balcony. *Directions:* The road into Sos passes directly below the parador. There is no shortage of parking just beyond the city ramparts.

*PARADOR DE SOS DEL REY CATÓLICO*
*50680 Sos del Rey Católico, Spain*
*Tel: 948-888-011, Fax: 948-888-100*
*66 Rooms, Double: €115–€125\**
*\*Breakfast not included: €13*
*Closed: Dec & Jan, Credit cards: all major*
*Region: Aragon, Michelin Map: 574*
*www.karenbrown.com/catolico.html*

The Hotel La Rectoral is a particularly nice, small hotel tucked into the remote countryside of Asturias. When you arrive in the tiny village of Taramundi, you will wonder if you could possibly be in the right town. However, follow the signs up a small lane and you will arrive at an 18th-century stone house, similar to those you have seen dotting the lovely, green countryside in the vicinity. But there is a big difference—this home (originally a rectory for the nearby church) has been totally renovated and now takes in overnight guests. The restoration has meticulously preserved the authentic, rustic mood. The bakery (with the old oven still in the corner) is now a small dining room with a skylight in the roof to lighten the darkened beams and thick, stone walls. The dining room is especially attractive with planked, wooden floors, stone walls, and heavy beams. Doors lead off the dining room to a wooden balcony where tables are set for dining in the warm summer months. The guestrooms are located in a new wing built in the same style as the original house, and are decorated in a most attractive modern style with built-in headboards. Ask for a room on the ground level with a terrace—while all the rooms offer stunning views of the valley these have the added attraction of terraces. Enjoy the well-equipped gymnasium and sauna. *Directions:* From the center of Pontenova on the N640 (Ribadeo to Luga road), take a country lane for the 6 km drive to Taramundi.

*HOTEL LA RECTORAL*
*Manager: Elena Valdes*
*32775 Taramundi, Spain*
*Tel: 985-646-760, Fax: 985-646-777*
*18 Rooms, Double: €130*
*Open: all year, Credit cards: all major*
*Region: Asturias, Michelin Map: 572*
*www.karenbrown.com/rectoral.html*

The Parador de Teruel sheltered from the busy N234 (the Cuenca to Zaragosa road) by a broad band of trees is of more recent construction than hotels that we usually include in this guide. We include it simply because this 3-star parador is the very best place to stay if you are visiting the city of Teruel and its surroundings. The hotel has the appearance of a large private home, built in Mudéjar style, with a warm-yellow façade and gently sloping tiled roofs. The unusual, somewhat formal octagonal lobby, with an antique table at its center, features marble pillars and a high, sculpted ceiling. A massive stone archway frames marble stairs leading up to the bedrooms. The sunny, glass-enclosed terrace off the dining room and bar has the feel of a conservatory with wicker furniture, making it an altogether inviting spot for cocktails or supper. The bedrooms are parador-large, with wood floors and woven earth-tone spreads on dark-wood beds. Behind a tall hedge in the grounds is a swimming pool. *Directions:* Leave Teruel in the direction of Zaragosa on the N234, stay in the right hand lane and exit for the parador just before the exit for the A420 to Alcañiz. (Arriving in Teruel from Zaragosa pass an area of light industry—with several car dealers—and the parador is on your left just after the A420 exit for Alcañiz.)

*PARADOR DE TERUEL*
*Carretera N234, Carretera Sagundo-Burgos*
*44003 Teruel, Spain*
*Tel: 978-601-800, Fax: 978-608-612*
*60 Rooms, Double: €95–€115\**
*\*Breakfast not included: €13*
*Open: all year, Credit cards: all major*
*Region: Aragon, Michelin Map: 574*
*www.karenbrown.com/teruel.html*

The Hostal del Cardenal, a former archbishop's summer home, is an absolute jewel. As an added bonus, it has a great location—on the northern edge of Toledo, with an entrance between the Puerta de Bisagra (the city's main gate) and the escalator that takes you up the hillside into the old town. Your introduction to the small hotel is through a dramatic 11th-century wall and into an enchanting garden with a reflecting pool. Climb the stairs on the right to reach the tiny foyer of the hotel. The stairway, the patio with its lovely fountain, and the cozy sitting rooms embellished with antiques all reflect the hotel's 18th-century heritage. The delightful guestrooms seem to blend into a tasteful whole. The rooms provide modern comfort with an unbeatable ambiance of past centuries. The breakfast room serves a delicious buffet breakfast. For dinner, consider the hotel's restaurant. Meals are served on the patios bounded by the ancient city walls, or inside in cold weather. The kitchen serves Castilian specialties such as suckling pig. The Hostal del Cardenal has a natural grace and authentic old-world charm frequently lacking in more deluxe hotels. With its gardens, excellent management, and lovely ambiance, this is definitely the finest place to stay in Toledo (and the price is good for value received). *Directions:* Arriving in Toledo you will find the hotel on the city wall adjacent to the tourist office and beside the main gates the Puerta de Bisagra. Parking is in front.

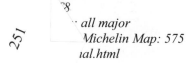

*HOSTAL DEL CARDENAL*
*Manager: Luis Gonzalez Gozalbo*
*Recaredo, 24*
*Spain*
*Fax: 925-222-991*
*€115.50\**
*all major*
*Michelin Map: 575*
*al.html*

251

*Places to Stay*

The Parador de Toledo has a choice setting on the hillside across the River Tagus from Toledo, one of the most beautiful ancient towns in Spain. If ever you're willing to pay extra for a view and a terrace, this is the place to do so. The bar and the restaurant also have terraces with a panoramic view across the deep river valley to Toledo which crowns the hill on the opposite bank so what you are paying for is privacy—your own balcony from which to the view. Watch the city change from golden brown to pink in the setting sun. In any case, you will be happy whichever room you have for they are all large, comfortable, tastefully decorated with gaily colored wooden headboards, red-tile floors with pretty rugs and have a terrace facing the city. The open-beamed ceilings are especially attractive. Indeed, the newly built, regional-style building is very handsome. The impressive, two-story lobby with its giant wood beams is magnificent when viewed from the gallery above, which leads to your room. Liberal use of colorful ceramic tiles and local copper pieces adds a delightful touch. There is also a pool surrounded by a pretty lawn. Drawback: you have to drive to town or take a taxi. *Directions:* The parador is on the southern bank of the river. It is easiest to find from the south: take N401 from Ciudad Real to Burguillos de T. (just south of Toledo), turn left to Cobsa, turn right (following signs to Toledo)—the parador is on your right just before you reach the city.

*PARADOR DE TOLEDO*
*Cerro del Emperador s/n*
*45000 Toledo, Spain*
*Tel: 925-221-850, Fax: 925-225-166*
*76 Rooms, Double: €145–€155\**
*\*Breakfast not included: €14*
*Open: all year, Credit cards: all major*
*Region: Castilla-La Mancha, Michelin Map: 575*
*www.karenbrown.com/toledo.html*

Unlike some of the paradors that are historic monuments, this one in Tordesillas should not be considered a destination in its own right. However, it certainly makes an excellent stop en route. The hotel is especially appealing during the hot summer months because in the rear garden, facing a lovely pine forest, is a very large, attractive swimming pool, with loungers set beneath the pines on the surrounding lawn. In the cooler months you can swim in the indoor pool and exercise in the gym. The Parador de Tordesillas was purpose-built in a traditional style and with many old-world accents such as hand-carved chests and grandfather clocks. The hotel faces directly onto the main highway into town, but a green lawn dotted with tall pine trees gives an appealing country air. To the right of the reception area is a large lounge with an enormous tapestry, a big open fireplace, and groupings of comfortable chairs and sofas. The dining room is bright and cheerful, with a wall of windows looking out to a lovely pine forest. The guestrooms are attractive, with traditional wood furniture, wrought-iron reading lamps, and gleaming parquet floors accented with colorful area rugs. In nearby Tordesillas you find the 14th-century Convento de Santa Clara with its Moorish arches and collection of musical instruments. *Directions:* Leave N6 at exit 179 (Salamanca) and follow signs for N620 (Salamanca). You will find the parador on the left about 2 km after leaving the freeway.

*ADOR DE TORDESILLAS*
*...silla, Spain*
*Fax: 983-771-013*
*...€145\**
*3*
*all major*
*...lin Map: 575*
*...llas.html*

253

*Places to Stay*

Mas means an old farmhouse, implying perhaps a simple place to stay. This is definitely not the case at the Mas de Torrent, a hotel of absolute luxury and stunning charm, idyllically set in the countryside near the beaches of the Costa Brava. The enchanted 18th-century, honey-toned, stone farmhouse remains and is enhanced by outstanding interior design. The walls and vaulted, stone ceiling are painted a delicate, muted salmon—an ever so appealing color scheme that is repeated in the fabrics and fresh bouquets of flowers. There are several cozy sitting areas, each tastefully decorated with antiques from the region. What was once the kitchen is now the bar, and you can still see the original, deep, stone well. In summer, the gourmet restaurant spills over onto the adjacent patio. The restaurant on the terrace above the swimming pool offers a sumptuous lunchtime buffet and is a more casual place to dine in the evening. Indulge yourself in the luxurious spa with its indoor pool, saunas, Turkish and ice baths, and massage and treatment regimes. Several exquisite bedrooms are found in the original farmhouse, but our favorites are the cottages on the grounds—all have totally private terraces and seven have private swimming pools. *Directions:* Just north of Girona, take exit 6 from the A7, signposted Palamós, and follow the Gi 652 Pals-Begur road to the hotel.

*MAS DE TORRENT*
*Manager: Xavier Rocas*
*Owners: Figueras family*
*17123 Torrent, Spain*
*Tel: 902-550-321, Fax: 972-303-293*
*39 Rooms, Double: €295–€665*
*Open: all year, Credit cards: all major*
*Relais & Châteaux*
*Region: Catalonia, Michelin Map: 574*
*www.karenbrown.com/torrent.html*

As you drive into Tortosa, you will see the Parador de Tortosa crowning a hill at the northern end of town. The location is significant, for this historic parador is nestled into the ruins of an ancient Arab fortress that guarded the city in former times. As you wind your way up the hill, the road enters through the ancient walls, which still stretch in partial ruins along the hilltop. Although the architectural style is that of a castle, most of the hotel is actually of new construction with a somewhat traditional hotel look. The dining room is very attractive and strives for an old-world feel with wrought-iron light fixtures and a beamed ceiling. The cuisine features specialties of the Catalan region. Each of the guestrooms is furnished exactly alike, with wood and leather headboards, homespun-style drapes and matching spreads, and dark-wood chairs and desks. Every room has a balcony and the views from this lofty hilltop setting are lovely in every direction, whether it be to the fertile Ebro river valley or the mountain massif. One of the nicest aspects of this parador is a romantic swimming pool tucked into a terrace framed by the ancient walls of the castle. There is also a children's play yard for those traveling with little ones. The bustling town of Tortosa is not terribly picturesque but the hotel, surrounded by acres of land, creates its own atmosphere.

※ ⚟ 🆑 👬 P ⑂ ≋

*PARADOR DE TORTOSA*
*43500 Tortosa, Spain*
*Tel: 977-444-450, Fax: 977-444-458*
*75 Rooms, Double: €115–€125\**
*\*Breakfast not included: €13*
*Open: all year, Credit cards: all major*
*Region: Catalonia, Michelin Map: 574*
*www.karenbrown.com/tortosa.html*

Restaurants, boutiques, and souvenir shops line the maze of narrow streets that spider-web back from Tossa de Mar's beach, but once you get to the water you enjoy a crescent of white sand beach curving to the base of the castle that once guarded the town. Most tourists opt for one of the modern hotels with swimming pool and up-to-date amenities on the outskirts of town. However, if you prefer location, the Hotel Diana has a lot to offer. The setting is prime: the hotel fronts right onto the main beach promenade and backs onto a charming little square. A bar with small tables is set along the beach promenade so that you can watch the action on the beach and people strolling by. Arched windows, dark-green trim, and a white exterior lend an atmosphere similar to a small villa. Within, the hotel has the character of a private home. Marble floors, antique furnishings, grandfather clock, painted tile decoration, inner courtyards, fountains, statues, and stained-glass designs all add to an old-world appeal. Bedrooms are not fancy, large, or air conditioned. We really liked the rooms with balconies, rooms 306, 307, 206 and room 207, which was our favorite because it is the largest. Room 107 is an especially large room without a terrace. We consider this simple hotel an especially good value for money. *Directions:* Arriving in Tossa del Mar, follow your nose to the seafront—we parked and walked to find the hotel.

*HOTEL DIANA*
*Owner: Fernando Osorio Gotarra*
*Plaza de España, 6*
*17320 Tossa de Mar, Spain*
*Tel & Fax: 972-341-886*
*21 Rooms, Double: €72–€149*
*Open: Easter week to Nov, Credit cards: all major*
*Region: Catalonia, Michelin Map: 574*
*www.karenbrown.com/hoteldiana.html*

Henri Elink Schuurman and his Spanish wife, Marta, are owners of a beautiful 19th-century farm (finca) with two granite houses, an olive press, a winery, and a house chapel 14 kilometers outside Trujillo (on the road between the lovely town of Trujilloto and Guadalupe). With patience and love they have tucked guestrooms into the various buildings, taking great care not to disturb the ambiance of the farm that makes a stay here so special. Henri (formerly a Dutch diplomat) and Marta, a talented artist and decorator, have created a beautiful ambiance of rustic simplicity. The entire farm is absolutely delightful. We really like all the bedrooms but if you want complete privacy, opt for El Palomar, a little cottage in the olive garden. Country-cute rooms are tucked into the former farm buildings overlooking the olive grove. Each has a private patio where you can sit out in the evening. We particularly loved Las Ciguanas, the grandest of suites in the farmhouse. An abundant breakfast and dinner are served in the "almazara" (wine press) or out in the vine-covered courtyard. There are two swimming pools and acres of grapes, olive groves, and cherry and almond trees. It's a paradise for birdwatchers. The dogs are always looking for guests willing to take them for a walk to the nearby village of San Clemente with its pretty little church. This is an ideal spot for visiting Trujillo and Guadalupe. *Directions:* The finca is on EX208 at signpost km 89.

*FINCA SANTA MARTA*
*Owners: Marta & Henri Elink Schuurman*
*Pago San Clemente, Por la carretera de Guadalupe*
*10200 Trujillo, Spain*
*Tel: 927-319-203, Fax: 927-334-115*
*15 Rooms, Double: €85–€120*
*Open: all year, Credit cards: MC, VS*
*Region: Extremadura, Michelin Map: 576*
*www.karenbrown.com/santamarta.html*

Installed in the 16th-century convent of Santa Clara, the Parador de Trujillo harmoniously blends with the Renaissance and medieval architecture in Trujillo. Enter through the outdoor stone patio, and be sure to notice the "torno" (revolving shelf) to the right of the doorway. The original residents were cloistered nuns, and it was by way of this device that they sold their homemade sweets to the town's citizens. Inside, bedrooms in the original nuns' cells retain their low, stone doorways (be careful not to bump your head). These rooms surround a sunlit gallery, whose walls are laced with climbing vines, overlooking a cloistered garden patio with an old stone well at its center. Equally attractive rooms surround a whitewashed courtyard and most of these have views out across the adjacent valley. It's a short walk into the beautiful town of Trujillo and you can launch expeditions into Extremadura, whose native sons launched their own explorations to the New World. *Directions:* The parador is well-signposted on the edge of the old town—follow signs very carefully if you arrive via the Plaza Mayor.

*PARADOR DE TRUJILLO*
*c/ Santa Beatriz de Silva, 1*
*10200 Trujillo, Spain*
*Tel: 927-321-350, Fax: 927-321-366*
*50 Rooms, Double: €130–€140\**
*\*Breakfast not included: €13*
*Open: all year, Credit cards: all major*
*Region: Extremadura, Michelin Map: 576*
*www.karenbrown.com/trujillo.html*

This parador is installed in a 16th-century palace on Úbeda's monumentally magnificent Renaissance main square. It features no less than three interior patios, one lined by slender stone arches and dotted with outdoor tables, another overhung with its original wooden terraces, and the third converted to a lovely garden. All but the five newest guestrooms are found at the glass-enclosed gallery level, up a massive stone stairway flanked by suits of armor. The hotel has several types of rooms from four-poster grand to spacious run of the mill. Our personal favorites are those overlooking the golden Plaza Vázquez de Molina and El Salvador chapel, largely furnished with antiques (room 112 is especially romantic, with a small corner balcony peeking out at the cathedral). The more recent additions are decorated in a modern style and are more spacious (one has a sitting room at an additional cost). Detailed attention to faithful historic preservation is obvious throughout the parador's public rooms, with the exception of the more modern restaurant. Don't miss the opportunity for a drink in the Taberna, a lounge/bar in the stone basement, whose decor includes huge, ceramic storage vats. *Directions:* On arriving in Ubeda follow the parador signs though the pedestrian only zone.

*PARADOR DE ÚBEDA*
*Plaza de Vázquez Molina s/n*
*23400 Úbeda, Spain*
*Tel: 953-750-345, Fax: 953-751-259*
*36 Rooms, Double: €145–€155\**
*\*Breakfast not included: €14*
*Open: all year, Credit cards: all major*
*Region: Andalusia, Michelin Map: 578*
*www.karenbrown.com/ubeda.html*

Four kilometers west of the sleepy town of Verín, its brooding stone towers visible from afar, stands the medieval castle fortress of Monterrey (the most important monument in the province of Orense) looking down on the nearby Parador de Verín. Reached by driving through green vineyards, the parador is constructed in the style of a regional manor, with a crenelated tower at one end. Perched atop a vine-covered hill, the parador has lovely views in all directions from its high vantage point. Just off the lobby, you find a lovely sitting room set in the old tower with its unusual fireplace. Bedrooms enjoy countryside or castle vistas. All are large and pleasantly decorated with wood floors and comfortable, contemporary Spanish furniture. The tranquil setting of this parador, along with its pretty pool in the middle of a green lawn, makes it an ideal spot for an overnight stay on the way to Santiago de la Compestella. Before you leave, drive up to the castle and its 13th-century church. Nearby bodegas sell local wine. *Directions:* Avoid the town of Verín by exiting the A52 at Verín oeste, and head cross-country towards the distant castle, closer to town the parador is clearly signposted.

*PARADOR DE VERÍN*
*32600 Verín, Spain*
*Tel: 988-410-075, Fax: 988-412-017*
*23 Rooms, Double: €95–€115\**
*\*Breakfast not included: €13*
*Open: Feb to mid-Dec, Credit cards: all major*
*Region: Galicia, Michelin Map: 571*
*www.karenbrown.com/verin.html*

It is easy to find this parador as it's incorporated into a huge, very old, stone tower—the only remaining fortification standing in Vilalba, which otherwise, apart from the few streets around the parador, has lost its medieval ambiance. In the tower, you find an elegant sitting room with a tall ceiling, and a few bedrooms accessed by a small elevator. Or, if you want some exercise, wind your way up the stairs to the various levels, peeking out through tiny, slit windows in the thick, stone walls. Windows in these historic rooms are so deep that you must actually walk into them to look out through the original tall and narrow slits. The heart of the parador is the adjacent stone building, built to look like a Galician palace and joined to the tower by a glass corridor. Between the two buildings sits a grassy terrace and a conservatory, where lunch and drinks are served. Dinner and breakfast are enjoyed in the spacious, dining room. Bedrooms are particularly attractive decorated in warm, pale colors, which go particularly well with the blond-oak furniture and doors. *Directions:* The parador is well-signposted as you enter Vilaba. Pull into the parador's parking garage on arrival, an elevator takes you up to reception and your room.

❄ 🏧 🐕 🛗 🏋 @ 🍷 P 🍴 🔔 🦽 🚶 👫 🏇

*PARADOR DE VILALBA*
*Valeriano Valdesuso s/n*
*27800 Vilalba, Spain*
*Tel: 982-510-011, Fax: 982-510-090*
*48 Rooms, Double: €115–€125\**
*\*Breakfast not included: €13*
*Open: all year, Credit cards: all major*
*Region: Galicia, Michelin Map: 571*
*www.karenbrown.com/vilalba.html*

La Posada del Torcal is a beautiful, traditional Andalusian cortijo (farmhouse) with 11 acres of almond groves occupying a hilltop setting beneath the crags of El Torcal National Park. This countryside retreat is an ideal touring base for exploring Andalusia. However, you may be as charmed by this idyllic spot as we were and, rather than rushing off sightseeing, content yourself with lounging by the heated pool, enjoying languorous lunches on the vine-covered patio, soaking in the stunning view of a broad, farm-dotted valley and the distant Mediterranean, enjoying a massage, bike riding on quiet lanes, horseback riding, or playing tennis. Inside, the hotel is as attractive as out, with plump sofas and chairs in the lofty beamed living room and 300-year-old beams in the dining room. The spacious king-bedded guestrooms are stylishly decorated with antiques and handmade ceramics and have under-floor heating, fireplaces, ceiling fans, and satellite TVs. The superior rooms have balconies or terraces. Because of the Torcal's location, it catches the breeze, so air conditioning is unnecessary. This is such an idyllic spot that you should plan to spend several nights here—use it as your base for forays to the coast and inland to Ronda, Córdoba and Granada (Michael can obtain Alhambra tickets for you). *Directions:* Facing the T-junction at the top of the town, turn left. After 2 km turn right, and the hotel is on the hill to your left after 3 km.

*LA POSADA DEL TORCAL*
*Owners: Karen & Geoffrey Banham*
*Partido de Jeva*
*29230 Villanueva de la Concepción, Spain*
*Tel: 952-031-177, Fax: 952-031-006*
*10 Rooms, Double: €115–€260*
*Open: Feb to Dec, Credit cards: all major*
*Region: Andalusia, Michelin Map: 578*
*www.karenbrown.com/torcal.html*

The bustling tree-lined town of Xàtiva is famous for providing two of the four Popes that were not of Italian descent. Set high on the hillside with sweeping views across the town and surrounding countryside, Hotel Mont Sant is a destination in its own right. The building was originally an Arabic palace, constructed in the late 1800s beneath the imposing castle walls that still border the property today. Converted to a hotel in the mid-1990s, it had been the summer home to the current owner's family for over 100 years. Rooms in the main building, the adjacent annex, and the wooden chalets in the gardens to the rear are all comfortably furnished with a contemporary theme, interspersed with a few antiques and archeological remnants discovered as work has progressed on the site over the years. There is a sunny pool and separate gymnasium. A major focus here is food. Director Javier Cifre presides over a glass-fronted, open kitchen that has been awarded three red rosettes by Michelin. Meals are served in the intimate formal dining room in one of the expansive conservatories or "al fresco" outside on the garden terrace. At night the property is illuminated with candles and the lights of the castle above, lending a romantic aura that is simply not to be missed. *Directions:* Arriving in Xàtiva on N340, follow signs for "castello" (castle that you see on the hill). Go through the city and climb upwards. The hotel is the left just before the castle gates.

❄ 🏊 CREDIT 🏋 P 🍴 🚭 🏊 🐾

*HOTEL MONT SANT*
*Manager: Javier Andrés Cifre*
*Subida al Castillo*
*46800 Xàtiva, Spain*
*Tel: 962-275-081, Fax: 962-281-905*
*16 Rooms, Double: €120–€200\**
*\*Breakfast not included: €12*
*Open: all year, Credit cards: MC, VS*
*Region: Valencia, Michelin Map: 577*
*www.karenbrown.com/montsant.html*

Cortés was the conquistador of the Aztec empire in Mexico in 1521. He was born in Medellín, east of Mérida, but was taken on as a protégé by the Duke of Feria, whose ancestors built this mighty fortress in the 15th century. Cortés actually lived here for a short time before embarking for Cuba as an ordinary colonist. The castle has been faithfully restored and put to use as a top-of-the-line parador. Virtually surrounded by towers, the exterior is somewhat intimidating, but the tiny plaza in front of it is charming and, once inside, you will love the lounges and public areas with antiques in every available space. There is a glorious chapel with an incredible golden cupola. The central patio, with its graceful stone columns, is equally enchanting. Bedrooms come in all shapes and sizes. All are attractively decorated with regional furniture and the traditional parador good taste. Three have a terrace and several have a special romantic decor. This parador affords a marvelous opportunity to lodge in an authentic castle without sacrificing a single modern comfort. To the rear of the castle is a grassy garden with a large swimming pool. You'll have no problem finding this imposing edifice at the heart of town.

*PARADOR DE ZAFRA*
*Plaza Corazón de María, 7*
*06300 Zafra, Spain*
*Tel: 924-554-540, Fax: 924-551-018*
*45 Rooms, Double: €130–€140\**
*\*Breakfast not included: €13*
*Open: all year, Credit cards: all major*
*Region: Extremadura, Michelin Map: 576*
*www.karenbrown.com/zafra.html*

The Parador de Zamora is a stately stone mansion built in the 15th century by the counts of Alba and Aliste on the tree-shaded Plaza de Viriato at the heart of the town. The exterior is somewhat austere, reflecting the style of the times, but inside, you will be charmed. The elaborate use of antiques (lots of coppers pots and several suits of armor) combined with regional furniture makes a terrific impression. The central patio, surrounded by glassed-in, stone-arcaded galleries, is wonderful. Masterful antique tapestries and chivalric banners abound on the walls, and many of the interior doorways have intricately carved façades. A clubby little bar opens to the back patio, which overlooks the pool. Bedrooms are found both in the old building and in a wing of rooms overlooking the pool. The tall-ceilinged traditional rooms have unusual "wavy ceilings" painted a shade of blue that gives the look of rippling waves. The newer rooms are decorated in a soft shade of lemon and are accented with greens and maroons—very smart. The town, often called "the pearl of the 12th century" is delightful and easily explored on foot. Don't miss the cathedral museum with its fine tapestries. *Directions:* Find your way to the "old town" and follow the one-way system up to the parador on the Plaza de Viriato.

*PARADOR DE ZAMORA*
*Plaza de Viriato, 5*
*49001 Zamora, Spain*
*Tel: 980-514-497, Fax: 980-530-063*
*51 Rooms, Double: €130–€140\**
*\*Breakfast not included: €13*
*Open: all year, Credit cards: all major*
*Region: Castilla y León, Michelin Map: 575*
*www.karenbrown.com/zamora.html*

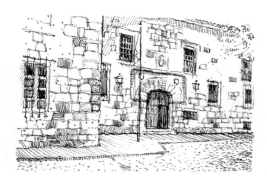

# *Index*

# C

272            *Index*

*Index*                277

KAREN BROWN wrote her first travel guide in 1976. Her personalized travel series has grown to 17 titles, which Karen and her small staff work diligently to keep updated. Karen, her husband, Rick, and their children, Alexandra and Richard, live in a small town on the coast south of San Francisco.

JUNE EVELEIGH BROWN'S love of travel was inspired by the National Geographic magazines that she read as a girl in her dentist's office—so far she has visited over 40 countries. June hails from Sheffield, England and lived in Zambia and Canada before moving to northern California where she lives in San Mateo with her husband, Tony, their two German Shepherds, and a Siamese cat.

LORENA ABURTO RAMÍREZ's lifelong travel to Mexico, her parents' homeland, and extensive travel throughout Spain have enhanced her love of the Spanish language and culture. Lorena is a native of San Mateo, California, and lives near San Francisco with her husband, Rafael, and her children Mariela and Alejandro.

CYNTHIA SAUVAGE was born in Denver and graduated from the University of Colorado where she earned a degree in Spanish and French. Cynthia has traveled extensively and has lived in Mexico, Spain and France. Cynthia lives in Denver, Colorado, with her sons, Evan and Michael.

BARBARA MACLURCAN TAPP, the talented artist who produces all of the hotel sketches and delightful illustrations in this guide, was raised in Sydney, Australia where she studied interior design. Although Barbara continues with architectural rendering and watercolor painting, she devotes much of her time to illustrating the Karen Brown guides. Barbara lives in Kensington, California, with her husband, Richard, and is Mum to Jono, Alex and Georgia. For more information about her work visit *www.barbaratapp.com*.

JANN POLLARD, The artist of the cover painting has studied art since childhood, and is well known for her outstanding impressionistic-style watercolors. Jann's original paintings are represented through The Gallery in Burlingame, CA and New Masters Gallery in Carmel, CA. *www.jannpollard.com*. Fine art giclée prints of her paintings are available at *www.karenbrown.com*.